GARDENING WITH SHRUBS

and

SMALL FLOWERING TREES

The white flowers of azaleas and rhododendrons are mirrored in
a small pool against a contrasting background of dark green
cryptomeria and the light trunks of deciduous trees.

Gardening with Shrubs

AND

Small Flowering Trees

BY MARY DEPUTY LAMSON

M. BARROWS AND COMPANY, INC.

PUBLISHERS   NEW YORK

PRINTED IN THE UNITED STATES OF AMERICA
AMERICAN BOOK–STRATFORD PRESS, INC., NEW YORK

To
VERNON

Foreword

LONG LISTS of common and Latin names with technical descriptions are available and essential in the reference library of a professional botanist, horticulturist or landscape architect. The home-owner seeks to know the familiar ways of and places for that fascinating and versatile group of plants known as shrubs, in order to enjoy them on his own piece of ground, whether square feet or acres. For him only is this book written, to share with him my own enthusiasm for the plants and their combinations.

The lists at the ends of the chapters are not all-inclusive, but indicate certain plants typical of the subject discussed, with easily recognized characteristics of each plant. The heights given are the useful landscape size for a period of fifteen to twenty years' growth but not necessarily the maximum which the plant may attain in its lifetime. There are sure to be differences of opinion as to the sizes, habits and usefulness of many of the shrubs and trees, and many omissions of other people's favorites.

The genus and species names follow the nomenclature of *Standardized Plant Names*, but the varietal and common names depart from it. This was done to facilitate the ordering of plants by using the variety names common to most nursery catalogs, and the English name familiar to the largest number of people.

The writing of the book has called for discussion with many amateurs and professionals in various fields, whose generous interest and help have been invaluable. My thanks go in particular to Dorothy H. Jenkins, Garden Editor of *The New*

York Times, without whose encouragement and help the book would never have been written; to my associates in the office, Barbara Capen, Maud Sargent, and Romaine Carpenter, for their patience, and care in both the preparation and revision of the manuscript, the lists and the drawings; to my clients who have allowed me to put into practice the ideas this book expresses.

MARY DEPUTY LAMSON

Contents

PAGE

Foreword   7

SECTION I: DESCRIPTION OF SHRUBS

I. Gardening with Shrubs   15
II. Shrubs without Leaves   22
III. Shrubs with Leaves   36
IV. Shrubs in Flower   49
V. Shrubs in Fall Color   76

SECTION II: PLACES TO PLANT SHRUBS

VI. Shrub Borders at a Distance   95
VII. Shrub Borders Nearby   109
VIII. Shrubs around the House   120
IX. Shrubs around the House (Continued)   127
X. Shrubs for Special Places   136
XI. Shrubs for Hedges, Fences and Walls   145

SECTION III: SHRUB GARDENS

XII. Shrub Roses   167
XIII. Green Gardens   173

PAGE

XIV. Fruit Gardens — 182
XV. Flower Gardens — 188

SECTION IV: HOW TO STUDY SHRUBS

XVI. How to Learn from an Arboretum, Park, or
Botanical Garden — 207
XVII. How to Visit a Nursery — 213
XVIII. How to Learn from Nature — 221
XIX. How to Learn from Friends — 229

SECTION V: HOW TO SELECT AND GROW SHRUBS

XX. How to Plan, Select and Order Shrubs — 237
XXI. How to Plant Shrubs — 247
XXII. Face-lifting the Shrub Borders — 258
XXIII. Care and Feeding of Shrubs — 269
Index — 283

List of Photographs

Evergreen Shrubs Behind a Pool   Frontispiece

FACING PAGE

I.   The Shrub Garden in Winter   32

II.   Winter Silhouette   33

III.   Early Spring Blossoms   48

IV.   Late Spring Blossoms   49

V.   Woodland Planting Near a Garden   128

VI.   Simple Foundation Planting   129

VII.   Flowering Crabapple as a Specimen   144

VIII.   A Sunken Garden   145

IX.   A Terrace Garden   152

X.   Trimmed Hedge as a Screen   153

XI.   A Formal Green Garden   176

XII.   An Informal Green Garden   177

XIII.   Shrubs at a House Corner   192

XIV.   Shrubs in the Flower Garden   193

ALL THE PHOTOGRAPHS EXCEPT NUMBERS I AND
III WERE TAKEN ON PLACES DESIGNED BY MARY
DEPUTY LAMSON.

SECTION ONE

DESCRIPTION OF SHRUBS

CHAPTER I

Gardening with Shrubs

SHRUBS properly chosen and planted are really the lazy man's, or more politely, the busy man's kind of gardening. They require little care and give constantly beautiful effects throughout the season and throughout the year. They are more adaptable and desirable in more places on the property and in more parts of the country than other plants.

In many locations trees will not thrive, in others almost no perennials will survive, but with few exceptions every section of this country has shrubs growing wild. The villages, towns, the countryside show unmistakably that it is shrubs which add the sense of permanence and well-being to our homes.

Many of us have had the experience of driving along a country road and seeing or smelling lilacs blooming in apparently wild land. If curiosity led to a little exploring, we probably found the foundations of an old house, or at least a cellar-hole where all other signs of man's habitation had long since disappeared, but the dooryard lilacs or flowering quince or sweet shrubs planted by a busy farm wife had persisted.

Twenty-five years ago there were many one-room houses in northern Minnesota which hardly kept out the weather, so recent was the settlement there. Yet frequently beside the door of these houses were a pair of spreading junipers, dug from the wild, or an arrowwood which may have volunteered near the house and been cherished by the farmer's wife. Around the farmhouses of the Middle West there are old roses and lilacs which started from a slip brought down the Ohio in a flatboat or overland in a covered wagon by the housewife accompanying her husband in the search for new land. Everywhere we go in this country we find shrubs native to the land, and promptly plant others.

Each dictionary and encyclopedia has a different definition of "shrubs," and few plantsmen agree with any one of them. The one thing they do agree upon is that shrubs are woody plants, meaning plants which produce wood, and have buds above the ground during the winter. This description also includes trees and vines, and it is very hard to decide when a plant is a tree, when a shrub, and occasionally when it is a vine. Sometimes shrubs act so much like perennials, in killing back to the ground level every winter, that we do not know quite where to class them.

Nursery catalogs, even technical plant lists, only add to the confusion. In looking up sources of supply, we frequently find the flowering dogwood, *Cornus florida*, listed as a tree in one catalog, as a shrub in another. The evergreen bittersweet, *Euonymus vegetus*, turns up as a small evergreen shrub in one list, as a vine in another; Buddleia comes under perennials in some northern catalogs and under shrubs in climates where it is hardier.

We may not be able to arrive at a completely acceptable definition, but to make things as easy as possible we may include as shrubs for the purpose of description and use all woody plants from one to twenty-five feet in height, regardless of whether they have many stems from the ground or a single trunk, branched low. This will exclude only the tall shade trees and the woody vines which always require support. This definition is based primarily on use, since the small flowering trees, like the dogwood and crabapples, are most often planted as shrubs; the trailing vine-like plants are interchangeable as either low shrubs or tall vines.

Since our purpose is to get satisfying outdoor pictures and since effect, whether in house decoration, clothes or plants is largely a matter of how they look as a whole, acquaintance with shrubs and description of them should not be on botanical or technical horticultural detail but on general appearance. In describing an individual, whether friend or foe, we do not go into anatomical dissection, feature by feature, but speak in understandable common terms, as blonde or brunette, tall or short, stout or thin, well-groomed or careless, easy-going or difficult. We may speak of outstanding virtues or faults, but rarely go into the blood pressure, bone structure, nervous system, skin texture or heredity. In the same way, details as to twig structure, leaf scars, cellular composition or family classification may be interesting to the scientist, but mean little to the person who is thinking primarily of quick identification for effect. Words like tall or short, upright or spreading, coarse or fine leaf, neat or untidy, tell what he wants to know to help him. The kind of familiar knowledge we need is that of an old lady of my acquaintance. When asked how she knew a plant at some distance was a crabapple, when it was neither in fruit nor in flower, she said firmly, "Why, don't be silly. It just looks like one."

This friendly recognition enables us to make pleasant compositions with shrubs. If you have been brought up in New England and build a shingle house in Florida, your instinct is for the same effect the lilacs gave at the corner of your former home. Since lilacs do not thrive in a hot climate you must substitute something that has the sturdy shape, the clean branching habit, the substantial leaf of the lilac, even though the flower may be entirely different. It may be one of the southern viburnums or perhaps the banana magnolia that reminds you most of your old lilacs. If you are familiar with northern woods where great white pines have a ground cover of blueberries, it is a little startling but interesting to see that the woods of Georgia and Florida look much the same, but to get that effect nature has used the turpentine pines and the ground cover of low native palmetto.

Wherever we garden shrubs appeal because of their ease of

upkeep. Wisely chosen and well placed, they require almost no further care or expense for years. There are fewer insects and diseases which are fatal to shrubs than there are to perennials and annuals. Even when the Japanese beetle is a problem, it is easier to spray the shrubs they like once or twice in a season than to protect all the flowers in a garden with almost daily sprayings.

The root systems of shrubs are deep and heavy, therefore they are usually more resistant to local or temporary drought or to cold weather. In the north a severe winter may almost wipe out a perennial border but in the spring the lilacs, spireas, hawthorns and laurels burst out in full garden glory. I remember after the bad winter of 1934, I asked a nurseryman who grows only native material if he had as much damage as many of the others did and he said, "No, you know my things have been growing up in northern New York state for a hundred years or more, or things just like them. So I don't worry about weather. Nature always has taken care of them and she still will."

Farther south extreme heat or drought may necessitate replacing annuals and perennials. But the jasmines, the camellias, crepe myrtles and the azaleas continue to bloom exquisitely.

Shrubs may need some pruning but much of it is because they are wrongly placed. If it is necessary, pruning annually is less trouble than the almost daily or weekly care demanded by other kinds of garden material. Removing the dead flower heads from the lilacs, laurels and rhododendrons is done only once a year, not every day or so as with annuals and perennials. Since the seed heads of the shrubs are large in themselves it is a fairly rapid job.

Shrubs and trees are a fine investment as they are almost the only thing connected with the home that increase in value rather than decrease. The first cost of good planting may be considerable but it is worth appreciating that the dollars spent on a coat of outside paint have to be spent all over again when, in a few years, the house becomes shabby. The same amount of money spent on shrubs around the new house never needs to be repeated, and as the plants grow they give greater beauty and create a more effective setting. A yew hedge planted along the street, a foot and a half to two feet high, possibly costs a hundred dollars but that same yew hedge, ten years later, is actually worth six or seven hundred dollars, if you were to buy it at the mature size.

Since most of us live in the same house twelve months of the year, the year-round beauty of shrubs is most appealing. Green lawns are wonderful in spring and fall but midsummer drought and winter cold make them look bare, brown and most uninviting. Flower gardens are beautiful during the blossoming season but in most parts of the country for six months of the year they are bare and uninteresting. With careful selection and arrangement gardens of shrubs or borders of shrubs can be attractive every month of the year. This need not necessarily mean that they are evergreen gardens. Certain deciduous shrubs have such beauty of form or interesting silhouette that even in their leafless season they are an addition to the landscape. There is not a month in the year when there are not attractive pictures to be made with shrubs.

To be sure of getting this year-round effect, you must know these plants in all seasons. An interesting experiment is a word test tried on garden friends. I asked several groups to write down the first word that comes into their minds when I say lilac, spirea, forsythia, dogwood, crabapple, trumpet vine, rose. At least 90% of the answers will be, "Lavender, white, yellow, pink, orange, red." Obviously they think of the shrubs only in bloom and identify them only by the color of their flowers. Yet with most shrubs the blossom lasts two or three weeks at the most, and we must look at the plants eleven months more. To use shrubs well we must know them completely unadorned as well as all dressed up with flowers.

Every year thousands of new homes are being built all over America. The first interest of their owners is in four walls and a roof, the house itself. Even before it is completed, while the builders' debris is still littering the yard, they start wondering how to take off the bareness and make the house belong to its surroundings. This is the first step in becoming gardeners, instead of only house-owners. Many have had no previous interest in nor knowledge of any kind of plant, except possibly a few house plants. In their eagerness to make the new home as attractive outside as it is inside, they will start looking around, reading, studying catalogs; trying to find out what to plant, how and where, and the first planting will almost inevitably be shrubs. Unfortunately a great many of these new home-owners plant far too many shrubs from a very limited list of varieties where they could get more effect and much less final expense and trouble by more thorough study and comprehension of the possibilities of this material.

In addition to the brand new houses which have to be planted, there are many others where time, money or labor scarcity make it difficult to do any work on the grounds, whether of planting or of maintaining existing planting. The result is likely to be a generally unkempt, down-at-the-heels look, or a jungle of badly crowded, over-grown plants, in decided need of over-hauling. Some of the trouble is obviously due to mistaken selection or layout in the first place, and we should try to avoid the same thing happening again.

The first step is to try to clear up the jungle. We should know which material is the most valuable, which will recover from neglect and still make a well-shaped and pleasant shrub, which ones grow so slowly that even a misshapen old one is probably worth salvaging because a new one would take too long to mature—all the fundamentally easy-to-recognize characteristics of the different shrubs. Otherwise we will have trouble in deciding which ones are worth moving, which ones should be discarded and which ones should stay where they are without trying to give them further shocks by moving.

Some years ago I saw an old place which in spite of fifteen years of neglect and unoccupancy needed very little drastic operation on the shrub borders and general planting. It had probably been planted about thirty years before but had been done with very fine material—magnolias, hawthorns, dogwoods, crabapples, lilacs—spaced so far apart that in spite of normal growth and neglect, the chief work needed was pruning out of dead entangling branches. Little transplanting of plants was needed.

I have known other neglected places where nothing but an axe or a jungle knife seemed to be indicated when we first went in. The fifteen-year-old planting had been done so badly and so tightly that it was completely impenetrable and all the shrubs looked practically worthless.

With the extraordinary range of material available nowadays, there is little excuse for bad or unimaginative shrub planting if you determine first the over-all effect you desire, the picture you wish to create, and then the general appearance of the material composing it. Observing shrubs at all seasons, knowing the qualities needed for various kinds of planting in different places, or for different purposes will enable you to select the right plants and to combine them for permanent beauty.

CHAPTER II

Shrubs without Leaves

THE LEAVES of a shrub are its clothes and, like our own, they may enhance its appearance or they may detract from it. The best time of the year to see the actual shape of a shrub is in winter when it is leafless. It is then that the real shape is completely visible and we can study its way of growth and its general character. For most plants it is the least attractive period of the year, so that it is important to know which ones are passable in the cold months, and which ones are pretty only when they have nice leaves or colorful flowers, and are definitely ugly in a winter landscape.

The manner of growth of the shrub is called its habit, and determines whether it can be described as upright or spreading; narrow or broad; open or dense; formal or picturesque. The direction in which the stems and branches grow, the number, spacing and arrangement of them are essentially the anatomy of a shrub and give it definite character and quality which leaves and flowers may conceal but do not change. If you recognize the true habit of a plant you can use it appropriately, taking advantage of its natural way of growth.

A shrub whose stems from the ground and main side branches grow in an almost vertical position even when very young will always tend to be a narrow, upright or columnar form. The stems are close together and the height of the shrub will be from four to eight times the width of it. A common shrub which assumes this form is the Rose of Sharon. Its branches hug the main trunk or if there are several stems from the ground, go up at not more than about a 10° angle from the vertical. As it gets older the side branches will change its straight columnar form somewhat, but in general even full grown, it is three or four times as high as it is wide. Hick's yew, *Taxus hicksi*, some of the cedars, *Juniperus*, and some of the arborvitae, *Thuja*, assume this form throughout their life.

In any nursery catalog when the word *columnaris* or *erecta* or *pyramidalis* is used, almost invariably it indicates a shrub whose height is considerably greater than its width and whose branches ascend almost vertically. These shrubs are useful as accents or a sort of exclamation point in shrub planting or in a very narrow space between a door and a window, where a tall vertical line is needed and where there is not room for sidewise growth.

The opposite of this type of growth is the one whose branches go out horizontally and whose growth is sideways rather than upward. These make the broad-spreading flat type of shrub particularly good for facing down taller plantings or for foundation plantings under windows or anywhere that height is not desirable and width is allowable. The names *horizontalis* or *prostrata* always indicate this habit of growth. In the nursery catalog if the price is quoted on the basis of spread rather than height, it is a sure indication that the shrub, even when young, is broader than it is high and that it will continue to assume that form. When full grown it may be seven or eight times as wide as high and it is important in planting that you know this characteristic so that you can allow for sidewise growth.

In the evergreens, *Pinus mugho*, *Taxus baccata repandens* or *Taxus cuspidata nana*, *Ilex helleri*, are characteristic. There are fewer deciduous shrubs of this habit but *Cotoneaster horizontalis*, *Cotoneaster divaricata*, some of the new dwarf flowering quinces, *Chaenomeles* hybrids, the native low blueberry, *Vaccinium angustifolium*, will always tend to be

wider than they are high. In the winter this habit shows up
very plainly as all the limbs and branches go out almost parallel to the ground and have few or no small twigs growing
straight up in the air. Without pruning these shrubs continue
low and broad. They rarely have a central upright stem or
leader.

The most violent pruning cannot make a shrub with a
strong central leader growing vertically, into a good horizontal
shrub or train a spreader into a vertical grower. An understanding of their natural habits will save mistakes that cause
hours of pruning and transplanting later.

There are other shrubs whose main stems grow vertically
or nearly so but whose side branches are horizontal or at an
interesting wide angle from the main stem. They incline to
make an open, picturesque plant and are particularly effective
in winter, because of the unusual shapes they assume. When
full-grown they are likely to be about as broad as high, sometimes a little broader. Among the small flowering trees the
Sargent crabapple, *Malus sargenti*, is the best example. Several of the other Japanese flowering crabapples have the same
habit but to a less marked degree. The hawthorns are likely
to branch at almost right angles from the trunk. *Styrax
japonica* has the same form. In that large and useful family,
the viburnums, the black haw, *Viburnum prunifolium*, and
the doublefile viburnum, *Viburnum tomentosum*, are characteristic. The winged euonymus, *Euonymus alatus*, has its main
stems fairly upright, but its side branches go out almost at a
right angle, so that it makes, when full grown, one of the
most picturesque and beautiful of all shrubs.

Looking at the manner of branching in the winter enables
us to decide whether a shrub is going to be too broad for the
space we can give it, or too low for the screen where we need
it. The horizontal branching habit always indicates width. A
central leader or vertical stems make for height.

Many shrubs are neither strongly upright nor strongly horizontal in habit, but have a general shape more or less round

or broadly oval. Most of them are inclined to be taller than they are broad, but the difference is not as great as in the other two forms. This is, in fact, the largest group of shrubs and in it are most of the ones we use in mass planting. Familiarity with this character will prevent too many of this rather undistinguished shape being used in large masses. Contrast is a valuable thing in any planting and interrupting the round shape with the tall spires of the columnar or with the spreading lines of the horizontal makes greater interest.

It is important to see whether the shrubs that you are planting are growing upright from natural habits or whether they are crowded into a place where they have to grow upright for light and air. More than once I have seen a tall, scraggy lilac that was practically a feather duster on the top of a tall stem. Had this lilac been properly taken care of and pruned and given room from the beginning, it would probably have been much more oval in shape, with foliage well up and down the whole shrub. I once rescued four fine English hawthorns from the back of a crowded border. When I found them they were about twenty feet high and no more than six or seven feet broad in the head. I put them out in full sunlight to mark the entrances to a garden. In the course of a few years their spread was almost equal to their height and they had once more assumed their natural picturesque vase-shaped head. The only way to observe the natural habit of any shrub is where it is uncrowded and where the pruning shears have not distorted it.

A more unusual form in shrubs is the weeping or pendulous type. These are usually some special sport of another variety, with a third name to indicate the special habit. The weeping cherry, *Prunus subhirtella pendula*, familiar all over the country, is a good example. The word *pendula* as a third name in a nursery catalog always indicates this manner of growth. Others which are not strictly pendulous or weeping are shrubs whose branches grow in great arches. Some of them are our most familiar shrubs and yet their graceful curves are often distorted by the pruning shears, instead of being utilized to full advantage. The wild rose of the prairie, *Rosa setigera*, has arching branches eight to ten feet long. Several of the other shrub roses have this same characteristic. The familiar spirea, *Spiraea vanhouttei*, or the Japanese barberry, *Berberis thunbergi*, are often pruned to make a round ball or at least a very ordinary upright shrub. Left to themselves they have long festoons which in flower or in fruit are outstandingly lovely. Shrubs with the true pendulous or weeping character are definitely for accent or for unusual places. Those with the arching or almost vinelike habit are particularly good on the fronts of borders, or on banks, where they cover the slope with their long branches much as vines would do, but with a little more height. They are also useful for training flat on walls or on fences. They come really in the shrub-vine group and should be used almost as large-sized vines.

One thing that is important in the winter appearance of shrubs is the number of stems or branches. The ones that look best in winter are almost invariably those that have one to four main stems from the ground and comparatively few side branches. If in addition to this they have large or interestingly shaped flower buds, the shrub is beautiful in silhouette in the winter. Most of the magnolias, the flowering dogwoods are of this type. A shrub which has innumerable stems from the ground and a thicket of side branches and twigs, looks like nothing but a brush-heap in the winter landscape and should be used at a distance, not nearby. The only way to keep such shrubs halfway tidy is by constant use of the pruning shears to thin them out from the ground. There is no reason for making any more work for ourselves than we need.

The winter is also the time to look for the shrubs with picturesque or irregular outline and habit. Our native highbush blueberry, *Vaccinium corymbosum*, is an outstanding example. Its branches are angular and interesting in color so that in winter the whole bush has a definite character and is a rather orangy-brown note in the landscape. The burning bush,

Euonymus alatus, with its queer bark, the fringetree, *Chionanthus virginica*, the flowering crabapples, the hawthorns, the flowering quinces, several of the cotoneasters are likely subjects for the photographer without their leaves because of their irregular branching at odd angles. They are excellent used close at hand so that you see them in detail.

Another valuable winter pastime is determining the rate of growth of shrubs. A few catalogs and books show the eventual height of the shrub and the rate of growth per year but it is easier to determine that for yourself by observation than to spend hours in the library. Shrubs grow generally in two ways: some of them throw up new branches from the ground each year and others grow at the ends of the existing branches or on side branches from the old trunk. Many do both.

The new wood is almost always a slightly different color from the old, so it is easy to tell which part is this year's growth. If the shrub is very dark gray in bark the new growth is likely to be a little greener and a little lighter gray. If the bark of the old wood is brown, the new growth is likely to be tan or at least a much lighter brown. The new growth is also rather shinier and has a less rough, hard appearance than the old bark.

If you look at a shrub which has been planted two years or more you can determine how much it can be expected to grow each year. (The reason for not examining a shrub that has been recently planted is, of course, that transplanting sets back the shrub and its rate of growth for the succeeding two years is slower than normal.) Where the shrub grows on the end of its old branches, or on side branches from the main one, there is a slight ring around the bark where the new growth starts, so that in the winter when the bark color is more noticeable than during the growing season, you can trace back from the tip of the branches to this ring and tell how much the shrub has grown the past year. True dwarf box, for instance, may grow only an inch a year on the side branches or the twigs from the branches. Many of the deciduous shrubs will grow as much as a foot to a foot and a half a year when they are well established.

In looking for the rate of growth it is well to trace it back for two or three years. An unusually dry season may make the growth less and an unusually wet one may cause it to grow much more. If you have kept any record of the number of seasons through which your own plants have lived, you can almost chart the kind of weather you had by the growth of the deciduous shrubs. Some of the famous drought years will show only four to six inches of growth on crabapples, viburnums and even the native plants in the woods and fields. An unusually wet season like that of 1945 in the northeastern states will show a foot and a half to two feet of growth on these same plants. If you know that one summer has been very dry and the previous one very wet, an average of the two will come close to the normal rate of growth for the plant.

A simpler way of finding out the rate of growth is to locate two shrubs whose age you know, and planted under more or less similar conditions. If one is three years old and three feet high and the other ten years old and eight feet high, the difference in height (5') divided by the difference in years (7 years) will give you the approximate yearly rate of growth (5/7 of a foot or 8½"). If it is a spreading shrub the difference in width is measured instead of height.

Unless you know also how large a shrub will be when full grown, you cannot tell without examination of the twig whether the shrub is now full size and will not get much larger, or whether it still has several years to go. In other words, you cannot tell whether the ten-year-old shrub was this size at six years or whether it has taken the full ten to get its mature stature.

On shrubs that grow only by new stems from the ground each year the rate of annual growth is likely to be very fast. Tender shrubs like buddleia, vitex, abelia, kill to the ground each year in the north so that growth on the old wood is unimportant but the height of the new shoots from the ground determines their space requirements. Others like stephan-andra keep main stems but kill back from the ends, so that the yearly rate of growth never increases the total size of the plant appreciably.

The rate of growth of any shrub is important because it enables you to decide how fast your plantings will mature so that you know how far apart to place them. Dwarf box and some of the other broad leaved evergreens whose rate of growth is from one to six inches can certainly be planted much closer together for effect than shrubs that grow a foot and a half a year. The evergreens will take ten years to crowd and the other shrubs will have to be moved out in three or four if they are planted for immediate effect. Observation can tell you not only what direction the shrub is going but how rapidly it is going to get there, so that you know how to plan for it.

To many gardeners the winter is the time when the only gardening possible is reading catalogs and working on paper. To the shrub gardener, however, it is a valuable season because it is then that he can really study his plants to the best advantage and learn them intimately and in the simplest form. It is the time when it is fun to walk through winter woods, or around the neighborhood and recognize at a passing glance all the various shrubs around us, just because of the general shape and habit of them. When once we can do that we are well on the way to being really good shrub gardeners.

LIST No. 1

SHRUBS FOR WINTER COLOR

BARK—The list of plants whose bark is brightly enough colored to count in winter landscape is small. These are the most conspicuous, although certain others can be found.

NAME	COLOR	HEIGHT	HABIT	PLACE TO USE
Betula pendula WHITE BIRCH	White	30′	Vase-shaped	Accent or woodland planting.
Cornus stolonifera RED OSIER DOGWOOD	Red	8′	Broad oval	Distant borders.
Cornus s. flaviramea GOLDENTWIG DOGWOOD	Yellow	8′	Broad oval	Distant borders.
Cytisus scoparius SCOTCH BROOM	Green	8′	Sprawling	Seashore planting at a distance.
Kerria japonica JAPANESE KERRIA	Green	6′–8′	Sprawling	Wall shrub.
Vaccinium corymbosum HIGHBUSH BLUEBERRY	Orange-brown	8′	Picturesque	Accent, nearby or native planting. Acid soil.

SHRUBS FOR WINTER COLOR

FRUIT—Hanging late, well into the winter or spring.

Name	Color	Height	Habit	Place to Use
Aronia arbutifolia RED CHOKEBERRY	Red	8'	Narrow oval	Distant borders.
* *Berberis thunbergi* JAPANESE BARBERRY	Red	5'	Broad oval	Nearby borders, banks.
* *Cotoneaster divaricata* SPREADING COTONEASTER	Red	6'	Arching oval	Near at hand, specimen.
Crataegus phaenopyrum WASHINGTON HAWTHORN	Red	25'	Vase-shaped tree	Accent, specimen.
C. nitida GLOSSY HAWTHORN	Red	18'	Spreading tree	Accent, specimen.
Ilex verticillata WINTERBERRY	Red	8'	Oval	Native planting, lowland.

List No. 2—Continued

Name	Color	Height	Habit	Place to Use
Ligustrum obtusifolium regelianum REGELS PRIVET	Black	5′	Picturesque	Nearby, accent or mass.
Malus Sieboldi TORINGO CRABAPPLE	Red	20′	Spreading tree	Accent, specimen.
Myrica pensylvanica BAYBERRY	Gray	4′	Mound	Near sea or sandy soil.
* Rhus glabra SMOOTH SUMAC	Red	10′	Awkward	Distant border, native.
* Rosa multiflora JAPANESE ROSE	Red	10′ spread	Arching	Distant borders, banks.
Symphoricarpos albus SNOWBERRY	White	6′	Untidy	Distant borders, shade.
Viburnum dilatatum LINDEN VIBURNUM	Red	8′	Oval	Nearby or distant borders.
Viburnum opulus EUROPEAN HIGHBUSH CRANBERRY	Red	12′	Vase-shaped	Nearby or distant borders.

* Other varieties of sumac, wild roses, cotoneasters and barberries have brilliant fruit. The ones given are typical.

Gottscho-Schleisner

1. The silhouettes of flowering dogwoods used as accents in a shrub garden stand boldly against the sky. The dark lines of trimmed evergreen hedges and the specimen cedar give contrast and depth to the landscape.

11. Against a late winter sky or a bare wall the branches of shrubs make picturesque patterns. This hawthorn is an outstanding example.

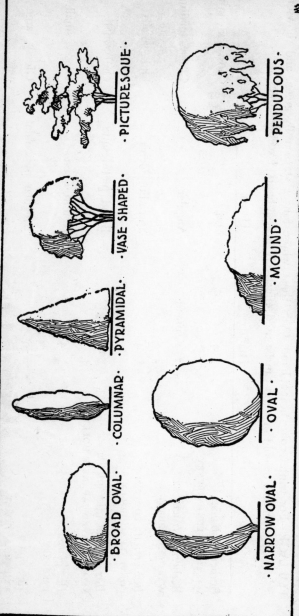

THE HABIT OF SHRUBS AND SMALL FLOWERING TREES. In the lists at the ends of the chapters the habit of the plants are usually described by the terms shown on this drawing. It is the characteristic form of the species or variety and can most easily be recognized by visualizing a string drawn around the outside of the branches of the plant.

SHRUBS FOR WINTER COLOR

FOLIAGE—For winter color near-at-hand. Only those whose foliage stays really green, and shows no effects of cold or wind can be used effectively near-at-hand. Excellent ones are:

Name	Height	Habit	Foliage
Berberis julianae WINTERGREEN BARBERRY	4′	Oval	Glossy, medium.
Berberis verruculosa WARTY BARBERRY	2½′ spread	Angular	Glossy, medium.
Ilex crenata convexa CONVEXLEAF HOLLY	4′	Spreading, dense	Dull, small.
Ilex crenata microphylla SMALL-LEAVED JAPANESE HOLLY	10′	Broad, picturesque	Dull, small.
Ilex glabra INKBERRY	4′	Round, open	Glossy, small.
Ilex opaca AMERICAN HOLLY	20′	Irregular, pyramidal	Glossy, large.

Plant	Height	Shape	Foliage
Kalmia latifolia MOUNTAIN LAUREL	6'–8'	Broad oval	Glossy, medium.
Pachystima canbyi CANBY PACHYSTIMA	12″	Mound	Glossy, tiny.
Pieris japonica JAPANESE ANDROMEDA	5'	Irregular oval	Glossy, medium.
Taxus cuspidata JAPANESE YEW		Depends on variety used	Dark, needled.
Taxus media HYBRID YEW		Depends on variety used	Dark, needled.

Rhododendron leaves curl and droop with cold, arborvitaes, *Thuja*, cedars, *Juniperus*, and English yews, *Taxus baccata*, burn or turn rusty in winter cold.

CHAPTER III

Shrubs with Leaves

THE TWO or three weeks of the year when buds are swelling
and new leaves emerging on shrubs and trees is an annual
glimpse into fairyland. The world of somber evergreens, relieved only by gray, black and brown is transformed almost
overnight by a soft haze of lavender-blue, with glints of yellow-
green here and there. The colored bark of the dogwoods and
broom, the twigs of the willow deepen in color so they are
vivid notes in the lowlands. The maples blossom in red and
yellow, some early shrubs—azaleas, forsythia, Cornelian cherry,
Nanking cherry, benzoin—burst into blossom before their
leaves unfold, special ornaments in an already lovely landscape.

The picturesque silhouette of the honey locust trees and
the light gray trunks of the beeches and ironwoods, slow to
unfold their new leaves, are clean lines in the pale green of
the elms, oaks, and maples and sharp contrast with the mass
of the undergrowth shrubs. Every day brings a little stronger
green and new flowers, so it is hard to go indoors even when
darkness comes.

The evergreens are late in putting out their new growth so
the soft greens and bronzes at the tip of their branches are
accent when other plants have lost the soft subtleties of
young leaf.

Sometimes the tints of the unfolding leaves, both the
deciduous and evergreen, suggest color schemes worth planning for in anyone's garden. The gray-green of certain shrubs,

particularly those whose second name is *tomentosum*, is almost like fog in spring dawn and twilight. The light underside of *Viburnum tomentosum*, *Cotoneaster*, *Ilex vomitoria*, *Eleagnus angustifolia*, silvers the whole plant just as the leaves are starting to unfold. The lavender flowers of *Azalea mucronulata* or the shrub daphnes have a quaint delicacy combined with the group. Other shrubs have a bronze tone to their new leaves. *Pieris japonica*, Japanese andromeda, has its own creamy racemes against soft bronze leaves, and with pale yellow primroses or a group of Breeder tulips in front of it makes an enchanting, subtle picture in bright spring sunshine.

A few shrubs have a reddish or red-purple cast to the leaves. Most of them keep their same color through the summer and are a little difficult to use in the general garden picture. They are useful for cutting for flower arrangement and if they must be planted on the place, it is well to keep all of them close together to make a purplish bronze picture from spring through fall. However they are used in indoor flower arrangement, they certainly look best outdoors if no other color than dark green or white is nearby. A few shrubs or small flowering trees (*Malus scheideckeri*, some of the Japanese maples and one or two of the flowering cherries) have this bronzy-red when they first open but lose it for a clear green during the summer. Even these must be used with great caution, as they are not part of the natural color palette of early spring, and must be kept away from the strong yellow-green or yellows that predominate at that time of year. The only season when they do not stick out like sore thumbs, in the midst of green or yellow-green foliage, is in the fall when the whole landscape has turned bronze and bronzy yellow and red so that their color looks at home and fits in with the world in general.

When the leaves on the shrubs are fully opened their color varies considerably and shades of green are infinite. Some of them are definitely gray-green, others are a very dark, almost bottle green, while most of them are what we commonly call leaf-green or medium dark blue-green color.

An occasional pause to absorb the over-all hue of the plant in full leaf is helpful in making pictures from your shrub borders. In general, the gray-greens, yellow-greens, reddish-greens should be used sparingly and for special purposes. The dark greens can make bays or shadowy recesses seem deeper, or the misty gray-greens can give illusion of distance, while the bulk of the planting is done with the ordinary leaf-green shrubs.

The size of the leaves is almost as important as the color. The Father Hugo rose has tiny little leaves, perhaps three-eighths of an inch long, while those of *Viburnum sieboldi* are tremendously heavy and long. Many of our most common flowering shrubs have almost similar leaves or at least similar in both color and size. The weigelas, syringas, deutzias, forsythias, look too much alike when not in flower to use in great masses.

In the south, the privets, the pittosporum, the smaller leaved magnolias, many of the other broad leaved evergreens have the same size and shape and color of leaf, so that there is a somberness and monotony about their wholesale planting in the border that is uninteresting. Varying such plantings with smaller-leaved evergreens that have a lighter quality makes a much livelier and pleasant-to-look-at group, even when they are not in bloom.

Too much fine, feathery foliage has an indeterminate quality about it that may be desirable in certain locations but not in too large masses. The contrast of a very fine-leaved shrub with a very coarse-leaved one gives variety, and this is enhanced if the color as well as the size of the leaves is different.

Another characteristic that makes the difference in the general appearance of the shrub is the way the leaves grow. This is part of the general branching habit of the tree and shrub and observed during the winter an open shrub like the *Styrax japonica* will appear more open because the light delicate leaves are placed not too thickly on the shrub. On the other hand, the *Viburnum sieboldi* has comparatively few branches but its heavy thick leaves give the appearance of a weighty dense mass. In general if the shrub has small leaves very thickly placed, the appearance of the whole is not quite as heavy and solid as the larger leaved plant of darker green, which actually carries fewer leaves. Yellow-green and gray-green shrubs with small leaves are lighter and more delicate than any of the dark green ones.

The color, the size and the placing of the leaves together make the quality that can be summed up in the artist's word *value*. It is really the darkness or lightness of the shrub as a mass in the landscape. It can best be judged by half closing the eyes and seeing which of the shrubs look the darkest in total landscape view. From my window a hillside mostly of native plants, with a few additions, is a good example. The cedars and the oaks are the darkest on the hillside. Then come the wild hawthorns and the flowering crabapples. The cherries and dogwoods are naturally lighter in over-all appearance and the sumacs and the wild locusts are only slightly darker gray-green than the field of young oats in front of the hillside. The mingling of these different greens and different darknesses makes for beautiful planting, with much more interest and much more liveliness than if the whole hillside were solid evergreens or solid deciduous material of exactly one color, shape and size.

Closer at hand is a shrub group near the house. At the back is the dark, heavy green leaf of hybrid lilacs. Immediately in front of it is the feathery slightly yellowish green of *Rosa hugonis* and facing down the foreground, the gray-green of *Daphne somerset* with small leaves light in quality, contrasting with the shiny pointed dark green of *Abelia grandiflora*. There is no time of day when this group is not a pleasure. When the early morning light filters through it, the delicacy of the *Rosa hugonis* and the Daphne catch the glimmer of the sun, the dark green of the lilacs give substance to the group, and the shininess of the abelia catches definite highlights. Each of these shrubs is beautiful in flower of course, but they need never blossom to make a satisfying and pleasant picture near the house door, seen every time we go in and out. The use of glossy leaves where sun only filters through is a great help in lightening a dark corner. The andromedas, abelia, many of the magnolias and mountain laurel all have a shine to their leaves which catches light and gives a certain sparkle that the dull evergreen leaves of rhododendrons would lose and make a planting mass seem gloomy.

Since in most parts of the country the world at large is made up of foliage for about six months of the year, with only occasional flower, it is certainly worth a great deal of thought to find out how to make this foliage world less monotonous with contrast and variety. Leaves are the everyday wardrobe of the shrubs and like our own, they are the most important and most frequently worn of all our belongings and should be most carefully chosen.

SHRUB VALUES

SHRUBS

DARK IN VALUE—Shrubs counting for a dark note in the landscape are usually compact, with fine twigs, bearing many dark green leaves, small or medium in size.

NAME	HEIGHT	HABIT	PLACE TO USE
Buxus sempervirens arborescens TREE BOX	20'	Vase-shaped tree	Specimen, frame, nearby.
Buxus sempervirens suffruticosa TRUEDWARF BOX	6"–10'	Round or broad oval	Hedge, specimen, formal planting.
Crataegus crusgalli COCKSPUR THORN	20'	Spreading tree	Nearby or distant, native planting, accent.
Cryptomeria japonica lobbi LOBB CRYPTOMERIA	25'+	Upright tree	Formal accent.
Ilex glabra INKBERRY	6'	Broad oval	Cultivated or native planting, light shade.
Kalmia latifolia MOUNTAIN LAUREL	8'	Broad oval	Shade, woodland planting, nearby or distant.
Taxus cuspidata in variety JAPANESE YEW		Depends on variety	Accent, foundation.
Thuja occidentalis douglasi pyramidalis PYRAMIDAL ARBORVITAE	20'	Pyramidal	Accent, nearby, cultivated planting.

See also the list of bold-textured shrubs.

SHRUB VALUES

SHRUBS

MEDIUM IN VALUE—The bulk of planting masses should be made up of shrubs in this group. It includes most of the familiar species, whose foliage is not conspicuous in color or texture. The examples given are distinctive largely because of the habit of the plant.

NAME	HEIGHT	HABIT	PLACE TO USE
Cornus florida FLOWERING DOGWOOD	25′	Picturesque tree	Accent, woodland edge, nearby border.
Crataegus oxyacantha splendens ENGLISH HAWTHORN	25′	Vase-shaped tree	Accent, nearby.
Juniperus virginiana RED CEDAR	35′	Columnar	Open meadow border, nearby or distant.
Juniperus chinensis pfitzeriana PFITZER'S JUNIPER	10′ spread	Low, horizontal	Accent, nearby.
Malus coronaria WILD SWEET CRABAPPLE	20′	Spreading tree	Specimen, sunny meadow border.
Pieris japonica JAPANESE ANDROMEDA	5′	Oval	Garden, nearby border, foundations.
Syringa vulgaris COMMON LILAC	12′	Oval	Near house or garden.
Viburnum tomentosum	8′	Horizontal, sym-	Near house or garden.

SHRUB VALUES

SHRUBS

LIGHT IN VALUE—Light green or grayish leaves, or those with lighter undersides, or medium green leaves widely spaced, or small leaves on plants open in habit, give the appearance of lightness needed for contrast or an illusion of distance.

NAME	HEIGHT	HABIT	LEAF COLOR	PLACE TO USE
Amelanchier laevis ALLEGHENY SERVICEBERRY	15′	Oval	Light green	Distant borders.
Betula pendula EUROPEAN WHITE BIRCH	30′	Vase-shaped tree	Light green	Accents in woodland setting. Specimen.
Cytisus scoparius SCOTCH BROOM	8′	Sprawling	Light green	Seashore.
Euonymus alatus WINGED EUONYMUS	10′	Picturesque	Green	Specimen, accent near house or garden.
Halesia carolina SILVERBELL	20′	Picturesque tree	Gray green	Long borders near or distant. Specimen.

LIST No. 6—Continued

NAME	HEIGHT	HABIT	LEAF COLOR	PLACE TO USE
Juniperus virginiana canaerti CANAERTS CEDAR	15'	Columnar	Gray green	Accent, nearby borders.
Kolkwitzia amabilis BEAUTYBUSH	8'	Oval	Gray green underneath	Nearby borders.
Lonicera korolkowi BLUELEAF HONEYSUCKLE	10'	Oval	Blue green	Nearby borders.
Magnolia stellata STAR MAGNOLIA	12'	Picturesque spreading	Gray green	Specimen, fragrant.
Malus sargenti SARGENT CRABAPPLE	8'	Picturesque	Medium green	Specimen. Foreground.
Rosa hugonis FATHER HUGO ROSE	6'	Arching	Light green	Near garden or house.
Styrax japonica JAPANESE SNOWBELL	20'	Open, picturesque tree	Light green	Specimen or accent.

See also the list of shrubs of fine texture, Chapter III.

FOLIAGE TEXTURE

FINE TEXTURE—Feathery and light in effect. The leaves are usually small, the habit of the shrub often open or picturesque. They are useful for contrast with bold, coarse foliage or for gaining an illusion of distance. They usually tell as light in value.

Name	Height	Character of Foliage	Place to Use
Acanthopanax sieboldianus FIVE-LEAVED ARALIA	8'	Dark green, glossy	Half shade, distant borders, banks.
Amelanchier canadensis SHADBLOW	20'	Light green	Distant borders or native planting.
Baccharis halimifolia GROUNDSELBUSH	8'	Gray green	Seashore.
Cotoneaster dielsiana DIELS COTONEASTER	6'	Dark green above gray below	Cultivated, nearby.
Daphne somerset GARLAND SHRUB	4'	Medium green, very narrow	Garden.
Eleagnus angustifolia RUSSIAN OLIVE	15'	Gray green	Screen, distance, seashore.

List No. 7—Continued

Name	Height	Character of Foliage	Place to Use
Exochorda racemosa PEARLBUSH	10'	Gray	Garden or nearby border.
Laburnum vulgare watereri WATERER GOLDENCHAIN TREE	20'	Light green, small	Specimen, accent, nearby border.
Nandina domestica HEAVENLY BAMBOO	6'	Green, lighter underneath	Nearby, for angular accent.
Robinia hispida ROSEACACIA LOCUST	6'	Blue green, compound	Distance, uncultivated mass planting.
Rosa hugonis FATHER HUGO ROSE	6'	Green, feathery	Nearby border or garden.
Sorbus aucuparia EUROPEAN MOUNTAINASH	30'	Medium green, compound	Accent, wild or cultivated border.
Stephanandra incisa CUTLEAF STEPHANANDRA	4'	Light green, delicate	Foreground, nearby.
Styrax japonica JAPANESE SNOWBELL	20'	Light green	Accent, nearby border.
Syringa persica PERSIAN LILAC	8'	Medium green	Garden, nearby border.

FOLIAGE TEXTURE

BOLD TEXTURE—The shrubs of bold texture usually have rather coarse, heavy leaves, dark in color, on large plants of open or picturesque habit. They are useful for contrast, for accenting points and making strong masses. Most of them also have large flowers and are dark in over-all value.

Name	Height	Flower Color	Place to Use
Aesculus parviflora BOTTLEBRUSH BUCKEYE	10′ spread	Pink	Specimen or accent.
Calycanthus floridus SWEETSHRUB	6′	Maroon	Half-shade, nearby borders.
Chionanthus virginicus WHITE FRINGETREE	20′	White	Accent, nearby borders, specimen.
Clerodendron trichotomum HARLEQUIN GLORYBOWER	6′	Pink and bronze	Distant border.
Cotinus coggygria SMOKETREE	12′	Cream	Near house or garden, accent, specimen.

Name	Height	Flower Color	Place to Use
Magnolia soulangeana SAUCER MAGNOLIA	25′	Pink and white	Accent or nearby border.
Magnolia tripetala UMBRELLA MAGNOLIA	30′	White	Accent, specimen, at distance.
Magnolia virginiana SWEETBAY MAGNOLIA	20′	White	Accent, at distance, nearby border.
Rhododendron maximum ROSEBAY RHODODENDRON	12′	Pink and white	Shade, middle distance, native woodland. In acid soil.
Rosa rugosa RUGOSA ROSE	5′	White to red	Seashore.
Syringa amurensis japonica JAPANESE TREE LILAC	20′	Cream	Accents, specimen, nearby border.
Viburnum sieboldi SIEBOLD VIBURNUM	12′	Cream	Large borders, or accents.

Richard Averill Smith

III. The golden bells of forsythia in a thickly planted border contrast with the unfolding yellow-green leaves of the trees behind. The narcissus in the foreground repeats the yellow of the shrubs for a gay spring picture.

Gottscho-Schleisner

IV. In late spring the horizontal branches of double-file viburnum
are a bold and handsome picture against the dark green of cedar.
The finer foliage and delicate flowers of enkianthus make a
group equally interesting close at hand.

CHAPTER IV

Shrubs in Flower

BLOSSOM TIME is the dressed-up period of the shrubs' year. Many of them are Cinderellas—they are inconspicuous for most of the year. Suddenly transformed by a mantle of beautiful color for two or three weeks, they sink back into obscurity to burst out again a year later. Others, beautiful in themselves throughout the year, are so ornamented that they are breath-taking for a short period. To take advantage of this transformation we must know when it takes place in a normal year, what color the dress is and its general effect in the landscape. Otherwise we may find that we have two colors together that clash, or at least do not add to each other's beauty, or that some shrub with very interesting but subtle flower is so far away we cannot even tell it has bloomed.

It is fun to keep a record of the time of bloom of the plants in your immediate neighborhood year after year. A five-year line-a-day diary is useful for this purpose as all you need to do is to write down the opening date, or the full bloom date of each thing as it comes along. Looking over my own I find, for instance, that the lilacs and apples were in full bloom on dates from April twenty-ninth to May twenty-fourth in the past ten years, but the average full bloom falls around the tenth to the fifteenth of May. A record over the period of a few years gives a very definite idea of the succession of bloom.

If yours is a week-end place in the north, you know that the shadbush blooms one week-end, the cherries the next, then the azaleas, the apples, and lilacs and dogwood, and finally the hawthorn. Of course nature may throw your calculations completely off as she did in the spring of 1945, in some sections of the country. In one great fairyland of bloom all the cherries, peaches, apples, crabapples, hawthorns, dogwoods, and lilacs flowered together for about ten days, early in May. The outdoors was almost like living in a florist shop. The unfortunate part of it was that it was so short that instead of having six weeks of successive bloom it all came in one great burst, too overwhelming to really appreciate the individual. If planting is not planned properly this same tremendous burst may occur every year because all the shrubs are the mid-May blossoming type, instead of flowering in succession from March through September giving time to appreciate each one.

In the southern sections of the country there are some shrubs in bloom every month of the year, and the effects that can be had from shrubs alone are almost incredible. One small place in Florida has no perennials or annuals whatsoever, except some hybrid hemerocallis on the edge of shrub borders, yet it is truly a flowering garden twelve months of the year and the house has cut flowers in it all of the time. We cannot do quite that well in the north and probably few of us would want to do without some of our more beloved annuals and perennials. But we can surely get a far greater effect than we do, by close study of the shrubs' flowering season and type and color of blossoms.

The general effect of a shrub in bloom varies considerably. Some of them, particularly those that flower before their leaves come out, seem like a solid sheet of color over the entire shrub. The forsythia, the early azaleas, *Azalea mucronulata, Azalea vaseyi*, the redbud, *Cercis canadensis*, the early flowering cherries, are a strong mass of color. On the other hand, shrubs which have their leaves fully formed before blooming are a little less conspicuous. Their beauty is in the contrast of their delicate pinks, whites, yellows, blues, with the green of their foliage and even though flowers are numerous, they are less of a solid sheet of color.

Still another type has relatively few blossoms in proportion to the entire mass of the shrub but the individual flowers are of very interesting form and subtle coloring so that they should be seen close at hand to be appreciated. The beautiful gordonia, *Franklinia alatamaha*, formerly native to the south and now introduced as far north as New York City, is an excellent example. Many of the magnolias have the same characteristics. The less familiar but beautiful stewartia is most delightful in flower but at any distance one hardly knows that it has blossoms.

The true color of the blossom of a shrub is important in making pictures. To say that most of the native azaleas, such as *arborescens, nudiflora, vaseyi, rosea*, are pink is just as accurate a description as saying that roses of certain varieties are pink. There are rose pinks and salmon pinks and to know which they are is important. *Vaseyi* is definitely a yellowish pink, *rosea* is a rosy pink, *arborescens* is pink and white so it registers as almost blush. In the yellows certain of the forsythias are a strong golden yellow, others are a pale yellow.

Viewing the shrubs in blossom time is important, in order to really make your own gradations of color. To dismiss lilacs as all purple or white is to miss an opportunity of making a most subtle and beautiful arrangement of colors outdoors, with this very common but much beloved shrub. They vary from very large snowy white to very dark almost black purple, through all the shades of pink-lavender, blue-lavender and reddish purple. Pink dogwood may be all pink but there is a great difference between the soft shell pink of certain specimens and the raw, almost watermelon pink of others. Part of this may be due to soil conditions but if you are planning to put in a pink dogwood it may be well to observe it the previous spring in the nursery to see what color its blossoms really are. It will probably not change too much when it gets to your own grounds.

Printed descriptions will help some in determining the general color of shrub flowers but no two people ever seem to see color exactly alike. My own notes of color combinations mean a great deal to me and make the kind of pink or the kind of yellow perfectly clear, but they would probably be of much less help to anyone else without considerable explanation. It is only through personal appreciation of subtle blends of color, subtle gradations in the same color, that interesting combinations can be made. First-hand observation is the best way of training this feeling for color and it is all important in using shrubs to their full advantage.

Aside from the amount of bloom on the shrub and the color of it, the general texture of the flower mass is interesting. Certain shrubs like the shadbush, the spireas, have small flowers but a multitude of them so that the effect is a feathery mass. Others like the Japanese snowball, the hydrangea, the camellias, the magnolias, have individual flowers of considerable size, so that the effect in bloom is bolder and stronger. Most of these individual flowered shrubs also have fairly large leaves, so that the whole mass of the bush is strong and bold. These are the handsome shrubs rather than the pretty ones.

Flowering shrubs should be used in exactly the same way that perennial and annual flowers are used to make garden pictures. Many gardeners know the satisfaction that comes from putting Madonna lilies and delphiniums together, to use a familiar example, or purple petunias and pink zinnias. It is perfectly possible and most satisfactory to make the same sort of bouquets out-of-doors on a much larger scale by combining shrub blooms so that they enhance each other and make outdoor flower arrangements in the landscape. It is important, however, to use the same care outdoors that we do indoors to give them a proper background. Inside we try to use flowers that bring out the color scheme of our room. Outdoors we ignore the general landscape all too often and make flower combinations with shrubs that fail of complete satisfaction because their background is bad.

If you have large Norway maples in the yard near your home or if the street trees are Norways, their greenish yellow bloom in the early spring is bound to be dominant. The yellows and whites of early spring bloom but none of the rose pinks or reds belong with them. The forsythias all look well in the same eye-full with the white of the early spireas, *Prunus tomentosa*, the early white cherry like *Prunus subhirtella* (it is such a pale blush that at a very little distance it looks like white), the white flowering almond, *Prunus amygdalus albo-plena*. If on the other hand, the maples are the swamp or red maple, *Acer rubrum*, forsythia swears at it and should never be in the same composition. Here is the setting for the shell pink of *Azalea vaseyi*, the pink flowering almond, *Prunus amygdalus roseoplena*, all of the whites, the pale pink and white cherries, with the strong yellows and oranges left out of the picture.

If you have a large copper beech, or a hedge of copper beech, whose tone in the early spring is a definitely reddish brown, it is a perfect place for the pale yellows, the orange and copper colors, but not for paler pinks which only look dirty in comparison with it. Nature has her own definite color scheme at every time of the year and the best we can do is to work with it, not against it. That is the reason that early flowering shrubs in magenta or rosy purple tones are much harder to use than they would be if they bloomed in midsummer when leaves are mostly dark green. The spring overall color is yellow green, and the rosy purple, unless skillfully used, is likely to look foreign and clash in the landscape. If it is used, it must be kept away from strong yellows and have nothing but the soft green of the opening trees and some white near it. Some of the daphnes, the magenta azaleas, the red-bud, all beautiful in themselves, are likely to look raw and obtrusive in the general color effect of early spring. It is better to trust to pure, clear colors for general use at a season when the world seems particularly fresh and clear in color.

Our own man-made background of houses, of fences or

walls, can make a great difference in the color schemes that
are beautiful. Near a white house almost any color shows up
to advantage except white. If the house, on the other hand,
is a red brick, almost all the yellows, the reds, pinks and rosy
purples look very ugly indeed. If they are used at all on the
grounds, they should be where you do not see the house behind them from any point of view. Sometimes even your own
house may not be as important as a neighboring house or
apartment. If there is a red brick building beyond your property line, you should not plant redbud, *Azalea hinodegiri*, or
any other rosy purple one, forsythia or other strong yellows
and oranges, so that you see them with the house behind. Of
course, if you are completely surrounded with red brick, the
only thing you can do with plants of these colors is to put a
strong green foliage mass behind them so that you see them
against the green rather than against the red. The same principle applies, of course, to fences or walls of difficult colors.
If your neighbor has a red brick wall on the property line you
must either resign yourself to having no reds, pinks, yellows
or oranges in front of it, or get permission to paint your side
of it white. Fences of lattice or boards, whether white or
weathered to a soft gray or brown, are an excellent foil for almost any color. A weathered gray fence with roses and hybrid
trumpet vines of apricot color climbing over it and flame-
yellow azaleas at the base, with here and there an interruption
of tall white lilac, is a lovely sight all spring and summer. The
same combination against red brick would set anyone's teeth
on edge. Against the brick only pure white is safe, and is,
indeed, most effective.

In planning flower combinations on the grounds it is important not to arrange them so that they give a polka dot
effect. This is particularly true with the earliest blooming
things of strong color mass, like forsythia, flowering quince
and some of the azaleas. They stand out so conspicuously in
the landscape that if they are used injudiciously they have an
unpleasant spottiness. Instead of admiring their general color

scheme in the landscape, you find your eye leaping from one to the other and almost counting them one—two—three. It is better to concentrate one flowering combination in one place than to repeat it or parts of it all over the visible landscape, making the whole thing restless and disjointed.

On the other hand, with some of the light feathery things, like shadbush or witchhazel and benzoin of our native plants, their general mass is so light and delicate that you can work them in here and there all through the planting. Of the cultivated shrubs, pearlbush and silverbell are the same type. It is very pleasant to see their mist of white in all directions. White dogwood, although it is a much bolder flower and a handsome tree, blends so well into the landscape that it can be used in great profusion, particularly if the property is big enough so that the distant views have the snow of the white dogwood in their composition. If the feathery rose of redbud is used with it, everyone familiar with the woodlands of Indiana knows how incredibly beautiful the wood's edge can be in May.

Everyone who has used shrubs for flowering combinations has his own pet two or three and every part of the country can make different ones. The same principles apply as in perennial color arrangements, that is, yellow, white and blue look well together. Strong yellow and strong pink should never be in the same picture. Different shades of yellow and yellow orange look well with the yellow green of opening leaves. Red looks best with white and with dark green as a background. Rose pink and yellow pink should not be used together and either one is improved by some use of white near it. A dark green background is excellent for the oranges and yellows or for a cool picture in hot weather as a foil for white. With all these ideas in mind here are some of my own proven combinations that are as lovely as any perennials in the garden.

SHRUBS WITH WHITE FLOWERS

IN ORDER OF THEIR BLOOM

NAME	HEIGHT	HABIT	WHERE TO USE
Magnolia stellata STAR MAGNOLIA	12'	Picturesque oval	Specimen, nearby.
Prunus tomentosa MANCHU CHERRY	6'	Mound	Distant border.
Prunus sargenti SARGENT CHERRY	30'	Upright	Specimen, nearby.
Magnolia soulangeana alba WHITE SAUCER MAGNOLIA	20'	Upright	Specimen, accent nearby.
Prunus shirotae (Mt. Fuji) WHITE FLOWERING CHERRY	20'	Upright	Specimen, accent nearby.
Amelanchier canadensis SHADBLOW	20'	Vase-shaped	Large distant border.
Spiraea arguta GARLAND SPIREA	6'	Oval	Cultivated border.
Spiraea thunbergi THUNBERG SPIREA	6'	Oval	Cultivated border.

Spiraea prunifolia BRIDALWREATH SPIREA	8'	Oval	Cultivated border.
Halesia carolina SILVERBELL	20'	Picturesque tree	Large borders.
Cornus florida FLOWERING DOGWOOD	25'	Picturesque	Accent, specimen in near or distant border.
Exochorda racemosa PEARLBUSH	10'	Oval	Cultivated border nearby.
Syringa vulgaris alba WHITE COMMON LILAC	12'	Oval	Near house or garden.
Syringa persica alba WHITE PERSIAN LILAC	8'	Oval	Near house or garden.
Spiraea vanhouttei VANHOUTTE SPIREA	8'	Arching	Nearby border.
Viburnum tomentosum DOUBLEFILE VIBURNUM	8'	Picturesque	Accent in nearby border.
Weigela wagneri candida WHITE WEIGELA	10'	Oval	Cultivated border.
Deutzia in variety DEUTZIA	3–6'	Oval, twiggy	Front of garden border.
Azalea indica alba WHITE INDICA AZALEA	5×8'	Mound	Shady cultivated planting, garden.

List No. 9—Continued

Name	Height	Habit	Where to Use
Chionanthus virginicus WHITE FRINGETREE	20'	Picturesque tree	Specimen or nearby border.
Rhododendron album elegans WHITE RHODODENDRON	8'	Compact oval	Shady border.
Cornus kousa CHINESE DOGWOOD	20'	Symmetrical tree	Specimen, accent in large border.
Rhododendron carolinianum album WHITE CAROLINA RHODODENDRON	5'	Round	Shady cultivated planting, garden.
Magnolia virginiana SWEETBAY	20'	Open, oval	Large borders.
Philadelphus in variety MOCKORANGE	4–10'	Oval	Nearby borders, cultivated distant borders.
Azalea viscosa SWAMP AZALEA	8'	Picturesque	Lowland, woodland borders, nearby.
Stewartia pseudocamellia JAPANESE STEWARTIA	25'	Neat, upright	Specimen, near house or garden.
Hibiscus syriacus Jeanne d'Arc WHITE ROSE OF SHARON	8'	Upright	Near garden.
Franklinia alatamaha GORDONIA	15'	Handsome bold	Specimen, near house or garden.

SHRUBS WITH YELLOW FLOWERS

IN ORDER OF THEIR BLOOM

NAME	HEIGHT	HABIT	WHERE TO USE
Hamamelis japonica JAPANESE WITCHHAZEL	12'	Picturesque	Large border, distance.
Cornus mas CORNELIAN CHERRY	15'	Large mound	Large border, distance.
Lindera benzoin SPICEBUSH	15'	Tall oval	Native planting, low land.
Forsythia in variety GOLDEN BELLS	8'	Vase fountain	Cultivated border, distant.
Ribes aureum GOLDEN CURRANT	5'	Mound	Nearby for fragrance.
Cytisus in variety BROOM	8'	Sprawling	Seashore, distant border.
Caragana arborescens SIBERIAN PEASHRUB	12'	Vase-shaped	Long border, distance.

List No. 10—Continued

Name	Height	Habit	Where to Use
Azalea obtusa kaempferi TORCH AZALEA	3'	Picturesque	Half-shade, near house or garden.
Azalea mollis CHINESE AZALEA	6'	Picturesque	Half-shade, near house or garden.
Rosa primula PRIMROSE ROSE	6'	Arching, broad oval	Near house or garden.
Rosa hugonis FATHER HUGO ROSE	6'	Arching, broad oval	Near house or garden.
Rosa harisoni HARISON YELLOW ROSE	4'	Tall oval	Near house or garden
Laburnum vulgare watereri WATERER GOLDENCHAIN TREE	20'	Vase-shaped tree	Accent, specimen nearby border.
Azalea calendulaceae FLAME AZALEA	8'	Picturesque oval	Half-shade, near house or garden.
Hypericum moserianum GOLDFLOWER	2'	Neat mound spreading	Garden.
Koelreuteria paniculata GOLDENRAINTREE	30'	Picturesque tree	Specimen.
Hamamelis virginiana COMMON WITCHHAZEL	15'	Picturesque	Large borders nearby or distant.

SHRUBS WITH BLUE OR LAVENDER FLOWERS

IN ORDER OF THEIR BLOOM

NAME	HEIGHT	HABIT	WHERE TO USE
Syringa in variety LILACS	to 20'	Tall cone or oval	Near house or garden, nearby borders.
Hydrangea macrophylla coerulea BIGLEAF BLUE HYDRANGEA	6'	Mound	Garden.
Hibiscus syriacus coelestis BLUE ROSE OF SHARON	8'	Upright	Near house or garden, nearby borders.
Buddleia in variety BUTTERFLYBUSH	7'	Vase-shaped	Garden.
Vitex agnuscastus HARDY CHASTETREE	8'	Tall oval	Garden, nearby borders.
Caryopteris incana BLUEBEARD	3'	Round	Garden.

SHRUBS WITH PINK FLOWERS

IN ORDER OF THEIR BLOOM

NAME	HEIGHT	HABIT	WHERE TO PLANT
Prunus subhirtella in variety HIGAN CHERRY	20′	Spreading tree	Specimen, lawn.
Prunus serrulata in variety ORIENTAL CHERRY	30′	Upright	Specimen, lawn.
Daphne somerset GARLAND SHRUB	4′	Upright mound	Near house in garden.
Viburnum carlesi KOREANSPICE VIBURNUM	6′	Neat, open	For fragrance.
Azalea vaseyi PINKSHELL AZALEA	8′	Picturesque	Half-shade against evergreens.
Malus halliana parkmani PARKMAN CRABAPPLE	12′	Vase-shaped, broad head	Specimen.

Name	Height	Form	Use
Malus spectabilis CHINESE FLOWERING CRABAPPLE	25'	Vase-shaped, upright tree	Specimen.
Cornus florida rubra RED FLOWERING DOGWOOD	25'	Picturesque tree	Specimen.
Robinia hispida ROSEACACIA LOCUST	6'	Spreading	Poor soil, banks.
Lonicera korolkowi BLUELEAF HONEYSUCKLE	10'	Oval	Nearby border.
Weigela florida OLD-FASHIONED WEIGELA	10'	Awkward, oval	Garden border.
Crataegus oxyacantha rosea PINK ENGLISH HAWTHORN	25'	Vase-shaped tree	Specimen.
Malus ioensis bechteli BECHTEL CRABAPPLE	25'	Like apple tree	Specimen.
Kolkwitzia amabilis BEAUTYBUSH	8'	Oval	Garden border.
Abelia grandiflora GLOSSY ABELIA	4'	Broad oval	Near house or garden.
Hibiscus syriacus in variety ROSE OF SHARON	12'	Narrow, upright	Garden border.

List No. 13

SHRUBS WITH ROSY AND PURPLE-PINK FLOWERS

IN ORDER OF THEIR BLOOM

Name	Height	Habit	Where to Plant
Azalea canadense RHODORA	3′	Round	Native planting, half shade.
Azalea mucronulatum MAGNOLIA AZALEA	6′	Spreading oval	With evergreens.
Daphne mezereum FEBRUARY DAPHNE	4′	Round	Against evergreens.
Magnolia soulangeana lenni PURPLE SAUCER MAGNOLIA	20′	Bold, free	Specimen.
Azalea obtusa hinodegiri KURUME AZALEA	3×5′	Mound	Specimen, filtered sunlight.
Cercis canadensis REDBUD	25′	Picturesque tree	Edge of woodland.

Malus eleyi ELEY CRABAPPLE	18′	Narrow tree	Specimen, bad color.
Malus niedzwetskyana RUSSIAN CRABAPPLE	25′	Narrow tree	Specimen, bad color.
Malus hopa HOPA CRABAPPLE	30′	Narrow tree	Specimen, bad color.
Malus atrosanguinea CARMINE CRABAPPLE	14′	Broad headed tree	Specimen, nice color.
Crataegus oxyacantha pauli PAULS SCARLET HAWTHORN	20′	Picturesque tree	Specimen.
Rhododendron minus PIEDMONT RHODODENDRON	8′	Loose mound	Half-shade, foreground of distant border.
Rhododendron arbutifolium ROCKMOUNT RHODODENDRON	4′	Low spreading	Half-shade, foreground of distant border.
Rhododendron catawbiense CATAWBA RHODODENDRON	6′	Spreading	Half-shade, distant border.
Spiraea bumalda Anthony Waterer PINK SPIREA	3′	Twiggy oval	Low hedge, magenta.
Rosa rugosa RUGOSA ROSE	5′	Upright	Seashore, hedge.

FLOWERING CRABAPPLES

IN ORDER OF THEIR BLOOM

Early May to late May in latitude of New York City

NAME	HEIGHT	HABIT	COLOR
Malus baccata SIBERIAN CRABAPPLE	20′	Compact, narrow	White.
Malus arnoldiana ARNOLD CRABAPPLE	15′	Spreading tree	Light rose to white.
Malus floribunda JAPANESE FLOWERING CRABAPPLE	20′	Spreading tree	Rose-red to white.
Malus halliana parkmani PARKMAN CRABAPPLE	12′	Vase-shaped, broad head	Rose-red.
Malus atrosanguinea CARMINE CRABAPPLE	14′	Broad head	Rose, non-fading.

Malus spectabilis CHINESE CRABAPPLE	25–30'	Upright, vase-shaped	Pale pink, coral bud.
* *Malus coronaria* WILD SWEET CRABAPPLE	20'	Spreading tree	Deep pink, non-fading.
Malus hupehensis TEA CRABAPPLE	20'	Broad tree	Blush white.
* *Malus ioensis bechteli* BECHTEL CRABAPPLE	25'	Like apple tree	Blush pink.
Malus sargenti SARGENT CRABAPPLE	8'	Picturesque	Coral bud.
Malus scheideckeri SCHEIDECKER CRABAPPLE	15'	Vase-shaped	Pale pink.
Malus spectabilis riversi RIVERS CRABAPPLE	25–30'	Vase-shaped	Pale pink, coral bud.
Malus toringoides CUTLEAF CRABAPPLE	18'	Narrow	White.

* Subject to cedar rust. Do not plant in vicinity of *Juniperus virginiana*.

FLOWERING CHERRIES, PLUMS AND PEACHES

IN ORDER OF THEIR BLOOM

Late April to mid-May in latitude of New York City

NAME	HEIGHT	HABIT	COLOR
Prunus sargenti SARGENT CHERRY	30'	Upright	Pink, single.
Prunus subhirtella Beni Higan HIGAN CHERRY	15'	Spreading	Blush, single.
Prunus triloba FLOWERING PLUM	10'	Spreading	Blush, double.
Prunus yedoensis YOSHINO CHERRY	20×20'	Spreading	Pink, single.
Prunus serrulata yedo zakura JAPANESE FLOWERING CHERRY	20'	Spreading	Light pink, double.

Prunus fugenzo (Kofugen) JAPANESE FLOWERING CHERRY	15′	Vase-shaped	Rose, double.
Prunus kwansan JAPANESE FLOWERING CHERRY	18′	Narrow tree	Deep pink.
Prunus takasago (Naden) JAPANESE FLOWERING CHERRY	20′	Vase-shaped	Pink to rose.
Prunus shirofugen JAPANESE FLOWERING CHERRY	20′	Spreading	Blush.
Prunus shirotae (Mt. Fuji) JAPANESE FLOWERING CHERRY	20′	Upright	White.
Prunus amanogawa JAPANESE FLOWERING CHERRY	12′	Columnar	Pink.
Prunus persica in variety FLOWERING PEACH	20′	Vase-shaped	Pink or white.

SHRUBS IN FLOWER

COMBINATIONS FOR BLOOM (season as of New York City)

APRIL

Name	Height	Color	Where to Plant
Forsythia intermedia spectabilis SHOWY FORSYTHIA	8'	Golden yellow	Nearby border as bold color accent, full sun.
Magnolia stellata STAR MAGNOLIA	12'	White	
Forsythia suspensa fortunei FORTUNE FORSYTHIA	8'	Canary yellow, bold	Distant cultivated border, for blossom mass, un-interesting foliage, full sun.
Spiraea thunbergi THUNBERG SPIREA	6'	Feathery white	
Lindera benzoin SPICEBUSH In front of	15'	Pale yellow	Native planting, edge of damp woodland.
Larix leptolepis JAPANESE LARCH	50'	Orange and yellow green	

Amelanchier canadensis SHADBLOW	20'	Feathery white	Native or nearby planting. Full sun.
Juniperus virginiana RED CEDAR	30'	Medium green	
Cornus mas CORNELIAN CHERRY	15'	Light yellow	Nearby, bold mass, light shade.
Ilex opaca AMERICAN HOLLY	20'	Dark green	
Chaenomeles japonica FLOWERING QUINCE	6'	Bright red	Nearby, full sun.
Prunus tomentosa MANCHU CHERRY	6'	White	
MAY			
Viburnum carlesi KOREANSPICE VIBURNUM	6'	Pink and white	Near the house or garden. Sun.
Daphne somerset GARLAND SHRUB	4'	Pink	
Pieris japonica JAPANESE ADROMEDA	5'	Cream	
Prunus subhirtella HIGAN CHERRY	20'	Blush	

List No. 16—Continued

Name	Height	Color	Where to Plant
Azalea vaseyi PINKSHELL AZALEA	8'	Pink	Nearby border.
Leucothoe catesbaei DROOPING LEUCOTHOE	4×5'	Green	
Syringa persica PERSIAN LILAC	8'	Lavender	Nearby, sun.
Rosa hugonis FATHER HUGO ROSE	6'	Primrose	
Azalea rosea ROSESHELL AZALEA	6'	Pink	Nearby, half shade.
Rhododendron carolinianum CAROLINA RHODODENDRON	5'	Pink	
Syringa macrostachya PINK LILAC	15'	Pink	Nearby, sun.
Syringa Ludwig Spaeth DARK PURPLE LILAC	15'	Purple	
Malus ioensis bechteli BECHTEL CRABAPPLE	25'	Pink	

Name	Height	Color	Location
Cornus florida rubra RED FLOWERING DOGWOOD	25′	Pink	Nearby, sun.
Syringa congo DARK PURPLE LILAC	15′	Purple	
Spiraea vanhouttei VANHOUTTE SPIREA	8′	White	
Halesia carolina SILVERBELL	20′	White	Cultivated distant or nearby border.
Cercis canadensis REDBUD	25′	Rose-red	

JUNE

Name	Height	Color	Location
Viburnum tomentosum DOUBLEFILE VIBURNUM	8′	White	Garden border.
Lonicera korolkowi BLUELEAF HONEYSUCKLE	10′	Rose	
Cornus kousa CHINESE DOGWOOD	20′	White	Edge of woodland planting, nearby or distant.
Azalea arborescens SMOOTH AZALEA	5′	Pink and white	
Rhododendron maximum ROSEBAY RHODODENDRON	12′	Rose, spotted green	

Name	Height	Color	Where to Plant
Philadelphus lemoinei LEMOINE MOCKORANGE	4'	White	Garden border.
Philadelphus lemoinei Mont Blanc MT. BLANC MOCKORANGE	4'	White	
Kolkwitzia amabilis BEAUTYBUSH	8'	Pink, yellow throat	
Rhododendron album elegans WHITE RHODODENDRON	8'	White	Half-shade or edge of woodland.
Azalea calendulaceae FLAME AZALEA	8'	Orange-yellow to scarlet	
Chionanthus virginicus WHITE FRINGETREE	20'	White	Large, sunny border.
Rosa multiflora JAPANESE ROSE	10' spread	White	
JULY AND AUGUST			
Rosa setigera PRAIRIE ROSE	15' spread	Bright pink	Near the house or garden.
Stewartia ovata MOUNTAIN STEWARTIA	15'	White	

Hibiscus syriacus roseus PINK ROSE OF SHARON	12′	Pink	In or near flower garden or near house walls.
Buddleia davidi Peace BUTTERFLYBUSH	8′	White	
Abelia grandiflora GLOSSY ABELIA	4′	White, flushed pink	
Hibiscus syriacus Jeanne d'Arc WHITE ROSE OF SHARON	12′	White	Near garden or house.
Hydrangea macrophylla coerulea BIGLEAF BLUE HYDRANGEA	8′	Blue lilac	Near garden or house.
Vitex agnuscastus HARDY CHASTETREE	7′	Lilac blue	In garden or for mid-summer border.
Clerodendron trichotomum HARLEQUIN GLORYBOWER	6′	White	Near garden.
Hypericum moserianum GOLDFLOWER	2′	Yellow	In flower garden or near house.
Caryopteris incana BLUEBEARD	3′	Lavender blue	Terrace.

CHAPTER V

Shrubs in Fall Color

HEADING NORTH in October is almost as urgent as getting out-doors the first warm spring days, wherever we live. The blazing color of the world in the northern parts of the country is something that once seen can never be forgotten. The reasoning of a small friend of mine in Minnesota expresses the feeling—since the winter was going to be so deathly cold, nature needed to warm it up with the color of fire before the leaves fall. It may be unscientific but it is perhaps as satisfactory as any other explanation. Many of us have for years taken a certain drive or a certain trip in the fall for the sheer pleasure of a particularly lovely spot of color along a roadside or a view of a brilliant world from the top of a high hill.

Too often this appreciation of the fall colors does not lead us to use it closer at home, so that we can enjoy its beauty without going out of our own house. The relatively short period of greatest brilliance is, of course, from foliage color. Certain parts of the country have very few shrubs that do turn color in the fall. Almost everywhere, however, there are some seasonal changes and there are always shrubs whose fruit is colorful. To know them and to use them wisely is to extend the garden season through another period.

In the northern climates where the color is most beautiful the big display is from the trees. In the lowlands early in the fall months the sweetgum, *Liquidambar styraciflua*, and sour-gum, *Nyssa sylvatica*, blaze with red and yellow. The elms turn only yellow and not a very clear one at that. The swamp maples are a blaze of red, the sugar maples red and gold. The oaks pick up the color scheme in the brilliant scarlet of the scarlet oak through to the dark red of the white and red oak. Here and there through the countryside the clear gold of the ash and the hickory and the green of the beeches still holding their leaves makes an unforgettable picture. Although the trees are the big show there are still many shrubs that carry on the effect and whose more frequent use is all important to those of us who like October best of any month in the year.

The first thing to notice about almost all of the shrubs is that they develop their full color only in good sunlight. If two identical shrubs are planted, one under shade and the other in full sun, the one in sun will color brilliantly while its sister shrub has only a tinge of color before its leaves fall. To avoid disappointment be sure you plant your own shrubs in the same kind of location that you saw them in originally or you will be badly disappointed. Only last fall I noticed a very good example of this. On the open lawn of a little church on Long Island is one of the finest and biggest burning bushes, *Euonymus alatus*, I have ever seen. For three or four weeks it was so brilliant that people stopped their cars along the street to look at it. It was almost a rosy red with tinges of bright scarlet here and there on the leaves. Just across the street were two others which had been planted at about the same time but were in the shade of a big privet hedge and an old ginko tree. The sun hit them only for two or three hours a day and they were green up to the time the leaves fell with only a tinge of color on the edges, as if they were trying to turn their right color but could not quite make it.

The colors we look for the most in the fall are certainly the flaming scarlet and gold which the maples and oaks represent in the larger trees. For this color there is nothing finer than the native blueberry. Aside from the interesting flower and the delicious fruit, I know of no better reason for planting the highbush blueberry on the home grounds than to see its flaming color in autumn. As a ground cover, the low bush blueberry is equally beautiful and the sight of a rolling hillside covered with the gold and red of these low bushes is worth a trip to the blueberry country or some nearby spot where you have picked blueberries in the summer but may have forgotten later.

Other shrubs with this same brilliance are the sourwood, *Oxydendron arboreum*, enkianthus, flowering dogwood and smoke bush. The black haw, whether the southern variety, *Viburnum rufidulum*, or the northern kind, *Viburnum prunifolium*, turn brilliant scarlet in the fall and stand out in any landscape.

There are a few shrubs which turn yellow in the fall but it is not the clear gold of the ash and hickories in the trees. The shrubs, also, count for comparatively little in the general color scheme. There is a much larger group that turn russet and purplish red in the fall to give the deeper tone which the oaks give in the skyline. Most of the viburnum family are in this group and some of the dogwoods. Among the cultivated shrubs, the lilac has a slightly purplish tone, the forsythia is russet and purple and the Japanese barberry is bronzy-red in leaf color.

Most of our commonest ornamental shrubs unfortunately to do not color appreciably in the fall. The weigelas, deutzia, syringas, spireas remain green or a rather dirty yellow and green until their leaves fall. While this green cast is needed to offset the brilliance of the other shrubs, it adds very little in itself to the whole color scheme—another very good reason for not limiting the planting entirely to the shrubs whose blossoms are most conspicuous. I have fancied sometimes that there is a connection in the fact that the shrubs which flower the most heavily and are the easiest to grow for their flowers, like the ones mentioned above, seem to exhaust themselves and not have enough energy left to turn brilliant in the fall. Perhaps one season of surpassing conspicuousness is enough for most plants.

This fanciful theory seems to be borne out also by the fact that some of the shrubs most beautiful in fruit are those whose flowers are so inconspicuous we hardly know they have flowered until they suddenly blaze out in the fall with brilliant berries all over them. Here again, one kind of beauty seems to be enough, for even in the fall the ones with brilliant red and yellow fruits usually have rather dull foliage, as if to show off by contrast and display the color of the fruit against the dull leaves.

Some of the best of the fruiting shrubs again are in the viburnum family. The highbush cranberry, *Viburnum opulus*, the doublefile viburnum, *Viburnum tomentosum*, and the linden viburnum, *Viburnum dilatatum*, all have brilliant red fruit, but with the exception of the doublefile viburnum, the flowers are quite inconspicuous. Unless you are watching for them you hardly know they are there.

In the dogwood family the little gray dogwood, *Cornus racemosa*, familiar in the hedgerows, has white fruit on bright red stems so that it gives a very interesting color combination as you drive along the country lanes. The flowering dogwood in an unusually heavy fruiting year is brilliantly red with berries, and its close relative, the Chinese flowering dogwood, has fruit all over it that looks almost like tiny red apples. The spicebush has small red fruit which is so attractive to the birds that we really have to keep our eyes open to see it at all. Many of the flowering crabapples are ablaze in the fall landscape with their brilliant fruit. Some are red and some are yellow and they vary in size from the pea size fruit of the *Malus floribunda* and *atrosanguinea*, to the very large almost apple size, or at least crabapple size of the *Malus niedzwetskyana*.

Again, in the flowering trees, the hawthorns are perhaps more conspicuous in their fruiting season than at any time of the year. One that is native in very large sections of the country, the Washington thorn, *Crataegus phaenopyrum*, has brilliant red fruit so that a drive through the country in the fall may make us stop our cars to see what that bright red spot in the landscape is. Almost all the hawthorns have red fruit but the Washington is much the most brilliant of all.

Among the lower shrubs the roses, particularly some of the native ones and one or two of the imported varieties are as brilliant in the fall as at their blooming season. The tough Rosa rugosa which grows even close to the seashore where few other shrubs can be counted on, is full of bright red very large rose hips in the fall. Arching branches of the Japanese rose, Rosa multiflora, are completely covered with thousands of tiny little red berries. Its tremendous sprawling habit makes it hard to use except where there is a great deal of space, but more than once I have worked hard to persuade a client to leave it when she was a little disdainful of the small white flowers that covered it in June. When they were succeeded by the bright red hips, it won its own place in the border and became the show of the fall garden.

A great many shrubs have blue or black fruits which are in themselves not at all conspicuous, but are interesting when seen close at hand. The nannyberry and several of the other viburnums, some of the dogwoods, the privet all have these dark fruits but in making a fall picture they are not particularly useful, unless like the nannyberry and some of the dogwoods they have interesting fall foliage color.

Other shrubs have seed pods that are beautiful, particularly for cutting to use in winter arrangements. Perhaps the most interesting of them is the native witchhazel. In addition to its delicate yellow mist in October when practically nothing else even thinks of blossoming in northern climates, the flowers are succeeded by curious and interesting seed pods. As children you may have eaten the little nuts, but as grown-ups you probably will want to use them for winter decoration. The seed pods of the sourwood and of the andromeda are also beautiful and a little research through the woodlands or in a botanical garden will show you certain things to plant close at hand where you can study their beautiful formation in the cold days of winter.

The brilliant red heads of sumac add a splash of color to the landscape and picked at exactly the right moment when they are most vivid last beautifully without fading most of the winter. Some of us still remember too vividly the stiff arrangements of straw flowers and dried cattails gathering dust in our grandmothers' parlors but if we can get over that prejudice, certain seed pod and fruit arrangements gathered from our own shrubs in the fall can give much more pleasure during the winter than the most elaborate bouquet from the florist.

Even in the parts of the country farther south or along the seashore where the color is less high than in inland and northern spots, there are always a few things whose leaf or fruit is worth having on your own place. If you have moved farther south and remember October with nostalgia, perhaps one bush of *Nandina* or *Ardisia* with bright red berries will help to satisfy the longing for a trip back home. If you are still in the north and the world around you ablaze, it is certainly very shortsighted not to make your own place the focal point of the brightest color you can find. The cold season is coming soon enough and to get all the brilliance and all the loveliness possible in the short period before the leaves fall certainly does help to get through the winter.

SHRUBS IN FALL COLOR

FALL COLOR FROM FRUIT—The red and orange fruits are most showy in the fall landscape, and many other varieties are available. The ones given are the most conspicuous of their species and of greatest landscape value.

a. RED AND ORANGE

NAME	HEIGHT	SEASON (As of New York City)	PLACE TO USE
Aronia arbutifolia brilliantissima RED CHOKEBERRY	8′	September, October	Native planting at a distance.
Berberis thunbergi JAPANESE BARBERRY	8′ spread	October to February	Large nearby borders.
Cornus florida FLOWERING DOGWOOD	25′	September, October	Accent or specimen nearby or distant edge of woodland.
Cornus kousa CHINESE DOGWOOD	20′	September	Accent or specimen nearby.
Cotoneaster apiculata CRANBERRY COTONEASTER	6′	September, October	Near house or garden.

Name	Size	Months	Use
Cotoneaster divaricata SPREADING COTONEASTER	6′ spread	September, October	Near house or garden.
Cotoneaster horizontalis ROCK COTONEASTER	5′ spread	September to November	Near house or garden.
Cotoneaster simonsi SIMONS COTONEASTER	6′	September, October	Near house or garden.
Crataegus crusgalli COCKSPUR HAWTHORN	20′	October, November	Accent or specimen, nearby or distant sunny border.
Crataegus intricata THICKET HAWTHORN	20′	October	Accent or specimen, nearby or distant sunny border.
Crataegus phaenopyrum WASHINGTON HAWTHORN	25′	October to December	Accent or specimen, nearby or distant sunny border.
Euonymus alatus WINGED EUONYMUS	10′	September, October	Accent or specimen nearby.
Ilex laevigata SMOOTH WINTERBERRY	6′	October, November	Lowlands, native planting.
Ilex opaca AMERICAN HOLLY	20′	November to February	Specimen nearby.
Ilex verticillata WINTERBERRY	8′	September to November	Lowlands, native planting.
Lindera benzoin SPICEBUSH	15′	October	Lowlands, native planting.

List No. 17—Continued

Name	Height	Season (As of New York City)	Place to Use
Lonicera korolkowi BLUELEAF HONEYSUCKLE	10'	August	Nearby border.
Lonicera maacki AMUR HONEYSUCKLE	8'	September, October	Nearby border.
Malus atrosanguinea CARMINE CRABAPPLE	14'	October	Accent or specimen in full sun, in large borders, nearby or distant sunny meadows.
Malus baccata SIBERIAN CRABAPPLE	35'	September, October	Accent or specimen in full sun, in large borders, nearby or distant sunny meadows.
Malus sargenti SARGENT CRABAPPLE	12' spread	September, October	Accent or specimen in full sun, in large borders, nearby or distant sunny meadows.
Malus toringoides CUTLEAF CRABAPPLE	20'	September, October	Accent or specimen in full sun, in large borders, nearby or distant sunny meadows.
Photinia villosa ORIENTAL PHOTINIA	12'	October	Large borders nearby or distant.
Pyracantha coccinea lalandi LALAND FIRETHORN	15'	September to November	Near house or garden as espalier.

Plant	Size	Season	Use
Rosa blanda MEADOW ROSE	5'	September to January	Banks or facing down hedgerows.
Rosa multiflora JAPANESE ROSE	8' spread	October to January	Nearby large borders, banks.
Rosa rugosa alba WHITE RUGOSA ROSE	5'	August to January	Seashore, nearby borders.
Rosa setigera PRAIRIE ROSE	10' spread	October to December	Slopes, sunny hedgerows, large nearby borders.
Rhus glabra SMOOTH SUMAC	10'	August to December	Native planting in full sun.
Sambucus racemosa RED-BERRIED ELDER	8'	September	Native planting in full sun.
Sorbus aucuparia EUROPEAN MOUNTAINASH	30'	August, September	Specimen.
Viburnum dilatatum LINDEN VIBURNUM	8'	September, October	Nearby borders, half-shade.
Viburnum opulus EUROPEAN HIGHBUSH CRANBERRY	12'	August to October	Nearby or distant borders.
Viburnum setigerum TEA VIBURNUM	10'	October	Nearby borders.
Viburnum sieboldi SIEBOLD VIBURNUM	12'	August, September	Specimen, screen, large nearby borders.

List No. 17—Continued

Name	Height	Season (As of New York City)	Place to Use
b. YELLOW FRUIT—Not effective at a distance of more than twenty-five feet.			
Chaenomeles japonica DWARF JAPANESE QUINCE	3′	September, October	Garden or foundation planting.
Chaenomeles lagenaria JAPANESE QUINCE	6′	September, October	Nearby borders.
Ilex verticillata chrysocarpa YELLOW-BERRIED WINTERBERRY	8′	September to November	Native or distant borders.
Malus arnoldiana ARNOLD CRABAPPLE	15′	September, October	Accent, specimen, open meadow.
Viburnum opulus xanthocarpum YELLOW CRANBERRY BUSH	10′	August to October	Nearby border.
c. WHITE FRUITS			
Cornus racemosa GRAY DOGWOOD	10′	September	Sunny hedgerows.
Symphoricarpos albus SNOWBERRY	4′	September, October	Shade, untidy habit.
d. BRIGHT BLUE OR PURPLE FRUITS			
Callicarpa dichotoma BEAUTYBUSH	5′	September	Garden borders.

Name	Height	Fruiting time	Location
Symplocos paniculata SAPPHIREBERRY	12'	September	Cultivated borders.

e. BLUE OR BLACK FRUIT—Interesting at close range but particularly useful for attracting birds.

Name	Height	Fruiting time	Location
Aronia melanocarpa BLACK CHOKEBERRY	9'	September, October	Woodland facing down.
Ilex crenata JAPANESE HOLLY	10'	October, November	Near house.
Ilex glabra INKBERRY	4'	October to January	Nearby, cultivated or native borders.
Ligustrum obtusifolium regelianum REGELS PRIVET	5'	October to December	Nearby borders or near house.
Rhamnus cathartica BUCKTHORN	10'	September	Large distant borders, screens.
Sambucus canadensis ELDER	10'	September	Sunny meadows, distant hedgerows.
Viburnum cassinoides WITHEROD	10'	August, September	Damp ground, large borders.
Viburnum lentago NANNYBERRY	20'	September to November	Distant or large nearby borders.
Vibernum prunifolium BLACKHAW	12'	September to November	Distant or large nearby borders.

SHRUBS IN FALL COLOR

a. RED AND RED-ORANGE FOLIAGE

NAME	HEIGHT	HABIT	PLACE TO USE
Aronia melanocarpa BLACK CHOKEBERRY	9'	Oval	Distant border.
Azalea kaempferi TORCH AZALEA	3'	Picturesque	Half-shade, against evergreens.
Azalea vaseyi PINKSHELL AZALEA	8'	Picturesque	Half-shade, near garden.
Berberis thunbergi JAPANESE BARBERRY	8' spread	Arching, mound	Nearby border.
Cornus kousa CHINESE DOGWOOD	20'	Symmetrical tree	Specimen, nearby border.
Cornus florida FLOWERING DOGWOOD	25'	Picturesque tree	Specimen, nearby or distant border.
Cotinus coggygria SMOKETREE	12'	Irregular oval	Specimen, near house or garden.

Cotoneaster foveolata GLOSSY COTONEASTER	8'	Open, upright	Large nearby borders.
Crataegus phaenopyrum WASHINGTON HAWTHORN	25'	Vase-shaped tree	Specimen, nearby or distant borders.
Enkianthus campanulatus REDVEIN ENKIANTHUS	12'	Picturesque, upright	Specimen, near house or garden.
Euonymus alatus WINGED EUONYMUS	10'	Picturesque	Specimen or accent, cultivated borders nearby.
Oxydendron arboreum SOURWOOD	25'	Slender tree	Distant borders, half-shade.
Rhus copallina SHINING SUMAC	5'	Mound	Sun, distant borders, native planting.
Vaccinium angustifolium LOWBUSH BLUEBERRY	12"	Picturesque sprawling	Ground cover.
Vaccinium corymbosum HIGHBUSH BLUEBERRY	8'	Picturesque	Specimen, accent, nearby or distant borders.
b. YELLOW FOLIAGE			
Calycanthus floridus SWEETSHRUB	6'	Oval	Near house.
Chionanthus virginicus WHITE FRINGETREE	20'	Oval tree	Specimen, large borders.

List No. 18—Continued

Name	Height	Habit	Place to Use
Clethra alnifolia SWEETPEPPER BUSH	6'	Symmetrical	Wild planting, moist ground, fragrance.
Ilex laevigata SMOOTH WINTERBERRY	6'	Oval	Distant borders, moist ground.
Lindera benzoin SPICEBUSH	15'	Oval	Distant borders, moist ground.
Spiraea thunbergi THUNBERG SPIREA	6'	Untidy, twiggy	Nearby borders, not too visible.
Zanthorhiza apiifolia YELLOWROOT	2'	Sprawling	Ground cover.
c. DARK RED TO PURPLISH BRONZE FOLIAGE			
Cornus amomum SILKY DOGWOOD	10'	Spreading oval	Large, distant borders.
Cotoneaster dielsiana DIEL COTONEASTER	6'	Arching, oval	Nearby borders or near house.
Cotoneaster divaricata SPREADING COTONEASTER	6'	Arching, oval	Nearby borders or over walls.

Name	Height	Form	Use
Franklinia alatamaha GORDONIA	15'	Neat and symmetrical, tree-like	Specimen, close at hand.
Forsythia intermedia BORDER FORSYTHIA	8'	Arching, oval	Large borders.
Prunus maritima BEACH PLUM	8' spread	Picturesque mound	Seashore.
Viburnum acerifolium MAPLELEAF VIBURNUM	5'	Straggly	Undergrowth in shady borders.
Viburnum carlesi KOREANSPICE VIBURNUM	6'	Open, vase-shaped	Specimen, near house or garden.
Viburnum dentatum ARROWWOOD	12'	Oval	Shade, distant native planting.
Viburnum lentago NANNYBERRY	20'	Oval	Native planting, large border.
Viburnum tomentosum DOUBLEFILE VIBURNUM	8'	Picturesque, horizontal	Specimen, nearby border.

SECTION TWO

PLACES TO PLANT SHRUBS

CHAPTER VI

Shrub Borders at a Distance

THE PLACE where shrubs are used in the greatest quantity if, unfortunately, not in quality is certainly the big shrub border at some distance from the house. All too often this merits the name that an old gardener of my acquaintance gave it. He insisted on calling it "the scrubbery." The borders well away from the house are usually there for one of four purposes. They may be to screen out objectionable objects or views; to act as a windbreak; to mark a property line; or to give privacy on one's own property or a part of it. In other words, they are usually primarily utilitarian and too often their practical purposes are so far in the foreground of our thoughts when we plant them, that we do not stop to appreciate the possibility of beauty as well as usefulness.

When we need a screen inside the house certainly few of us would choose an ugly three-panel one of plain wall board in preference to a beautifully decorated one, or photo-mural panels of our favorite views. There may be a great variation in price among the different kinds of decorative screen but outdoors uninteresting, ugly screen plants cost just as much as beautiful ones and there is no reason for putting dull shrubs without beauty at any time, when we could have those that have one season of great beauty and often two or three when they are effective in the distance. As the intrusive object that we want to hide is likely to be fairly large, quick growing material is usually desirable. Unless we live in the warmer

95

parts of the country or have just a summer place in the north, we need plants that are presentable all year round.

This usually means a certain proportion of evergreens and it is all-important here to choose those that will like the location and grow as rapidly as possible without handicap. To be sure most evergreens are a little slower growing than deciduous material but the winter effect is worth waiting for. If the objects or the view to be screened have a fairly wide expanse it is certainly better to use evergreens. The pines and hemlocks, firs and spruces are broader than most of the arborvitaes and red cedars. If the object is fairly high, it is well to remember that many of these evergreens are pyramidal in shape so that the width will be near the ground where the deciduous material will screen it anyway and the point of the tree will be up in the top where we need width. The firs and spruces remain narrow at the top, while the hemlocks and pines broaden out early in life, if they are well planted and given any kind of care.

When planting time comes the evergreens are put in place before any of the other plants. They are most conspicuous for many months of the year and need to be located so as to make a pleasant composition in the winter landscape. If they are not well arranged they are likely not only to fail in their utilitarian purpose as a screen, but stick out like green blots on a delicate picture.

It will probably be advisable to put a few high-headed deciduous trees in such a border. Young oaks, maples, elms, honey locusts are all fairly rapid in growth, and placed strategically through the border they will do much to make it count for something even in its early stages. Since the object is to blot out as much as possible with as few plants as possible, the broad-spreading flowering trees like the hawthorns, the crabapples and the speading shrubs, most of the viburnums and dogwoods, and the witchhazels, are very useful. All the plants used in such a border should be reasonably fast growing, easily taken care of or almost self-sustaining, and varying in height and shape so that the border is not monotonous even from a distance.

If the shrub border is primarily for a windbreak, it is of course obvious that it should be made up of things that will stand high winds. Evergreens like the hemlocks which burn badly in wind or the arborvitae which turn brown if the wind hits them too strongly in the winter, certainly do not belong in a windbreak. The front part of them may be all right but the side toward the wind is sure to be very thin and likely to be entirely bare. This border calls for really tough, wind-resistant material. Many of our native plants are the best of all for such a location and a little study of windy hillsides in the neighborhood may give you ideas.

Among the cultivated shrubs, honeysuckle, *Lonicera*, buckthorn, *Rhamnus*, Siberian-pea, *Caragana*, and the Russian olive, *Eleagnus*, are all well adapted to strong wind. They can be used here and there through the borders where the winds are strongest. This sort of planting should be thicker even at the time it is done than most borders, because you want an impenetrable mass there to break the wind. Near the seashore where the wind is a constant problem the native scrub oak, scrub pine, bayberry and beach plum form a durable as well as beautiful and appropriate windbreak.

Most of the material for this purpose, if it is not evergreen, should have many twigs and branches to break the force of the winter wind. The leeward side of a brush-heapy shrub like spirea, or honeysuckle is a great deal warmer than the leeward side of two or three trunks of hybrid lilac. For the same reason the hawthorns and crabapples are usually better in a windbreak than the cherries or dogwoods whose habit is much more open.

It is important in planning such a windbreak that you know very surely which season you want the wind broken. It is easy to cut off the summer breezes that mean a great deal to your comfort, in an effort to make a windbreak which you may need very slightly in the winter. You may also be piling up quite a snow problem for yourself if you place windbreaks so that every snowfall in the winter drifts across a much-used path or driveway, or piles up against the garage or the house wall. Quite often a few sections of snow fence are a much simpler solution for winter protection than a shrub border which unfortunately cannot be removed in the summer when you want the breezes.

Perhaps the commonest use of all for shrub borders is that of marking the property lines. There seems to be a firm belief that once you have a property line you must put something on it to show very clearly that this is exactly as far as you own and no further. In many cases we sacrifice pleasant views and a feeling of spaciousness by such definite demarkation. Unless you are really on unfriendly terms with the neighbors there is no reason why the space in front of your house and all your neighbors' houses should be cut up into square little boxes. Sometimes there are local restrictions that prevent this but all too often I have seen individually pleasant lawns, neatly hedged in with shrubs or hedges or fences when throwing it all together would have made the street an entirely different and more spacious place.

There is one long avenue in a suburb of New York City where the zoning laws have required the houses to be set back quite deeply in the lot. Many of the existing big trees were left, fortunately, and whether by agreement or ordinance, the property owners have all kept their front lawns uninterrupted by property line markers of any sort. The effect is that of a beautiful big English park. One misguided owner could easily ruin it if he were determined to plant along every property line.

Again, if a golf course or a park adjoins your property or is across the street from it, there is no earthly reason for not taking advantage of it and pretending visually that it belongs to you. A small place that I was called in to help with some years ago had grounds that were a little too small for the size of the house. It felt crowded and closed in. A heavy shrubbery border was along the back property line and in wading through it to explore the possibilities of thinning it out, I discovered that a beautiful golf course was immediately behind it. There was a section of rough immediately beyond the client's grounds with a slight roll to the land, so there was very little danger of stray golf balls or golfers wandering up into their property. There was, on the other hand, a beautiful view across the course to distant hills. We very promptly started marking shrubs to be transplanted or discarded from this heavy border, leaving only a few fine specimens of flowering trees in groups here and there to give shape to the lawn. The result was that we actually gained not only fifteen feet of ground space on our own property, but completely took away the shut-in, crowded air that was almost giving the owner claustrophobia. So before obeying that impulse to mark every property line, look around and be sure that you are not shutting out something that you might as well claim visually if not legally.

If it is necessary to plant on the property line for privacy it should usually be done as lightly and sparsely as possible. If it is in a crowded neighborhood, each neighbor probably has some planting next to his line. Quite often I have seen fifteen feet of planting on either side of the property line, when with a little smart thinking, thick planting on one side could have been balanced with very thin planting on the other, so that each person gained in space. Of course there is the objection that someone else may buy the property and change the planting but that can always be overcome by a little heavier planting on your side.

Sometimes it is even possible to take advantage of the neighbors' planting to make color schemes of your own. If just next to your line there are two beautiful purple lilacs, it will mean very little for you to add another purple one but if you add a white one or a white weigela, you have made a color scheme by buying one bush instead of three. If the neighbor has a swamp maple near your line you certainly cannot blot it out even if you wanted to. That means you need to put your forsythia in some other part of the property and to use that line for planting the whites and the pale pinks that bloom early in the spring, or for the heavily, brilliantly colored plants in the fall, to make that the brightest spot in the neighborhood.

If your property is in less heavily settled territory and is from two to five acres, your lines are likely to be old boundary lines and have some kind of native hedgerow along them. When this is true, it is a wonderful opportunity to do good naturalistic planting with native material. It is certainly extravagant and inappropriate to rip out all these fine local things that give character to the place, and replace them with an indiscriminate shrub mass of flowering deutzias, syringas, weigelas, and other things that can be grown almost anywhere and that have nothing to do with your particular locality.

On a real farm there are probably fences separating the farm proper from the "yard" or the grounds immediately around the house. It is all too easy to think of these fences almost as property lines and, in an effort to dress up the yard, make it look much smaller and as if it might be in a suburb instead of open country. An occasional flowering tree or group of native plants along the fence, or in one corner, leaves the view to the pastures or the meadows open and keeps the place in character. Chicken-houses, or ugly buildings may have to be concealed or at least made less obtrusive, but the flowering trees or large plants of kinds native to the locality are in excellent proportion and appropriate to the open vistas that are the charm of the country. A tight mass of cultivated shrubs is likely to be too obvious a screen to be successful.

The shrub borders at a distance from the house are the great opportunity for most of us to do native planting. Some of the finest plants in the nursery are actually native to your own part of the country and should be used much more than they are. Certain of them look well in either wild or cultivated settings, and some cultivated plants blend in well with the native plants. This is largely a matter of association perhaps, although cultural conditions have something to do with it.

All of us would recognize the incongruity of walking through a sunny lane and suddenly in the midst of the elders, sumacs, little gray dogwoods and cedars along the roadside, find weigela, syringa, beautybush, spirea suddenly bursting forth. We would have no doubt whatsoever that man had been working on that planting, and the whole point of native planting is to make it look as if nature did it and you had nothing to do with it. Almost all of the common garden shrubs are traditionally associated in our minds with man's handiwork; in other words, they belong near the house, and in very few cases do they ever look well in the midst of natural surroundings. If they are planted, it is an artificial setting, man-made, for a garden.

On the other hand, there are many shrubs which are close relatives of certain native shrubs and look enough like them that they seem perfectly at home in our own landscape. There are good examples of this in the small flowering trees. We have three or four crabapples native to various parts of this country but most of the Asiatic varieties, except the purple-leaved ones, look perfectly at home used with the native crabapples. The hawthorns, except possibly the English hawthorn which has a very different leaf and flower, fit in with our own wild kinds. The Chinese witchhazels look enough like our witchhazels to be at home. The rule is not infallible but it is fairly safe to say that if there is another member of the group native to your locality, you can use a different variety near it, without causing a false note in the landscape. If the first name is the same—*Malus, Crataegus, Hamamelis*—all the species and varieties (the second and third names) will fit together.

Since it is seen at a distance, the general mass and skyline of the planting are very important. If it is made up of shrubs which when full grown are all about the same height, it might almost as well be a hedge. If, on the other hand, there are light lacy heads high above low dense foliage, with definite form seen against the sky, it is interesting—even if too far away to distinguish what any of the plants are. The distant border is the place for silhouettes that are unusual. If there is a slight rise in the land so that one wild crabapple or hawthorn can stand alone, its winter silhouette is beautiful. The exclamation points of cedars, high on a windy hillside are most satisfying on a winter day. The clean lines of the dogwoods with their buds held out as if at the tips of their fingers stand out surprisingly against either the sky or an evergreen background.

A point to keep in mind on borders at a distance from the house is that they will almost inevitably get less care than the area immediately at hand. For that reason they should be plants well adapted to the environment in which you are putting them, free from pest and disease, well fitted for a certain amount of struggle for survival. For future care the rank growers must be carefully used. Otherwise they will choke out all the finer things which are a little less vigorous in habit. If it is far enough away that you almost never see it close at hand, a certain amount of jungle is permissible and even desirable, particularly if it is native planting. But just as in the perennial border feverfew and physostegia can crowd out all the delphiniums and aquilegias in no time at all, a few rampant growers like sumacs or clammy locusts or honeysuckle can completely swamp the finer witchhazels and viburnums, sweet fern or even flowering trees.

In planting for color in distant borders only bold color masses are at all effective. The sparse bloom of the viburnums and most of the cornuses shows not at all at a little distance. Only the true flowering dogwood, Cornus florida, and its Chinese cousin, Cornus kousa, are even noticeable when in bloom. On the other hand the flowering crabapples and hawthorns are heavy enough in bloom and in fruit that they tell even at a distance of two or three hundred yards. If it is a border of cultivated shrubs it is a fine place for the bold yellow masses of forsythia, contrasted with the fine feathery mass of *Spiraea thunbergi*. The mock-oranges, the weigelas, the deutzias are excellent in such a border, just far enough away that their rather twiggy and untidy habit in winter and their uninteresting leaf are not so important and the bold mass of bloom shows stunningly in the spring months.

For fall color the borders at a distance are the place to really go berserk on the most brilliant colors in both foliage and fruit. The sumacs, the blueberries, the black haws, sourwood, can be used in really satisfying quantities. The red berried shrubs will be effective even at a considerable distance and you will have the added satisfaction of knowing that they, with their blue and black berried cousins, are in a location where even the shyest of the birds can enjoy them. I know of one border only a hundred feet from the house which was planned primarily for food for the birds. It has been thoroughly satisfactory to them but it is a joy to see in the autumn because most of the things the birds like are also highly decorative in their fall color.

The borders at a distance from the house are perhaps the easiest of all places in which to use shrubs. You do have to keep in mind the silhouette and the winter appearance of the skyline but you can go into really large scale use of color both in flower and in fruit and the subtleties of texture, fussy arrangement and finicky care are less important there than anywhere else on the place. Even if you do make a few mistakes it is far enough away that they do not stare you in the face every time you come around the house or look out of the window.

SHRUB BORDERS AT A DISTANCE

BOLD FLOWER MASSES—Shrubs with numerous or large flowers effective from a distance of 75 to 150 feet may be chosen from either the best-known garden varieties for cultivated borders or from material native to our meadows and woodlands. They are particularly effective in wide, long borders where they have room to develop and are seen across a meadow or lawn.

a. Cultivated borders.

Name	Height	Habit	Color
Azalea calendulaceae FLAME AZALEA	8'	Picturesque	Yellow.
Azalea indica alba WHITE INDICA AZALEA	5×8'	Broad mound	White.
Azalea mollis CHINESE AZALEA	6'	Picturesque	Salmon, orange yellow.
Azalea obtusa japonica in variety KURUME AZALEA	3×5'	Broad mound	White, pink, rosy red.
Azalea obtusa kaempferi TORCH AZALEA	3'	Angular oval	Yellow to red.

Botanical / Common Name	Size	Form	Flower Color
Azalea vaseyi PINKSHELL AZALEA	3×5'	Picturesque	Pink.
Chaenomeles lagenaria FLOWERING QUINCE	10'	Picturesque	Pink to white.
Cornus florida FLOWERING DOGWOOD	25'	Picturesque	White.
Crataegus oxyacantha rosea ROSE FLOWERING HAWTHORN	25'	Vase-shaped tree	Rose.
Deutzia gracilis SLENDER DEUTZIA	3'	Round	White.
Deutzia lemoinei LEMOINE DEUTZIA	4'	Round	White.
Exochorda racemosa PEARLBUSH	10'	Open, oval	White.
Forsythia intermedia BORDER FORSYTHIA	8'	Arching	Gold-yellow.
Kolkwitzia amabilis BEAUTYBUSH	8'	Oval	Pink.
Lonicera korolkowi BLUELEAF HONEYSUCKLE	10'	Broad oval	Rose.
Malus atrosanguinea CARMINE CRABAPPLE	14'	Broad	Rose non-fading.

LIST No. 19—Continued

NAME	HEIGHT	HABIT	COLOR
Malus ioensis bechteli BECHTEL CRABAPPLE	25'	Like apple tree	Blush pink.
Malus floribunda JAPANESE FLOWERING CRABAPPLE	20'	Spreading tree	Rose-red to white.
Malus hupehensis TEA CRABAPPLE	20'	Vase-shaped tree	Pink buds, white bloom.
Prunus shirofugen JAPANESE CHERRY	20'	Spreading tree	Blush.
Prunus subhirtella HIGAN CHERRY	20'	Spreading tree	Pink.
Prunus yedo zakura ZAKURA CHERRY	20'	Spreading tree	Delicate pink.
Philadelphus grandiflorus BIG SCENTLESS MOCKORANGE	10'	Upright	White.
Philadelphus lemoinei Mont Blanc MT. BLANC MOCKORANGE	4'	Compact, oval	White.
Spiraea van houttei VANHOUTTE SPIREA	8'	Arching	White.
Viburnum tomentosum DOUBLEFILE VIBURNUM	8'	Picturesque	White.

b. Native or wild planting at a distance, property line, in edge of meadow or open country. Full sun.

Crataegus crusgalli COCKSPUR HAWTHORN	20′	Spreading tree	White.
Crataegus phaenopyrum WASHINGTON HAWTHORN	25′	Broad, vase-shaped tree	White.
Malus arnoldiana ARNOLD CRABAPPLE	15′	Spreading tree	Pink.
Malus coronaria WILD SWEET CRABAPPLE	20′	Spreading tree	Deep pink, non-fading.
Malus floribunda JAPANESE FLOWERING CRABAPPLE	20′	Spreading tree	White, rose-red bud.
Malus sargenti SARGENT CRABAPPLE	8′	Picturesque	Coral bud.
Malus spectabilis CHINESE CRABAPPLE	25–30′	Vase-shaped tree	Pale pink coral bud.
Rosa setigera PRAIRIE ROSE	15′	Arching	Pink.
Rubus flagellaris AMERICAN DEWBERRY	5′	Spreading oval	White.
Sambucus canadensis AMERICAN ELDER	10′	Vase-shaped	Cream.

c. *For edge of woodlands or shaded borders.*

NAME	HEIGHT	HABIT	COLOR
Amelanchier canadensis SHADBLOW	20'	Vase-shaped	White.
Azalea calendulaceae FLAME AZALEA	8'	Picturesque	Yellow, vermilion.
Azalea nudiflora PINXTER AZALEA	8'	Picturesque	Pink.
Cercis canadensis REDBUD	25'	Vase-shaped tree	Pink.
Cornus florida FLOWERING DOGWOOD	25'	Picturesque tree	White.
Kalmia latifolia MOUNTAIN LAUREL	8'	Broad oval	Pink, white.
Rhododendron maximum ROSEBAY RHODODENDRON	12'	Broad oval, leggy	Pink, white.

CHAPTER VII

Shrub Borders Nearby

ANY MASS planting that is within seventy-five feet of the house or the flower garden can be called a nearby border. It is constantly seen at close range so that you are conscious of its detail at all times of the year. For that reason it is one that must be done most carefully. Not only must every shrub in it be considered for its own worth but it must also be thought of in relation to the other shrubs nearby, so that there is not an inharmonious note in the entire planting. It should be planned as carefully as any perennial bed but it is perhaps even harder to do because the perennial groups are, after all, primarily to give bloom for about five months in the year. The shrub border is to give beauty twelve months in the year and usually serves some utilitarian purpose as well.

On the small property, of course, all the shrub masses are nearby and in most cases each one has not only one useful purpose but is likely to have three or four. It may screen the neighbor's garage, give privacy in your grounds, shut off traffic noises and give a background for a flower garden, all with the same group of plants. This of course means that every shrub has to do double or triple duty, usually in much less space than the faraway border on the larger place and frequently with more difficult conditions for growth. (One of the worst suburban conditions is that in which the builder leaves the subsoil from the basement, with a slight admixture of brick-bats, lime, lath, plaster and anything else that has to be dis-

posed of. It is very poor growing soil for shrubs and unfortunately it is what we are very likely to find even clear out to the
property line on new places.)

The skyline of this nearby border is just as important as on
the faraway one but, since it is closer at hand, the perspective
on it changes. Where at a distance of five hundred feet you
need really high-headed shade trees and tall evergreens to give
the high points in the skyline, the nearby border can do the
same thing with small flowering trees and much lower evergreens or shrubs. A hill close at hand looks as tall as a mountain twenty-five miles away. But it is important to have high
points and low points in any border more than twenty-five
feet long, so that it does not look like a hedge of miscellaneous
shrubs.

Winter silhouette is just as important as it is in the faraway
border but instead of being silhouetted against clear space,
the shrubs in this border are likely to be silhouetted against
the neighbor's house or against his hedge or fence or miscellaneous plant masses. If you do find a clear space where
nothing can interrupt the silhouette against the sky, by all
means choose the shrub picturesque in habit and interesting
without its leaves. The general winter effect should be interesting and varied. The evergreens, even though they be few,
should be placed so they do not look spotty in the winter
landscape and the rest of the shrubs should be mingled as to
habit and form, not restricted to either the very open or the
very twiggy type.

A border that consists entirely of plants like forsythia,
spirea, barberry, weigela, mockorange, seen close at hand in
the winter is likely to look like nothing in the world so much
as a large brush-heap, ready for a match to be set to it. Even
on the small place most of us want some of these shrubs for
their lovely bloom, but they can and should be limited in
number and set at the back of the planting, with something
of a different habit in front of them and adjoining them, so

that their general twiggy mass is hardly noticed in their un-attractive leafless season.

This nearby shrub planting is likely to be seen all in one eyeful as it is not often longer than the width of the property and the eye takes in fifty to seventy-five feet in length very easily. For that reason, the color scheme when in bloom must be most carefully studied. If you want to have strong yellows at a certain season be sure there are no pinks in that same border that might fight with them. If there are rose-pink flowering cherries or rose-pink English hawthorn, it is no place for either the fiery red flowering quince or orange *Azalea calendulaceae*. In the faraway border it is very easy to have some yellow at one end and rose-pink at the other but in any planting within seventy-five feet of the house, the whole must be considered as a unified scheme, not in isolated patches. Thinking of it as one color group, just as you do a flower garden, will help avoid the spottiness of too many islands of color in an otherwise green mass, at any one season.

I remodeled a border some two or three years ago which was a hundred and twenty-five feet long, on a back property line. When I first saw it in early spring the only thing I could think of was a piece of polka-dotted gingham or calico. There was one polka-dot of yellow, then ten feet further on a polka-dot of white, then a polka-dot of bright red, then yellow, then white, then bright red, and so on for the entire length of the border. They were, of course, forsythia, early spirea and flowering quince.

Examination of the border showed that the shrubs for succeeding seasons would have exactly the same polka-dot effect. It had apparently been done on the tit-tat-toe principle, so that every twenty-five feet had exactly the same shrub in exactly the same position. We solved that particular border by taking the flowering quince out entirely, using it elsewhere on the property, grouping the forsythias at either end with the spireas adjoining them, so that we had two strong flower-ing groups that really counted for something and were a mass

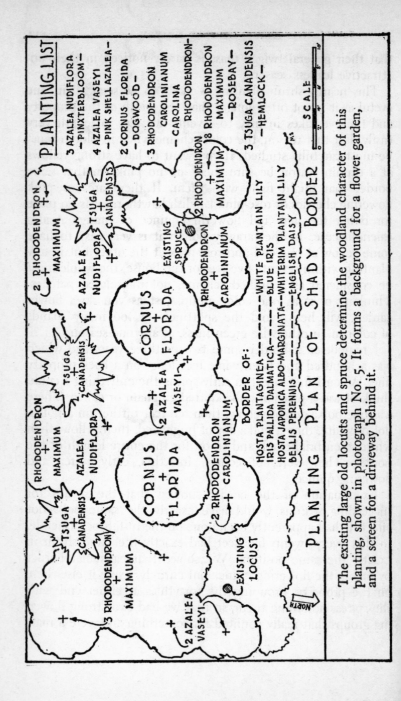

PLANTING LIST

3 AZALEA NUDIFLORA — PINXTERBLOOM —

4 AZALEA VASEYI — PINK SHELL AZALEA —

2 CORNUS FLORIDA — DOGWOOD —

3 RHODODENDRON CAROLINIANUM — CAROLINA RHODODENDRON—

8 RHODODENDRON MAXIMUM — ROSEBAY —

3 TSUGA CANADENSIS — HEMLOCK —

BORDER OF:

HOSTA PLANTAGINEA——— — WHITE PLANTAIN LILY
IRIS PALLIDA DALMATICA———————— BLUE IRIS
HOSTA JAPONICA ALBO-MARGINATA—WHITERIM PLANTAIN LILY
BELLIS PERENNIS ———————————— ENGLISH DAISY

PLANTING PLAN OF SHADY BORDER

The existing large old locusts and spruce determine the woodland character of this planting, shown in photograph No. 5. It forms a background for a flower garden, and a screen for a driveway behind it.

of color. The same rearrangement of combinations was needed for every season.

In the constantly seen border we must appreciate that it does not take six forsythias to make a spring effect and give us the pleasure of their early bloom. One well-grown and spreading, with two spireas near it, can give more pleasure than a golden jungle and at the same time will leave room for effects later in the season. The number of shrubs of one kind must be limited to the effect you want to get, the total room you have and how important that season is to you. Large shrubs with the bolder blooms need be used only in ones, twos, and threes and not in large masses. One handsome doublefile viburnum is outstanding, ten in a group have little distinction, except as a mass of white. Delicate small things like tender azaleas, abelia, daphne, dwarf quince should have enough in a group so the mass counts for something, usually three to six at least.

On the other hand, one serious mistake that is often made is to try to get one of everything you like into the same border. The result is not a planting scheme, it is merely a collection of shrubs. Just as you cannot possibly get all the flowers you like into one flower bed, you cannot possibly get all the shrubs you like into one shrub border. As a practical consideration, not all shrubs like the same growing conditions. There are shade-lovers and sun-lovers, there are lime-enduring and lime-disliking shrubs, some like wind, others need protection. Most important of all, you are trying to make a picture and every element in it must be considered and chosen to contribute its part in the whole scheme and to fit with its neighbors in effectiveness and harmony.

I have frequently had the experience of having new clients come in with a list of shrubs that they had on their place to be moved, and another list almost equally long of the ones that they would like to add. In many cases they would have had to buy at least two adjoining lots to get them all in as far as space alone was concerned. It was a question of eliminating certain of their existing ones, of which they had too many or of which they were not particularly fond, and then choosing which of the new ones they really wanted the most. Far too many people see some shrub that they like, go to a nursery and buy it, take it home and then wonder what in the world to do with it. They finally end by sticking it somewhere in an existing shrub planting, where it may or may not thrive and usually does not have a chance to do anything for the whole effect of the border.

I am appalled when I see advertisements for collections of shrubs, either one of a kind or three of a kind, that will plant so many square feet of border. It is entirely too much like a recipe for beef and kidney stew that reads, "One beef and one kidney." There is no allowance made for the size of the different shrubs, for the bold or delicate effect, for their cultural preferences or anything else. As a matter of fact these collections are quite often made up of the things easiest to grow in the nursery or on which there is an over-stock. This is very rarely stated in the advertisement and the reader is all too likely to consider it a genuine offer of things suitable for any border.

The only time a collection of shrubs may be valuable is when they are different varieties of a certain kind of shrub, as for example, azaleas or camellias or lilacs. For the beginner some of these collections may be very useful in helping him to get his own group of them started. Usually, however, he will find that there are one or two in any collection whose color he does not like or which do not blend well with the rest of his planting. Therefore, as his collection enlarges, he weeds them out and the collection is no longer a bargain.

A successful border seventy-five feet long, ten feet wide may consist of two or three flowering trees, for height and skyline, five or six evergreens of one kind for depth of color and winter effect, two or perhaps three kinds of large shrubs of the general size of lilacs or viburnums or the flowering garden shrubs, and perhaps a dozen or a dozen and a half of two varieties of low shrubs to face down. The effect in general has continuity and careful bloom combination, with room to grow and effectiveness at all seasons.

Another border, however short, somewhere else on the place can have an entirely different combination. Perhaps one flowering tree, two large sized shrubs of the same kind and half a dozen lower shrubs to blend with them. With such selective groupings we avoid both monotony and restlessness and make each group worth a particular look to enjoy its own special beauty.

A pitfall to be avoided in the constantly visible shrub border is the use of any shrubs that demand certain soil conditions. For example, however fond you may be of the shrubs of the azalea and laurel group which like acid soil, the lime regions of the Middle West are unsuitable for them. They dislike lime intensely and in order to grow them well the soil must not only be prepared for the first planting but must be constantly treated to keep it on the acid side. In a mixed shrub border this is not only practically impossible but is very hard on the other shrubs. Also success is questionable if the work is neglected for a year. If you must have some of these for sentimental reasons, if no other, they should be isolated as specimens in some rather concealed spot where you can treat them as a horticultural *tour de force* and baby them along as they must be.

Again, if you have a wet spot on your property you must make up your mind to select for the border at that point shrubs that like wet soil. Otherwise a major drainage operation is unavoidable. Sometimes the necessity for choosing special plants for special soil conditions can make for a more interesting shrub border and much more varied than if the border had just the usual amount of dryness or wetness throughout its length. The larches, the benzoins, the swamp azaleas, the elders all like low ground and will make an unusual plant group very different from that of your neighbor who is on high ground and has no particular reason to use these shrubs.

On your own place you may have one spot on which all the water collects and another where it runs away faster than the hose can supply it. This offers a real chance to make a sound choice of plants suited to those conditions and with a great deal of contrast between the two parts of the border. Since the nearby border must at all times be presentable, it is certainly wiser to chose things that will adapt easily to the existing conditions and thrive with very little care, than it is to either go to great expense to change the conditions or constantly to nurse along unsuitable shrubs to make them attractive.

For the same reason it is better to rule out of the nearby border any shrub or group of shrubs that is known to be subject to a certain disease or certain insect pests in your neighborhood, unless you are perfectly sure that you have the knowledge and the time to control the trouble. For example, if you are in a wet, humid climate where mildew is prevalent, lilacs close at hand are very unlikely to be presentable.

The rose chafer is extremely fond of any white-flowering shrub that blooms just at its season, so if you know there are many rose chafers present in your neighborhood it is better to skip all the white blooming shrubs at that particular period. We tried for years on one place to get the "smoke" on the smoke bush or berries on the *Viburnum dilatatum* with absolutely no success because the rose bugs always ate the flowers in June. We finally substituted *Magnolia glauca* for the former and *Cornus racemosa* for the latter, and hoped that the rose bugs were properly disappointed the following year.

While the combination of bloom in a border close by is important and must be planned for most carefully, it is actually less valuable for the rest of the year than the texture of leaf or foliage. This border is close enough that you actually see the fine gradation between a coarse-leaved shrub and a fine lacy one and the contrast of gray green and light green leaves against very dark ones is a daily satisfaction. The high lights on shiny leaves and the softness of tomentose or hairy leaves make interesting pictures when there is very little or no bloom anywhere in the border.

When the list for such a border is finally made up it is well to check it with the following questions:

1. Is everything in this border presentable twelve months in the year?
2. Is there contrast of foliage both in texture and color?
3. Are the brilliant seasons of bloom and fall color taken account of, so it is outstandingly interesting at those seasons?
4. Is the skyline varied and in proportion to the nearness of the observer?
5. Is every plant in it harmonious with its neighbor and pa.ι of the general picture?

If the answer is "yes" to all of these points you are certain to have a completely satisfying and effective garden picture.

SHRUB BORDERS NEARBY

FRAGRANT SHRUBS

NAME	HEIGHT	SEASON	PLACE TO USE
Azalea viscosa SWAMP AZALEA	8′	July	Near pool or in lowland.
Clethra alnifolia SWEETPEPPER BUSH	6′	July, August	Lowland, along path.
Daphne somerset GARLAND SHRUB	4′	May	Garden or house plant.
Lonicera fragrantissima FRAGRANT HONEYSUCKLE	6′	March, April	Bank or slope near drive or path.
Lonicera morrowi MORROW HONEYSUCKLE	8′	May, June	Near house.
Magnolia stellata STAR MAGNOLIA	12′	April	Specimen, near house or garden.
Malus coronaria WILD SWEET CRABAPPLE	20′	May	Accent, sunny border.

Plant	Size	Bloom	Location
Philadelphus coronarius FRAGRANT MOCKORANGE	10'	June	Near house or garden.
Ribes aureum GOLDEN CURRANT	5'	June	Under kitchen windows, or near path.
Rosa centifolia CABBAGE ROSE	6'	June	Garden.
Rosa helenae HELEN ROSE	12' spread	June	Nearby shrub border.
Rosa rubiginosa SWEETBRIAR ROSE	6'	June	Near window or path.
Rosa spinosissima SCOTCH ROSE	3'	May, June	Nearby shrub border.
Syringa vulgaris COMMON LILAC	12'	May	Nearby shrub border or near house.
Viburnum burkwoodi BURKWOOD VIBURNUM	8'	April, May	Specimen, garden or house.
Viburnum carlesi KOREANSPICE VIBURNUM	6'	April, May	Specimen, garden or house.

CHAPTER VIII

Shrubs Around the House

WHEN I look at the planting around a great many houses I think of the famous epigram on Lady Hamilton's taste, "There is so much of it and all of it bad." Almost invariably the first place that gets planted on any new property is the foundation of the house. Almost as invariably, at least twice as many plants are set around a foundation as are needed, so that from then on it is a race of pruning, transplanting, removing and trying to keep the house from being submerged. All too often it is a case not only of too many shrubs but of the wrong kind wrongly placed.

The first thing to remember is that the purpose of foundation planting is to emphasize and accent the architecture of the house and to tie it to the surrounding landscape, so that its location seems right and inevitable. Unless the house is a complete architectural monstrosity, concealment is not a primary virtue. We are all familiar with the houses that seem to be set, not on a good firm concrete or brick or stone foundation, but on an indeterminate and indiscriminate mass of plants—a soft, green featherbed. This may come from the old days of building when houses were set two or three feet out of the ground on ugly foundations, or often only on piers at the corners with lattice between. In order to hide this ugly base, shrubs were massed all the way around it.

Any number of houses built in the '90's and early nineteen hundreds have foundations so ugly and so high that almost the only thing one can do is to conceal them. Most houses today, however, are set very close to the ground and their foundations are low or so unobtrusive that there is no reason for making a tremendous effort to cover them up. If the house is of brick, stone, or stucco, the house walls probably go directly to the ground. Even with a frame house, with low brick foundation, perhaps nine inches to a foot above grade, it is not an eyesore and should not be covered up as if it were a disgrace to the family.

An areaway also is a perfectly frank architectural necessity. Putting a lump of shrubs around it not only calls attention to it and makes one wonder why this sudden excrescence of greenery, but at the same time destroys the reason for the areaway, letting in light and air to the basement. If the areaway is flush with the ground, there is no reason for trying to hide it and it will be much less conspicuous left level with the lawn than it will be treated so that everyone wonders what is behind the screen.

The only foundation planting most houses need is something at the door entrances to make them more important, possibly something at the corners or occasionally a screen for certain service quarters of the house. A few full-size flowering shrubs or flowering trees or evergreens properly used will do a great deal more to give an immediately finished effect to a house than any number of small ones of great variety, jammed in together to make a solid and monotonous band of green.

In certain settings and on certain houses, practically no foundation planting at all is necessary and in some cases, any at all is actually undesirable. For example, if a log cabin is set down in the midst of woods, nature does a complete enough job by herself, with her tall tree trunks and undergrowth coming close to the house, to do away with any severe break or any necessity for tying the house down to the ground. In that case, the house itself is inconspicuous and the native setting predominant. Definite foundation planting looks rather silly.

On the other hand, if in the midst of a wood a large clearing is made in order to build a house, there must be some kind of transition between the approaching woodland, the lawn around the house, and the house itself. In such a case the foundation planting should be simple, probably of native material, so that the change man has made in nature's landscape is as unobtrusive as possible and the house looks appropriate to its setting. Very heavy solid foundation planting in such a situation looks as if the clearing job were not complete and nature had tried to reclaim her own in a band immediately around the house, then got discouraged and left a clear space before the forest took over again.

In more open country where the house is on an estate or on a farm, the old builders had the right idea. Frequently some of the lovely New England farmhouses have only a bush on either side of the front door and great clumps of fragrant lilacs or philadelphus or honeysuckle near the windows of the living room or beside the kitchen door. The houses stand foursquare and handsome in a green lawn with great trees arching over them and only an occasional shrub against the house to give interesting accent and contrast of green against white. The same houses restored by modern owners often are smothered and their dignity destroyed by masses of planting all around them so that the clean, square architectural lines of the house are completely lost in a fluffy green mass.

A house high on a hill-top looks bare and as if it might slide into a new location with a good push. A thick planting all around the house walls will not relieve the bareness. The place still looks as if the house might have been dropped from a giant airplane onto the hill-top, complete with a green ring. It is better to plant an old apple at one side and an elm or two arching over the top of the house, with occasional lilacs or snowballs at the corners. These immediately lower the house and anchor it in its natural place in the landscape by making its size fit between equally large plant groups.

When we come to houses in groups, whether in country villages or in suburbs of big cities, we have a more difficult foundation planting problem. There, in addition to trying to tie the house down to its land, many people do foundation planting in an effort to get privacy. Evergreens high above the living room windows will certainly keep passersby from seeing in. They will, however, also cut out all the air and light and feeling of spaciousness from inside the house and are probably much harder on the family than they are on the passersby. Under these circumstances it is well to remember that the closer the screen is to the observer, the more effective it is. A small sheet of paper held in front of your face does more screening than a bill board some twenty-five feet away. In other words, a shrub border out by the sidewalk need not be as thick nor as high as one immediately in front of the window. At the same time it allows all of the property between the house windows and the sidewalk to belong to the home-owner rather than to the public and allows his living room windows to look out on his own home grounds without loss of privacy, air or light.

In most surburban communities one of the great faults of foundation planting is that it is all so much alike. Many streets look as if all the owners had bought their foundation planting by the running foot as Pattern No. 1. A small Colonial cottage, a large Georgian and a stucco house all have exactly the same plants, placed in almost the same position and doing the same inadequate job. Unless houses are exactly identical, it is safe to say that planting should never be identical. Each house should have its individuality brought out, not its common features emphasized.

A few years ago this uniformity in planting was so common and done with such unsuitable material that a friend of mine nicknamed it "the 57 varieties." That was in the days when energetic but non-horticultural salesmen went through a neighborhood and sold a cartload of assorted evergreens to go around the foundation. Neither the salesmen nor the owner knew what they were or anything about how tall they grew, how wide they got, what kind of conditions they liked. They varied in color from yellow green to dark green. Fortunately about half of them died the first year so that the jungle was not quite as bad as it might have been. But the whole planting looked more like a series of pincushions, question marks, exclamation points and dashes than it did like planting.

Perhaps it was word-of-mouth reporting of one friend to another, of the disastrous results of this tail-of-cart-selling, or perhaps the gas shortage helped to cut it down, but at any rate there is very little of that being done today. There is still too much inclination for the builder or the new owner to go out and buy a lot of assorted shrubs and stick them around the house just to have something green there. It never results in satisfaction, either immediately or in the course of years. The material available is for the most part better than formerly—longer lived and of finer quality—but the effect is no more pleasing than if we bought a lot of beautiful assorted buttons and sewed them all on the front of the same dress.

The qualities to look for in good foundation planting are first of all that it be in proportion to the size of the house. In other words, a cottage should have planting material which when full grown is still small and does not dwarf the house. A very tall building, on the other hand, needs very large size shrubs or trees—small ones are about as effective as a blade of grass or a well grown weed at the base of a thirty or forty foot house or a public building.

The ultimate size of the plant material should be the determining factor in selection, and not the size when planted. All too often the innocent planter puts in small hemlocks, small pines, small red cedars, when in reality these are forest trees. As soon as their roots get established they start making tall growth and from then on it is a case of either moving them out where they have room to grow or constantly chopping their heads out, deforming a naturally beautiful tree and never quite accomplishing the results of good foundation planting.

If the house is low or if there are windows within three feet of the ground, it is always wiser to use material which the catalog says is three or four feet in eventual height. This usually means the spreading type of material like the coton-easters, the dwarf quinces, the low-growing ilexes, and rules out all the upright growers and the taller relatives of the low types. When there is a blank or a bare corner, a flowering tree or small shrub is appropriate and then can be allowed to grow its full size and height without interference from the pruning shears. If constant pruning to keep in bounds is necessary on any planting, but particularly foundation planting, it means that the wrong-size shrub has been used.

A second quality which is most important in any material near the house is that it look well in all four seasons. There is probably no one spot on the property where planting is so frequently visible as the plants immediately in front of the house or near doorways. This means that you and all your neighbors see them four seasons a year, day in and day out, and that any plant which has a very shabby season is ruled out for such close and frequent inspection.

The third quality is that they are plants which have extreme hardihood, both as to winter hardiness in northern climates, drought in hot dry climates, insect pest and disease. Boxwood in Virginia looks beautiful all year round, but in Connecticut or north of New York City certainly burlap covers or cornstalk protection are no ornament all winter and yet without them the boxwood is likely to look burned, if not half dead, in the spring.

In warmer parts of the country where most of the plant material is broad-leaved evergreens—magnolias, privets, viburnums, jasmines—deciduous material, for some reason, instead of merely looking bare as it does in the north, looks dead in the winter. At a distance this is interesting and gives lightness but close at hand around the foundations of the house it always makes me want to dig up the shrub and put in something with leaves on it.

Near the shore where salt winds and salt spray burn the leaves of many plants the flowering tree at the corner of the house might much better be hawthorn than dogwood. Unfortunately the dogwood leaves almost invariably are half brown and very deformed looking for midsummer and are an unpleasant sight close at hand and seen constantly.

Another point to consider is that the material should be suitable for the side of the house on which it is placed. For .example, certain broad-leaved evergreens are likely to burn very badly in full south sun, with the added glare reflected from the house wall, so make bad foundation planting for the south side of the house. On the other hand, the broad-leaved evergreens and the yews like the shady north side and grow luxuriantly and handsomely. On the shady side in a temperate climate there are not many flowering shrubs which will even survive, much less bloom or look thrifty. In southern heat certain favorite plants which like a cooler climate may do very well on the cooler north side of the house, and give up entirely in the tropical climate of a hot south wall.

One point which is hard to define but which makes the difference between individuality and monotony on different houses is that planting should be in keeping with tradition. Observation of old towns, either in this country or abroad, teaches us much about their way of planting so that they look right. Just as lilacs seem to belong to the New England farmhouse or the New England cottage, boxwood to the Southern plantation home, the small cottages of England and France are likely to have almost no foundation planting except vines and an occasional shrub near the door. The houses of Italy and Spain suggest cypresses in the landscape. The large houses of England make one think of yews and holly.

In transplanting these forms of architecture to different climates, it may not be possible to use exactly the same material. All we can do is to select something the same color, texture, shape and eventual size so that it recalls the planting of the old houses without actually reproducing the material that gives the feeling. On the so-called modern or functional architecture of today there is, of course, no tradition. It is such a specialized field that special attention must be given it in the next chapter, with specific recommendations.

CHAPTER IX

Shrubs Around the House (Continued)

FOUNDATION PLANTING separates easily into certain locations where planting may be needed against the house, at doorways, on corners, on chimneys, under windows, and as screens. Few houses need it in all these places. Each position has its particular requirements, and its appropriate kind of plants.

Near doorways, particularly the front door, perhaps the most important requirement is that of year-round effect. This is the place where untidiness, offensive color of leaf or flower, or ugly awkward habit is a daily or almost hourly source of irritation. The plants for doorways must look well 365 days in the year, with a minimum of attention or nursing, and are worth all the time and money that can be spared in selecting just the right ones. Next to their beauty of form, foliage and flower, their scale or proportion is vital, in relation to the size and type of doorway.

On houses of Colonial, Cape Cod, Georgian, Italian ancestry, the doorway is usually in the center, or at least symmetrically balanced on the face of the house. This usually calls for a matched pair of shrubs, almost as architectural accents. Their final height should be determined by both the size of the house as a whole and by the size of the doorway or the entrance porch which they frame. If there are hall windows or outside lights on either side of the door, they should certainly not be blocked by tall-growing shrubs. If the door has a blank wall on either side of it, upright or columnar shaped plants give the accent needed and soften the bareness of the wall. This planting should rarely be higher than the top of the doorway, however, or it will make the entrance look too overpowering for the rest of the house.

In the more informal, or at least more unsymmetrical architecture of the English-type house, the doorway is likely to be off center and so needs a much more subtle type of balance in the planting. If it is near the corner of the house, one side of the doorway planting may actually be both corner planting and doorway planting. In such position one picturesque flowering tree like dogwood, or hawthorn meets all requirements. On the other side of the door where a longer wall space is probable, a lower group of plants, or an entirely different kind of shrub makes the entrance more interesting. Here a heavy mass of holly, *Ilex opaca* or *crenata*, with a sprawling cotoneaster or two give contrast in both height and character with the picturesque quality of the tree silhouette.

On the side or back doors, porch doors, all secondary exits from the house, the same qualities of effectiveness at all times and of proportion apply, but these doors should have a slightly less important planting, in keeping with their function. A matched pair of yews, box, privets, hollies by each door looks more like polka-dots all around the house than like thoughtfully considered planting. After all, you prefer people to know which is the front door.

The corners of the house are the one other location where planting is likely to be needed. This does not mean that every time we see a corner, in must go a plant or group of plants. If the corner needs strengthening or extending, planting can do it, but if the house has too many corners, as on some of the older houses with many jogs, emphasizing certain corners and ignoring others will help to straighten out the line. Again, if a large tree is near the corner of a perfectly symmetrical house it will take a fairly heavy mass of lower planting at the opposite corner to balance it. No planting will be necessary near the tree itself.

The only rules to be sure of in corner planting are that it

Richard Averill Smith

v. The shade of existing spruce and locusts makes a natural setting for a woodland planting of dogwoods, carolina rhododendrons, and azaleas. The foreground of plantain lilies, primroses, and spring bulbs recalls the near-by flower garden.

vi. A pair of dwarf box on either side of the fine doorway, a lilac near one corner, and an apple tree for balance are appropriate for a house of simple dignity and excellent proportion.

can usually be higher than the plants at the entrance, but should be restricted to one fine big specimen, or a well-spaced group of three to five shrubs or one or two varieties, rather than a large and indiscriminate mass of various kinds of plants, however beautiful in themselves. On a low house the corner planting should not come much above the eaves, except in the case of a single flowering tree, and on a tall house the second story windows are a good stopping place.

There are sometimes certain groups of windows under which it is pleasant to have planting. Here is the place where the eventual height of the shrub is all important. The physical energy spent in chopping the tops off shrubs shooting up to cut off light and air would astonish foot-pound calculators. Plants under windows must be chosen from the 3'-4' high group unless the house is high on its foundation. If they can also be fragrant the open-window season gains in pleasure. To keep the height in proportion, shrubs whose width is greater than their height are the best choice.

Slow-growing shrubs are also helpful. For example, dwarf English box, *Buxus suffruticosa*, grows ten or fifteen feet high but at the rate of an inch or two a year. The American box, *Buxus sempervirens*, gets the same height but does it at six inches or more a year. The spreading yews, *Taxus baccata repandens*, or *cuspidata nana*, grow at the same rate as the upright forms, but the first grows sidewise, and the others grow upwards. A new shrub, *Daphne somerset*, promises well, as its rate of growth is moderate and its final height is about five feet. It has the faint daphne fragrance so delightful in its familiar garland flower cousin, *Daphne cneorum*. Unfortunately the list of low shrubs is small, but there are few groups of windows, too, so the right choice is always possible.

An outside chimney on a house can be an opportunity, not an eyesore. It is the ideal spot for the flat-trained shrub of a rare variety, or a fine vine. Since the chimney itself projects from the house, the planting should not add to the mass but be as tight and flat as possible. While it is possible to buy ready-made trained fruit trees, there are many other plants well suited to more informal training. The firethorn, *Pyracantha coccinea Lalandi*, is glorious in bright orange berries, the star magnolia, *M. stellata*, several of the jasmines, *J. nudiflorum, fruticans, humile* (where hardy), *Forsythia suspensa*, are adaptable and there are many others still to be tried. The wall shrubs are discussed in greater detail in a later chapter.

Screen planting near the house is difficult. In screening the kitchen windows from the front door or the living room terrace it is all too easy to use a heavy mass of tall shrubs that might as well have a sign on them saying, "Something hidden here!" That sort of mass also usually cuts out all the light and air and is most unpopular with the cook. One single flowering tree strategically located can do the work of a collection of shrubs. On one place where the dining terrace stared into the kitchen windows at dish-washing time, and had a fine view of the laundry below, we unpaved enough of the corner of the terrace to put in a dogwood. It is a joy from the dining room window, the *pièce de résistance* of the terrace and no one notices the utilitarian purpose it really serves.

Any attempt to screen a faraway eyesore by planting close to the house is likely to be unsuccessful. The sacrifice of air, light and dignity at hand is too great for the ends gained. It may take a heavier, taller screen a little farther away, but is worth it.

A very special kind of foundation planting may be needed where the lines of the house need help. A house too tall for its length can be greatly improved by a clipped hedge extending the line of the house at both ends. A house with an over heavy wing on one end can be brought back into balance with a tall hedge or a combination of vines on posts and connecting chains with a lower hedge between the posts. An L-shaped house can have a secluded enclosed garden by matching the wing with a tall line of shrubs, to give the feeling of complete privacy and intimacy an old walled garden has. This use of shrubs as architectural lines is foundation planting only in that it starts at the foundation.

In all these locations for foundation planting, one to three or five plants are all that are needed. With so few plants and so few locations there is really little reason for the pseudo-arboretum that surrounds many houses. If foundations are so high or so ugly they must be covered up, a flat green band of vine like ivy or euonymus or a trimmed square hedge makes a more substantial and tidy base for a house than a miscellany.

On the house of "modernistic" design the same principles of restraint, order and selectivity apply, but with greater force. Since its beauty is in clean line, plain surfaces, generous window openings, there is no excuse for cluttering it up with messy planting. Shrubs or small trees can be set where they form changing shadow patterns on the flat walls. An occasional picturesque plant form like a gnarled hawthorn or crabapple makes the geometric lines of the house more interesting by contrast. Vines or shrubs can be trained to accent certain house lines or break up over-large blank walls. Too much repetition of the square straight lines of the house by square hedges or distorted topiary work usually leads only to monotony and gives the place a cut-out-of-cardboard feeling with no relation to its outdoor surroundings.

Whatever the kind of house and wherever it is located, it gains in beauty only by careful selection of important material for as few places as possible immediately around the walls.

SHRUBS AROUND THE HOUSE

FOUNDATION PLANTING—The plants suggested for planting near the house include those that best represent the qualities of good all-year-round appearance, hardiness, disease resistance. The evergreens are usually more formal in effect and best suited to the symmetrical type of house.

EVERGREENS

PLANT MATERIAL	HEIGHT	HABIT	PLACE TO PLANT
Azalea indica alba INDICA AZALEA	5′	Broad oval	Underplanting in group, matched pair by door.
Berberis julianae WINTERGREEN BARBERRY	4′	Oval	Upright hedge under windows.
Berberis verruculosa WARTY BARBERRY	2½′ spread	Angular	Interplanting with deciduous in groups.
Buxus sempervirens suffruticosa TRUEDWARF BOX	2′–10′	Broad oval	Specimens, matched pair.
Ilex crenata microphylla SMALL-LEAVED JAPANESE HOLLY	10′	Narrow oval	Specimen, natural or sheared.

Name	Height	Shape	Use
Ilex glabra INKBERRY	4'	Round	Group planting, or specimen.
Ilex opaca AMERICAN HOLLY	20'	Broad pyramid	Specimen.
Juniperus virginiana RED CEDAR	25'	Columnar	Tall accent for large house.
Kalmia latifolia MOUNTAIN LAUREL	8'	Broad oval	Group planting, shade.
Rhododendron arbutifolium ROCKMOUNT RHODODENDRON	4'	Spreading oval	Group planting, shade.
Rhododendron catawbiense Boule de Neige DWARF WHITE RHODODENDRON	6'	Oval	Group planting, shade.
Taxus cuspidata capitata UPRIGHT YEW	5'–20'	Pyramid	Specimen, natural or sheared.
Taxus hunnewelliana HUNNEWELL YEW	2'–8'	Broad oval	Specimen, by doors.
Thuja occidentalis pyramidalis PYRAMIDAL ARBORVITAE	25'	Columnar	Tall accent, for large house.

FOUNDATION PLANTING

DECIDUOUS

PLANT MATERIAL	HEIGHT	HABIT	PLACE TO PLANT
Azalea vaseyi PINKSHELL AZALEA	8′	Picturesque	Picturesque group, semi-shade.
Calycanthus floridus SWEETSHRUB	6′	Oval	Corner, specimen, semi-shade.
Chaenomeles japonica DWARF FLOWERING QUINCE	4′	Picturesque mound	Low informal pair at door.
Chaenomeles lagenaria JAPANESE FLOWERING QUINCE	10′	Picturesque oval	Informal pair at door.
Cornus florida FLOWERING DOGWOOD	25′	Picturesque	Specimen for silhouette and flower.
Cotinus coggygria SMOKETREE	12′	Irregular oval	Specimen, on corner.
Cotoneaster divaricata SPREADING COTONEASTER	6′	Arching oval	Light mass in group.
Crataegus oxyacantha ENGLISH HAWTHORN	25′	Vase-shaped tree	Specimen on corner.
Euonymus alatus WINGED EUONYMUS	10′	Vase-shaped, picturesque	Specimen on corner.

Name	Height	Shape	Use
Hibiscus syriacus ROSE OF SHARON	12′	Narrow upright	Specimen at corner, or door of tall house.
Laburnum vulgare watereri WATERER GOLDENCHAIN TREE	15′	Narrow tree	Specimen for tall house.
Magnolia soulangeana SAUCER MAGNOLIA	25′	Broad oval tree	Specimen on sunny corner.
Myrica pensylvanica BAYBERRY	4′	Broad oval	Formal mass near door, seashore.
Rosa hugonis FATHER HUGO ROSE	6′	Arching broad oval	With lilacs for corner.
Syringa amurensis japonica JAPANESE TREE LILAC	20′	Narrow tree	Tall specimen on corner.
Syringa villosa LATE LILAC	12′	Oval	Corners of house.
Syringa vulgaris or varieties COMMON LILAC	12′	Oval or vase-shaped	Corners of New England house.
Vaccinium corymbosum HIGHBUSH BLUEBERRY	8′	Picturesque	Specimen.
Viburnum carlesi KOREANSPICE VIBURNUM	6′	Oval	Specimen, by door or under window.
Viburnum sieboldi SIEBOLD VIBURNUM	8′	Oval	Specimen on corner, large house.
Viburnum tomentosum DOUBLEFILE VIBURNUM	8′	Oval	Specimen on corner.

CHAPTER X

Shrubs for Special Places

ONE OF the very special places where shrubs are almost always needed is at the driveway entrance to any property. Here the shrubs must be chosen with an appreciation both of the use of the plant and its beauty. From a practical point of view they serve to mark the entrance to the place, making it easier to find, and in northern climates quite often serve as a barrier, to keep the snow from drifting across the entrance of the road. The looks of this planting can and should indicate the kind of place inside this entrance, whether it is formal or informal, of woods or meadow atmosphere, or one large flower garden on a small suburban place.

If the driveway leads to the front door so that it is primarily the entrance for family and friends, it should certainly show the hospitality and invitation to enter which the attractive and well proportioned front door itself does. If it is, as on many small suburban places, only a driveway directly to the garage, its planting should be simple so as not to call too much attention to it and to indicate, as far as possible, its purely utilitarian purpose.

Although the planting should indicate the character of the place, this does not mean that it need be a sample ground. Many driveway entrances seem to have been planted with an idea of having one of everything that is inside the property line, shown at the entrance, including some of the flowers. This is much more likely to look like the sales display of a nursery office than it is the entrance to a private home. The same kind of restraint and careful selection are needed at the entrance of the property as at the entrance to the house itself and a great many of the same principles of selection apply.

The driveway entrance is the front door to the grounds. It is most important that all the planting be chosen for year-round effect. Not only do all the people who actually come in pass it frequently but the public at large can get a very good idea of the kind of family living there by the condition of the front entrance planting at all seasons of the year. With this constant visibility it must not only have beauty at all times but it must be as nearly care-free and insect- and disease-free as is possible. Even on a fairly quiet road there is a certain amount of handicap from traffic dust and fumes, and also the hazard of the wandering flower picker, those careless or thoughtless people who do not realize that in breaking off showy blooms from shrubs along the roadside, they are damaging not only the looks but the health of the planting. If the entrance planting is too attractive in bloom, it may unfortunately be too attractive to some of these casual passersby, with their queer sense of property rights.

The eventual size of the planting at the entrance is all important from the purely practical standpoint of not blocking vision as you come in and out of your own driveway. Too many people have planted three to four foot shrubs close to a driveway entrance and found that in two or three years it was the choice of either ripping them out, crashing into passing cars or spending the summer pruning back shrubs. For safety's sake, it is imperative that when the driveway comes directly from a main traveled road the driver, coming in or out of it, must be able to see at least fifty feet up and down the highway and at least thirty feet inside the driveway. This means that either the shrubs must be small flowering trees, pruned high enough so the driver looks under their heads up and down the road, or must be very low shrubs, which without the aid of pruning shears will never get higher than the hood of the car.

If the property inside the entrance consists largely of beautifully kept, open lawns with formal hedges and formal gardens or with a generally manicured look, certainly the entrance planting should have the same characteristics. For such planting, a pair of trees, one on either side of the driveway, of a formal and symmetrical shape, or groups of plants which are completely symmetrically placed, such as yews, cedars and broad-leaved evergreens, will give a foretaste of the formality inside.

If, on the other hand, the property is approached through a fruit orchard or through a native woodland or meadow, the planting at the entrance should be part of this natural setting. It may be man-made but it certainly should not look it, so that there is a feeling of disappointment or shock on being led to believe that you are coming to formality and then find yourself in more casual surroundings too abruptly. If the grounds inside the entrance have an apple orchard as one of the chief features, the entrance planting may very well have a pair of flowering crabapples or even a pair of apples at the entrance.

If the home is in rolling meadow country, certainly native planting of the flowering crabapple, the elders, the sumac and other plants that fill the hedgerows and the roadsides should be represented at the entrance. A roadside planting of these native things may terminate at the driveway entrance with a particularly fine group of crabapples or magnolias or holly, or whatever is in the native roadside planting that is particularly effective at all seasons of the year.

One home in beautiful Connecticut woodlands has an entrance I have always thought particularly well-chosen. An old stone wall marks the front boundary to the property and just where the driveway enters, the owner has cleared away enough of the woodland to let two fine dogwoods on one side come close to the road as specimens, and on the other, planted a younger dogwood against some already existing and very handsome hemlocks. This entrance gives you a pleasant foretaste of the open woodland you drive through as you come to the house, some three hundred feet away.

If the place and the house itself are small and unpretentious, certainly the driveway entrance should not lead you to expect a mansion after you get past it. Large stone piers, elaborate fence or gate treatment belong to the big house. So do large, heavy formal masses of over-groomed and ostentatious planting. For some reason all evergreen plantings or plantings of solid evergreen have a certain opulence and luxuriance that makes them seem over-full, inappropriate to the small property. There can be some evergreen in the entrance planting for winter effect but it should always be mixed with deciduous material.

The planting problem is entirely different when the driveway leads only to the service quarters or to the garage. There it is not a question of calling attention to the driveway and making it easier to find but rather a question of making it less conspicuous from the front door of the house. This is a purely utilitarian driveway and like all utilitarian areas should be minimized without having its usefulness impaired. It is just as important to have the visibility good from this driveway, of course and perhaps more so, as big delivery trucks need more room to maneuver and more visibility for distance in which to stop. If this driveway is visible from the front door, however, it should certainly not be the chief feature of that side of the property. One excellent planting scheme is to have two or three flowering trees to bloom at different seasons and whose attraction is in the head of the tree rather than down near the ground. In that way, the eye is called up in the air and the paved surface of the driveway is made less conspicuous, even though it is actually visible.

If the planting or treatment of the service entrance is made too important or too attractive you may be embarrassed to find that certain acquaintances land in your garage court and the kitchen door instead of parking their cars out in the street and walking to the front door. If the property is big enough so that it has both a service drive and a main entrance drive, it should not require signs to tell which is which, any more than it does to tell which is the front door and which is the kitchen door of the house.

Another place where shrubs are very useful is at the entrance of the garden or some special decorative area on the property. These should be plants which are interesting enough to lead the observer to go see them and to tempt him on into the area beyond. Here is the place for a matched pair of flowering trees, whose heads can arch together and form a frame through which the bright color of a flower garden is seen. The magnolias, the dogwoods, hawthorns, crabapples, cherries, are especially good for this purpose, if they are leading to an area which is symmetrical and where you want the eye to follow a strongly defined line.

If, on the other hand, the garden is below the house so that you look down onto it, you will not want the high heads of tall trees or shrubs to interfere with the view. In such a case you may want a pair of low plants that are beautiful in form and interesting in bloom or fruit color just as an accent to mark the entrance to a certain area. This is the place for some very special shrub, like *Daphne somerset*, or *Ilex crenata convexa*, or low-growing yews, the fine evergreen azaleas or *Pieris japonica*. It should not be growing elsewhere on the place so that its very rareness makes it interesting, and of course it must be something that looks well at all times without too much pampering.

There is one special use of shrubs that has been so badly abused that it is almost dangerous to suggest it. This is the planting of shrubs or small flowering trees as specimens. Too often we have seen lawns spotted here and there with shrubs with no reason for their existence except sheer perfection of growing a horticultural specimen. They not only do nothing for the looks of the place as a whole, but break up the lawn and give it a restless, cluttered-up feeling. With this in mind it is safe to say that occasionally there are places where a specimen shrub may be not only allowable but necessary.

There are certain characteristics of a specimen shrub that should always be taken into account. It must, first of all, be fairly uniform in growth or else particularly picturesque in its habit. It should be unusually beautiful at one season, but completely presentable at all seasons, and it should be immune to almost anything that might damage its beauty. Most of the small flowering trees will qualify as specimens but among the shrubs themselves very few will.

Any of the many-twigged shrubs like the spireas, forsythias, weigelas, deutzias, philadelphus will grow terrifically as single specimens on a lawn but when they are grown they only look like a larger brush-heap, with even less excuse for their untidy existence than when they are partly concealed by distance or by other more interesting shrubs nearby. They may be beautiful when they are in bloom for two weeks, but there are eleven and a half months when you still have to live with them. On the other hand, the burningbush, *Euonymus alatus*, when it is alone and very old is so gnarled in habit, with its corky bark, its brilliant fall color and its nice leaf, that it can be used as a specimen in certain places. Many of the hollies can, also, and others of the broad leaf evergreens whose habit of growth is particularly nice. The tree lilacs, the flowering quince, the fringe tree, the silver bell all make intriguing old specimens, if they are in exactly the right place.

The places where specimens are justified are very few. One is on the small suburban property where there is not room for a large shade tree but where some sort of tree is needed to cast a shadow across the lawn, to shade a terrace, or to frame the house from the street. A fine magnolia, any one of the flowering crabapples or cherries, or hawthorns, an interesting old apple tree will have room and opportunity to develop its interesting character and beautiful shape, and still be in more correct proportion to the size of the place than an oak, an elm, a beech, or a linden. This is particularly true of the small property and the small house, where too many big trees dwarf it and trees fifteen to twenty-five feet high are much more in character.

Any entrance is, of course, an opportunity for specimens, whether to the driveway, the house itself or the garden. As accents in the flower garden itself fine specimens may be invaluable. If an old, gnarled apple or pear, a big magnolia, a huge old lilac or a tremendous handsome yew or holly is in the vicinity of your garden site, it can be the focal point of the entire area, so that the garden has an interest and character that no amount of new planting could ever give it. If a big one does not exist it may be worth while to import one from a nursery or from somewhere else on your own place, to get the feeling of age and charm that only old shrubs give. In the very formal garden, however small, symmetrically placed, trimmed shrubs like yews or privet or box may mark the important crossings of the paths, or the axes of the garden.

Another use of specimens is to tempt the eye and the feet to explore more or less concealed parts of the place. For example, if you have a path which is particularly lovely in early May, with spring bulbs and flowering shrubs, one big handsome flowering tree near it calls attention to that part of the ground and makes you and all your friends want to go down and see it, and thence be led into the path naturally without verbal coaxing. If you have a fruit orchard however small, of which you are very proud, a specimen fruit tree near the entrance to the area gives an interesting foretaste of the beauty just beyond and makes everyone want to go to see it. Woodland paths, even on the smallest property, can be made inviting by one single fine specimen dogwood calling the eye to the entrance to the path.

Frequently specimens can be used to give an illusion of greater distance or of greater depth to planting. For example, if the shrub border cannot be made very wide and you want to give the illusion of having a deep bay, a flowering tree or a handsome specimen of some shrub placed slightly in front of the border will give the same illusion as a genuinely deeply curving border. The specimens for this use should be bold in habit and striking in color in as many seasons as possible. Of the shrubs, things like the burningbush, flowering quince, highbush blueberry are excellent. Of the small flowering trees, the hawthorns and crabapples and dogwoods are perhaps the best. Specimens must be regarded as very special ornaments and therefore used very sparingly. Too many of them make the grounds as restless as a room with a mirror every ten feet, or a woman with so many diamonds that your eyes are dazzled and bewildered.

While very few people grow shrubs for the sole purpose of cutting them for the house, there are certain ones that are particularly good for that purpose. The requirement for such shrubs is that they do not shatter too quickly and easily after cutting, that their bloom is heavy enough in proportion to their leaf that they tell as a flower mass when cut, or that their bold color in itself is interesting and useful for arrangement.

Most of the shrubs with many flowers on the stem, such as the bridalwreath, may be effective in big containers in the house but they are likely to be very messy as far as housekeeping is concerned. Their petals keep falling and it is a nuisance to have to keep dusting the table and the floor near where they are every time a breeze blows through the house. The philadelphus, weigelias and deutzias have this same unpleasant characteristic, although they are beautiful cut. On the other hand, the bolder flowers, like the lilacs, the buddleias, the magnolias, the crabapples, dogwoods last well in the house and are handsome for several days after picking. The shrub roses are all good for bouquets if you can wear heavy enough gloves to stand the briars.

Of the foliage shrubs, the purple leaved ones like *Prunus pissardi*, the purple leaved barberry and some of the purple crabapples are very popular in arrangements. Even some of the green and white variegated leaved things may be useful but hardly worth the space they take up, unless the property is a big one.

When flower branches are cut it is advisable to strip off most of the leaves or as many as possible without completely destroying the character of the plant, using the leaves separately in the bouquet as needed. Then the stems of the shrubs should be either mashed or slit so as to allow more water to get up into the branches. It takes a certain amount of experimenting with any shrub to find out just how to handle it when cut, but these two precautions will help.

If shrubs are used for bouquets for the house, the cutting should be done as part of the general pruning of the shrub and done properly. It is just as easy and certainly a great time saver to prune your lilacs to use for the house and not have to go over the whole bush later to repair the damage you did in ruthless cutting. With the flowering crabapples and magnolias, the interfering branches which have to come out anyway can just as well be used for house bouquets, without spoiling and, in fact, with improvement of the general shape of the shrub. The shrubs that are cut for forcing in the house like the forsythias, the flowering quince and the crabapple can be pruned on the wood which will need to come out anyway at the end of flowering.

At the corner of a stone wall I have bittersweet and a flowering quince which would have fought it out to the death of one or the other long since, except that every fall I cut almost all the bittersweet off for huge bouquets for my own apartment and my friends', and every spring cut all the interfering branches on the flowering quince for forcing. It is a very good example of one of the rare times when ruthless pruning is not only necessary but a very happy thing to do because I can use everything I prune. If you prune carefully and according to the proper treatment for that particular shrub every time you cut flowers for the house, you will find that not only do you have more flowers but you also have much less work later and a much finer shrub as a result.

VII. A single specimen of flowering crabapple against a simple picket fence needs only a few tulips and forget-me-nots near by for effectiveness. More shrubs would detract from the picturesque quality of the tree.

Gottscho-Schleisner

viii. A pair of styrax frame the view of a sunken shrub garden. The shrubs at the end are rhododendrons and evergreen azaleas with rock cotoneasters hanging over the small pool. Two sweet gums give dark vertical accent.

CHAPTER XI

Shrubs for Hedges, Fences and Walls

ALMOST EVERY place, whether large or small, has some spot where a fairly narrow line of planting is needed. This usually means a hedge. A hedge is really a living fence, or a wall of live plant material instead of wood, iron, stone or brick, and certain qualities are important in the choice of the material for such a purpose. It is usually needed where space is more or less limited or where a definite geometric line is appropriate in the general design, rather than a soft irregular mass.

TRIMMED HEDGE

The obvious hedge for such purpose is a sheared or trimmed line of plants. The first thing to determine is exactly how much room you can give to this hedge when it is full grown. Too often a small hedge of a very free-growing material is planted without regard to its natural size or habit of growth. In a few years it is impossible to keep the hedge within bounds, either in height or in width, so that it all has to be ripped out and replaced with some more suitable.

In choosing a hedge a list of plant material which gives total height, width or general habit and the rate of growth will be invaluable. The hedge shape should conform to the general shape of the plants used. That is, a tall broad plant grown free-standing will make a tall broad hedge. A tall slender plant will make a tall slender hedge and a low broad plant will make a low broad hedge. Failure to take this into account almost invariably means either that you have a hedge that is wrongly shaped for your purpose, or that you spend your life trying to make a plant conform to an unnatural habit.

If there is no more than two and a half feet between the property line and a path, a hedge of hemlocks three feet high may fit when they are planted but no amount of drastic shearing will ever keep them in bounds ten years later. All that would be left would be the trunks of the hemlocks with little green around them. On the other hand, if the space is six to seven feet, three foot hemlocks may look pretty puny when they are first started, but as they grow they can be sheared lightly and make a graceful, green wall, ten or twelve feet high and six or seven feet broad. In the narrow space, a line of yew or small leaved holly, or arborvitae can give the same dark green line with less trouble in constant pruning to keep the path open.

The rate of growth is important in the amount of pruning that the hedge needs. Any plant which grows wildly two or three feet a year, is difficult to keep in bounds. If, on the other hand, it grows only five to six inches a year, it means that the pruning needs to be done much less often and so the hedge will demand much less upkeep. This rate of growth, however, should be checked in your own vicinity, not taken from a list of plant material in some different part of the country. In general the same plants will grow much faster and many more inches a year in the more southern limits of its range than at the extreme north of its range. A longer growing season obviously means more prunings a year to keep in bounds than the northern season of five to six months.

Another quality that is most important is the natural branching habit of the shrub. The ones that make the best thick hedges are those with many twigs and branches from top to bottom and broader at the ground than at the top. Of the larger growing plants this form is typical of hemlock and arborvitae of the needled evergreens; *Ilex crenata*, or in the south *Ilex vomitoria*, of the broad-leaved evergreens; beech, hawthorn and privet in the tall deciduous plants; barberry, and *Euonymus alatus compactus* in the smaller deciduous shrubs. All prune well and can be kept to a tight, thick hedge for many years.

The shrubs with open rather coarse branches like *Viburnum sieboldi*, most of the magnolias, do not have enough side branches to be thick or close in habit as a trimmed hedge should be. It is not invariable but in general any shrub which is particularly good for specimen use because of its open, picturesque habit, is a poor choice for trimmed hedges.

In order to keep a hedge uniform and attractive the plants must be of some variety that is tough and hardy in your locality, fairly free from pest and disease, and reasonably uniform in growth. The use of any half-hardy or temperamental material will only result in certain plants thriving and others doing badly, so that the hedge always looks like the little boy who has lost part of his teeth. Far better to have a sturdy, uniform, solid hedge of common material like privet or barberry, than a rarer and infinitely more expensive one of box where the winters are severe so that part of it is burned or winter snows break out great branches.

The trimmed hedge is most useful where space is limited but enclosure is needed or where from the standpoint of looks alone, a straight, hard line or a perfectly geometric curve is demanded. A low hedge surrounding the beds gives the garden a tidy and formal appearance that no irregular perennial edges can attain. A taller one around the outside of the garden gives the same feeling of intimacy and privacy that a vine-covered wall does. A house which is unsymmetrical can sometimes be brought into much better proportion by a long straight hedge at one end, extending the line of the house.

Trimmed hedges usually have a feeling of formality about them and are therefore not appropriate in open farm country or native woodland, except immediately adjoining the house.

Since they are obviously man-made, they belong in places where the landscape as a whole is obviously man-made, not that of nature. In the city or in suburbs or in small towns they look appropriate and are very useful.

One great disadvantage of the trimmed hedge is that it is a large item in the total upkeep of the place. Almost any hedge to look well has to be trimmed at least twice a year and some of them four times to keep them neat and healthy. Anyone who has ever tried to trim a perfectly square tall hedge knows that it is no job for an amateur and that it takes many hours to do. Badly trimmed, it is an eyesore with an irregular top and bulges on both sides. Trimmed too infrequently it looks ragged and untidy. Trimmed well and frequently it is likely to be a major upkeep problem on the place. It should be used with great discretion and restraint, and often an untrimmed hedge can be substituted to advantage.

UNTRIMMED HEDGES

Some of the most beautiful hedges in existence are straight lines of plants but kept that way with very light or no use of pruning shears. These are the untrimmed hedges of old gardens which even years of neglect have not hurt too much. They may be either evergreen or deciduous but the same qualities of hardihood and natural size apply. If they are of evergreen material such as hemlock or holly, some trimming is probably needed to keep them thick and handsome. This usually consists only of taking out the tops, so that the growth is thrown into the side branches, and trimming at the ends of the branches lightly, not shearing them back to a very hard line as for a real trimmed hedge.

Some of the more open materials are well adapted to the untrimmed hedge. For big hedges, white pine, hawthorn, beech are more beautiful if left slightly irregular and loose in outline than if trimmed to a hard, sheer, wall-like line. They will, of course, be broader and take up more room. A long lane of lilacs, probably topped back a little to keep them from getting too leggy, and with many of the suckers left in at the base, is beautiful near a New England house, or back of an informal garden. For lower hedges some of the very floriferous shrubs are most attractive. Around a garden an untrimmed hedge of *Rosa hugonis*, or *Spiraea van houttei*, needs very little attention from the pruning shears and has a chance to show its great arching branches of flowers to full advantage.

If any of these flowering shrubs are used for a tightly clipped hedge all the benefit of the flower is likely to be lost as the two or three times a year pruning is bound to hit one of the seasons when the flowering wood is being developed. Flowering hedges are very effective with green lawn in front of them so that their mass of flower is contrasted with the green carpet. They are also excellent for enclosing a flower garden so that at the season of their bloom the whole thing looks like a great corsage with a frill around it.

Certain of the low spreading evergreens are well adapted to the untrimmed hedge. Any of the andromedas have fairly uniform growth, enhanced by the lily-of-the-valley like flowers in the spring. *Pieris japonica* is probably the best of them but either *floribunda* or *nitida* (now called *Lyonia lucida*) is excellent. The dwarf holly like *Ilex crenata convexa* or *Ilex helleri* need only the end branches trimmed out when they get a little ragged. Certain of the upright growing yews, like *hicksi*, *hatfieldi*, or *hunnewelliana* need only very light shearing for a good hedge. Of course dwarf box, *Buxus suffruticosa*, is ideal low untrimmed hedge in sections of the country where it is hardy. Its growth is so slow that even without trimming it is many years before a little six or eight inch box plant gets too big for its place as an edging.

Where space is limited and there is room for only one row of shrubs, the untrimmed hedge is far more effective than a mixed border of shrubs. Its very uniformity when it is not in bloom gives a feeling of repose and continuity. When it is in flower it is a stunning mass and has none of the polka-dot

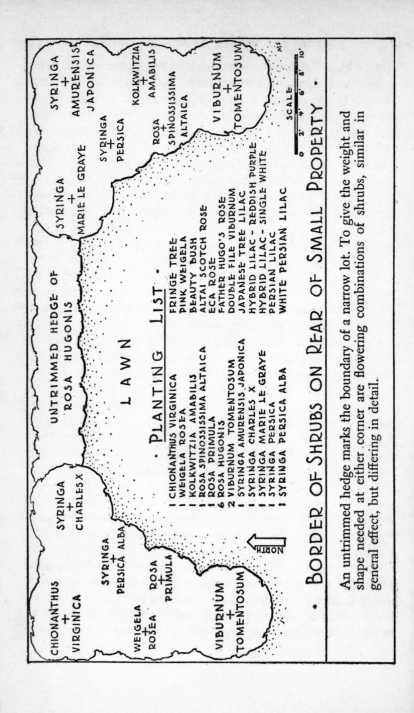

CHIONANTHUS + VIRGINICA

SYRINGA + CHARLES X

UNTRIMMED HEDGE OF ROSA HUGONIS

SYRINGA + MARIE LE GRAYE

SYRINGA + AMURENSIS JAPONICA

SYRINGA + PERSICA ALBA

ROSA PRIMULA

SYRINGA + PERSICA

KOLKWITZIA AMABILIS

WEIGELA + ROSEA

ROSA + SPINOSISSIMA ALTAICA

VIBURNUM + TOMENTOSUM

VIBURNUM + TOMENTOSUM

LAWN

NORTH

SCALE
0 2' 4' 6' 8' 10'

· PLANTING LIST ·

1 CHIONANTHUS VIRGINICA   FRINGE TREE
1 WEIGELA ROSEA   PINK WEIGELA
1 KOLKWITZIA AMABILIS   BEAUTY BUSH
1 ROSA SPINOSISSIMA ALTAICA   ALTAI SCOTCH ROSE
1 ROSA PRIMULA   ECA ROSE
6 ROSA HUGONIS   FATHER HUGO'S ROSE
2 VIBURNUM TOMENTOSUM   DOUBLE FILE VIBURNUM
1 SYRINGA AMURENSIS JAPONICA   JAPANESE TREE LILAC
1 SYRINGA CHARLES X   HYBRID LILAC - REDDISH PURPLE
1 SYRINGA MARIE LE GRAYE   HYBRID LILAC - SINGLE WHITE
1 SYRINGA PERSICA   PERSIAN LILAC
1 SYRINGA PERSICA ALBA   WHITE PERSIAN LILAC

· BORDER OF SHRUBS ON REAR OF SMALL PROPERTY ·

An untrimmed hedge marks the boundary of a narrow lot. To give the weight and shape needed at either corner are flowering combinations of shrubs, similar in general effect, but differing in detail.

effect that a long single row of two roses, two spireas, two flowering quinces, two lilacs, two mockoranges would give. An untrimmed hedge on the far property line with a group of shrubs at either end of it, can give the effect of a broad and pleasantly shaped curve at the back of the lawn without taking up the room that a wider border of mixed shrubs does, to make the same shape. In the country the untrimmed hedge has a charm that no hard straight line of a trimmed one can give. Its simplicity is particularly appropriate to the small informal home in country or town. (See Drawing No. 3, p. 150.)

FENCES OF SHRUBS AND SMALL FLOWERING TREES

Visitors to Gardens on Parade at the World's Fair in New York may remember fruit trees trimmed to form a tight narrow fence. With plenty of time, patience, determination and sharp pruning shears, a living fence can be made from shrubs and small trees. Where a straight line is desirable but there is not even room for a hedge, such a fence may be made of plants which have a single trunk or at most, three branches from the ground. The branches themselves must be sturdy and stiff enough to hold shape after they are trained but pliable enough when young to train easily and without too many small twigs from the main stem.

The general characteristic of the apple and pear trees should be kept in mind in selecting shrubs for such purpose. They must be started very young and of course will require posts with wires run between them for the first few years in order to have something to tie the branches to, while they are being trained. One form consists of small plants set about a foot apart and trained to V shape. The V's overlap each other making a diamond shaped lattice. Another form is of a single leader with branches opposite each other at regular intervals, horizontally trained.

Openly branched shrubs and small trees are the only ones suitable for such work. The flowering crabapple, particularly

Malus sargenti, can be trained to form a fairly high fence. Of the shrubs, *Viburnum sieboldi* or *tomentosum* are excellent for the purpose. For a lower fence, flowering quince, *Chaenomeles japonica*, and dwarf winged euonymus, *Euonymus alatus compacta*, train satisfactorily.

Since the pruning and training require a great deal of time, this fence certainly should be used only in small quantities. Twenty-five or thirty feet of such fence is possible, a hundred feet would demand so much attention and time that it would be completely out of proportion to the effect. Even the gasps of admiration and ill-concealed envy of your friends will hardly compensate for the gardening time spent on such a tour-de-force.

WALL SHRUBS

Closely related to the use of shrubs as a fence in themselves is that of training them flat against a masonry wall or a wood or wire fence. It is familiar to anyone who has seen the fruit trained against walls abroad but the potentialities in other shrubs has been explored in only a few places in this country. In the newer houses, with their wide wall spaces unbroken by windows, this kind of planting has infinite possibilities and great appropriateness. On the more traditional types of houses there is usually some blank wall between windows or an outside chimney breast where a decorative accent is needed and where a shrub trained flat would be more interesting than a vine left to ramble at its own will.

The more familiar type of trained or espalier shrubs is the one which is trained to a definite pattern, usually either fan-shaped or U or double U form. These have a certain formality even when trained of informal plant material like fruit trees. They should, therefore, be used in the more tailored parts of the place, that is, on a garden wall, on the wall adjoining a paved terrace, around a formal entrance court—in other words, in the man-made part of the place and of a rather prim and formal type place at that.

Richard Averill Smith

IX. A lightly trimmed hedge of dwarf yew is a handsome setting for white calla lilies and ageratum on the house terrace. The tightly clipped hedge of privet on the street gives privacy and dignity, without shutting out the interesting dunes in the background.

Gottscho-Schleisner

x. The service areas are screened by the loosely sheared hedge of English beech on the left of the path. The creamy flowers of Siebold's viburnum make a bold background for the delicate purple of Persian lilac and primrose of Father Hugo's rose on the right.

For this kind of training it is essential that the plant chosen have a fairly sturdy branching habit, without too many side twigs. It should not be too rampant a grower, so that the severe pruning which such training requires will not result in a wild mass of soft sucker growth at each cut. If fruit trees are used for such purpose they must be on dwarf root-stock. Full sized apple or pear trees soon get out of bounds and are impossible to keep to any reasonable size or shape.

Possibly more interesting and certainly less usual are the shrubs or small trees trained flat against the wall or fence, but with no set shape to the training. The same qualities of sturdy branching habits so that the main stems of the training can be held firmly to the support is necessary as for the formally trained shrub. Here, however, shrubs of more picturesque and gnarled habit are interesting. Shrubs with unusual bark and twigs make arresting pictures. *Euonymus alatus* with its corky wings is one of the best.

Shrubs which have a single leader from the ground and no suckers or numerous branches coming up from the root train nicely. Otherwise, pruning back of the main part of the shrub may encourage so much new growth and such vigorous growth from the ground that it will be a constant battle to keep any kind of flatness in the training. The eventual natural height of the shrub is important in relation to the space to be covered. If the space is only six feet wide by ten feet high, a shrub whose total height when grown free-standing is in the eight to ten foot class will fit. If a twelve to fifteen foot shrub is put in there it will require such constant cropping back to keep it in bounds that the top of it is likely to be an ugly mass of stubbed-back growth.

One drawback to fruit trees trained flat is that the number of sprays they require to produce good fruit in most parts of the country makes a problem of staining the house or wall behind them and of actually giving the plant enough coverage on the spray to get good fruit. This indicates one essential of shrubs chosen for such purpose. They should be as nearly as possible disease- and insect-free, tough and hardy, in fact immune to almost anything that can happen to a shrub. Pruning and training takes too much work and too much time to risk losing one whole side of a plant and spoiling the shape, with a dry summer or a hard winter, or having the house or wall behind it constantly stained with the spray material which the shrub needs to thrive but makes it anything but an ornament.

Other desirable qualities to look for in shrubs to be used flat are unusual fruit or flower which is born close to the main stem, unusual color in bark or twig, attractive leaves throughout the growing season. In the south there are many evergreen shrubs which are well adapted. In the north, almost none. The half-vine, half-shrub group like the weeping forsythia, *Forsythia suspensa*, or winter jasmine, *Jasminum nudiflorum*, are naturals for this kind of work, as they need support, so cannot be called real vines, but are too floppy for general shrub use. In milder parts of the country some of the old roses, even the hybrid perpetuals, many of the shrub roses can be used this way. In the south there are many half-climbing evergreens that are invaluable.

The low wall around a garden gains in interest if occasional panels have a trained shrub for accent rather than having all of them covered with vines. A niche in a garden wall where a seat is built can have shrubs trained flat on the wall behind the seat to very excellent effect. The end of a path may lead to a particularly picturesque example of trained shrubs on either side of a gate. An inexpensive fence of either vertical or horizontal boards is much more decorative when it serves as a background for trained shrubs than if it is covered with rampant-growing vines.

All these shrubs should be at least eight inches to a foot away from the wall or fence so that provision must be made for some sort of support, at least while they are young. In a brick or stone wall wood plugs should be set into the wall for expansion bolts to hold wires or rods at the proper placings for the shrubs. On a wood house or fence some form of trellis must be extended from the house. All supports must be sturdy as it takes a certain amount of pulling and tying firmly to keep the shrub in the shape to which you want it to grow. The list of shrubs useful for this treatment is only indicative of types. There are many others which have not been tried which would probably be most effective.

SHRUBS FOR HEDGES, FENCES AND WALLS

TRIMMED HEDGES—While many plants can be trimmed to hedge shape, those suggested are the ones that can be kept to handsome tight hedge over a period of many years, with a minimum shearing. Twice a year should be often enough for shearing. The heights and widths given are those of useful landscape value for permanent effect.

b. LOW HEDGES

Plant Material	Height	Width	Characteristics
Carpinus betulus EUROPEAN HORNBEAM	8'–12'	5'–6'	Deciduous, spreading hedge. Resembles beech hedge but hardier.
Crataegus crusgalli COCKSPUR HAWTHORN	6'– 8'	4'–5'	Thorny barrier, near house or flower garden.
Fagus sylvatica EUROPEAN BEECH	7'–12'	4'–6'	Traditional with English house. Leaves persistent.
Ligustrum ovalifolium CALIFORNIA PRIVET	6'–10'	3'–5'	Inexpensive, excellent near salt water or in city.

Maclura pomifera OSAGE ORANGE	6'–10'	5'–7'	Thorny barrier, hard to trim, exposed location.
Rhamnus cathartica BUCKTHORN	6'– 8'	3'–5'	Cold climates, exposed locations.
Taxus cuspidata capitata UPRIGHT YEW	4'– 8'	3'–5'	Darkest evergreen, semi-shade, for garden enclosure.
Thuja occidentalis EASTERN ARBORVITAE	6'–10'	3'–4'	Narrow evergreen hedge, not for windy location.
Tilia cordata SMALL-LEAVED LINDEN	10'–12'	6'–8'	Broad, deciduous hedge
Tsuga canadensis CANADIAN HEMLOCK	7'–12'	4'–5'	Rich evergreen screen or accent line. Light shearing, light shade.
Tsuga carolina CAROLINA HEMLOCK	6'–10'	3'–4'	Finer texture than Canadian, slightly less hardy, shade.

SHRUBS FOR HEDGES, FENCES AND WALLS

TRIMMED HEDGES

b. LOW HEDGES

PLANT MATERIAL	HEIGHT	WIDTH	CHARACTERISTICS
Berberis thunbergi JAPANESE BARBERRY	2½'–4'	2½'–3'	Thorny, broad hedge, inexpensive.
Berberis thunbergi erecta TRUEHEDGE COLUMNBERRY	1'–4'	1½'–2'	Only top shearing needed. Berries effective.
Buxus sempervirens COMMON BOX	2½'–4'	1½'–2½'	Shears well, subject to miner.
Buxus sempervirens suffruticosa TRUEDWARF BOX	1'–4'	1½'–3'	Little shearing necessary unless height is to be restricted. Richest green, slow-growing.
Euonymus alatus compactus DWARFWINGED EUONYMUS	2'–4'	2'–3'	Compact deciduous hedge.

Ilex crenata convexa CONVEXLEAF HOLLY	1½'–2½'	1½'–2½'	Compact low line, hardy.
Ilex crenata microphylla SMALL-LEAVED JAPANESE HOLLY	2'–5'	2'–3'	Narrow evergreen line in formal area.
Taxus cuspidata nana DWARF JAPANESE YEW	2'–4'	2½'–3½'	Easy to shear, evergreen.
Taxus hicksi HICKS YEW	2'–4'	2'–3'	Narrow upright hedge, good evergreen color all winter.
Taxus hunnewelliana HUNNEWELL YEW	1½'–4'	2'–3'	Berries effective if not sheared too tightly.
Taxus media hatfieldi HATFIELD YEW	2'–4'	2'–3'	Compact, fine dark green.

SHRUBS FOR HEDGES, FENCES AND WALLS

UNTRIMMED HEDGES

a. FIVE TO TWELVE FEET

PLANT MATERIAL	HEIGHT	WIDTH	CHARACTERISTICS
Berberis thunbergi JAPANESE BARBERRY	To 6'	6'	Broad arching hedge for fall color of leaf and fruit.
Chaenomeles lagenaria JAPANESE FLOWERING QUINCE	To 6'	5'	Picturesque flowering hedge, may get leggy.
Hibiscus syriacus ROSE OF SHARON	To 12'	5'	Narrow tall hedge for mid-summer effect in flower.
Rosa hugonis FATHER HUGO ROSE	To 6'	6'	Delicate texture, for light, broad garden hedge.
Rosa rugosa alba WHITE RUGOSA ROSE	To 5'	3'	Hardy, coarse effect, near sea-shore.
Spiraea vanhoutei VANHOUTTE SPIREA	To 8'	6'	Light textured, arching effect for leaf and blossom mass.

Syringa vulgaris COMMON LILAC	To 12'	6'	Traditional in country places, or near old-fashioned garden.
Vaccinium corymbosum HIGHBUSH BLUEBERRY	To 8'	5'	Fall color, picturesque habit.
Viburnum opulus HIGHBUSH CRANBERRY	To 12'	6'	Fall color in fruit, bold texture.
b. ONE TO FIVE FEET			
Berberis verruculosa WARTY BARBERRY	To 2'	2½'	Evergreen, sprawling line.
Buxus sempervirens suffruticosa TRUEDWARF BOX	To 5'	4'	Slightly formal, slow growing.
Chaenomeles japonica DWARF FLOWERING QUINCE	To 4'	3'	Picturesque flowering hedge.
Deutzia lemoinei LEMOINE DEUTZIA	To 4'	3'	Twiggy hedge for location not visible in winter.
Euonymus alatus compactus DWARFWINGED EUONYMUS	To 6'	3'	Fine fall color, picturesque bark.
Pieris japonica JAPANESE ANDROMEDA	To 5'	3'	Loose evergreen mass, early flower.
Vaccinium angustifolium LOWBUSH BLUEBERRY	To 1'	2'	Fall color, picturesque habit.

SHRUBS FOR HEDGES, FENCES AND WALLS

WALL SHRUBS

PLANT MATERIAL	SPACE	TYPE OF TRAINING	WHERE TO USE
Acanthopanax sieboldianus FIVELEAVED ARALIA	To 10′× 8′	Irregular	North wall, for leaf texture.
Chaenomeles japonica DWARF FLOWERING QUINCE	To 12′× 6′	Picturesque	Full sun, not against red brick.
Chionanthus virginica WHITE FRINGETREE	To 20′×12′	Fan-shaped	Semi-shade, bold texture against stone or brick.
Cornus kousa CHINESE DOGWOOD	To 25′×10′	Fan or formal	Against stone or brick, semi-shade.
Cotoneaster divaricata SPREADING COTONEASTER	To 4′× 6′	Horizontal	Fine texture, against white.
Cotoneaster francheti FRANCHET COTONEASTER	To 4′× 6′	Horizontal	For fruit color against white or gray.
Euonymus alatus WINGED EUONYMUS	To 10′× 8′	Irregular fan	For bark and fall color, not against brick.
Forsythia suspensa	To 15′×15′	Irregular	Full sun for large spaces.

Plant	Size	Form	Notes
Jasminum nudiflorum WINTER JASMINE	To 3′ × 6′	Horizontal	Not against brick, for winter twig color, tender.
Kerria japonica JAPANESE KERRIA	To 4′ × 4′	Horizontal	Not against brick, for winter color.
Lycium chinense CHINESE MATRIMONY VINE	To 10′ × 6′	Irregular	Against frame or stone, for brilliant fruit.
Laburnum vulgare watereri WATERER GOLDENCHAIN TREE	To 20′ × 10′	Formal	Large spaces for delicacy of leaf and flower.
Magnolia soulangeana SAUCER MAGNOLIA	To 20′ × 15′	Irregular fan	Against stone, or white.
Magnolia stellata STAR MAGNOLIA	To 12′ × 8′	Horizontal	Against stone or brick for flower mass.
Malus ioensis bechteli BECHTEL CRABAPPLE	To 20′ × 10′	Like fruit or in fan	Against white or gray, large spaces.
Malus hupehensis TEA CRABAPPLE	To 20′ × 10′	Like fruit or in fan	Against white or gray for delicate flower effect.
Pyracantha coccinea lalandi LALAND FIRETHORN	To 15′ × 8′	Picturesque	On stone or frame, not red brick, for fall fruit.
Symplocos paniculata TURQUOISEBERRY	To 15′ × 8′	Irregular fan	Large space, for fall fruit.
Viburnum carlesi KOREANSPICE VIBURNUM	To 6′ × 4′	Open fan	Near door or window, exquisite blend of gray-green leaf and pink flower.
Viburnum sieboldi SIEBOLD VIBURNUM	To 12′ × 8′	Open fan	Bold effect in large spaces, foliage and silhouette.

SECTION THREE

SHRUB GARDENS

CHAPTER XII

Shrub Roses

AN OLD GARDENER once told me, "You know, miss, some folks like peonies, other folks like pansies, but all folks like roses." The truth of his observation seems borne out by the word association game. If you ask ten people to name the first flower that comes into their head, eight out of the ten will probably say, "Rose." In spite of this universal love of roses, too many people deny themselves the pleasure of growing them because they do not know that they are as easy as spirea or forsythia. They think only in terms of the lovely but temperamental Hybrid Teas or the long-stemmed beauties of the florist shop, and do not realize that there is a great group which are both excellent shrubs and excellent roses.

This lack of appreciation of shrub roses is all the more surprising when so many of us remember certain lanes in the middle west, in June, covered with the long arching sprays of the pink wild rose, *Rosa setigera*, or masses of the lovely Cherokee rose of the south. There are so many species of wild roses native to North America that there is at least one adaptable to and at home in every part of our country.

Most of our native roses are pink, ranging from very pale pink of *blanda* in northeastern North America to the deep rose and red of *laevigata*, the Cherokee rose of the south, originally from China but now wild in this country. Some of them, like *blanda* and *palustris*, grow in swampy land. Others like *virginiana*, *setigera*, *carolina*, and *acicularis*, grow along fairly dry country lanes and even in dry rocks. All of them have single flowers, disease-resistant foliage and most of them are brilliant with red hips in the fall. They are excellent for covering banks in difficult locations as they need no care and, with the possible exception of *laevigata* and *setigera*, will grow in rather poor soil.

From across the world come other shrub roses of even greater beauty and usefulness than our own native ones. If I could have but one shrub rose it would certainly be Father Hugo's, *Rosa hugonis*, from China. As a shrub it is vigorous, graceful in habit, with arching branches, delicate in foliage and free from pests. As a rose it is an exquisite primrose yellow and so prolific in bloom that the bush is almost entirely covered. It prefers poor soil and the only attention it needs is pruning out the old heavy canes after blooming. My only complaint is that it lasts only for ten days to two weeks in full bloom.

Two other natives of China resemble it and prolong the enjoyment. They are *Rosa primula* and *Rosa xanthina*. Other Asiatic roses which belong in the same shrub group are *Rosa helenae*, a tremendously strong grower, which has small single fragrant white flowers in clusters, and *spinosissima altaica*, a native of Siberia. A group of these five roses will give delicate yellow and white single blossoms for several weeks, and a clean light foliage for the rest of the summer. They are all vigorous growers so should be planted six to eight to ten feet apart, even though the plants are very small when they come from the nursery.

One very familiar shrub rose is the yellow one that was taken all over the country by pioneer women traveling westward by flatboat or in covered wagons. It still persists in abandoned farmyards and around old farm houses. It is Harison's Yellow and with very little care—only light thinning out of the old wood—it is a beautiful shrub. It is a relative of the Scotch rose, *Rosa spinosissima*. Several others in that group have the same quaintness and interest.

Here in the yellow and copper group are three of my favorite roses all belonging to the Austrian briar class. They are Austrian Copper which has single flowers of intense copper red, with the reverse of the petals golden yellow, Austrian Yellow and Persian Yellow with smaller flowers. They are the ancestors of the modern yellow Tea and Hybrid Teas and are perhaps not quite as sturdy and fool proof as the other shrub roses mentioned. Anyone who likes Talisman or the other copper and yellow roses in the florists' windows will certainly want one Austrian Copper. Placed in front of Rosa hugonis or near the white rugosa roses or with the coppery leaves of andromeda nearby, it is a fine strong color note.

The very name of sweetbriar rose, the eglantine of Elizabethan days, has romance. Its arching branches are jeweled with single or half double flowers, but perhaps its greatest charm is the fragrance of the young leaves when they are wet with morning dew or after a shower. During the last of the 19th century Lord Penzance of England crossed the sweetbriar, Rosa rubiginosa, with other species, and the names of the hybrids, taken for the most part from Scott's romances, are almost enough reason for growing all of them.

My favorites are probably Lord Penzance with fawn flowers, delicately tinted ecru, and Lady Penzance, with bright copper colored flowers. Some of the other hybrids come in red (Anne of Geierstein and Lucy Bertram) and in pink (Julia Mannering and Brenda) but all of them have kept the fragrant foliage. Some of them also have fragrant flowers and all of them have bright red hips in great quantities in the fall.

The only care this group needs is thinning out the old wood. They are roses to plant along a sunny path or near a door where the fragrance of the foliage can be a constant joy. Lord and Lady Penzance grow only about four feet high while many of the others will make a bush seven to nine feet high and five or six feet across.

Another old rose with romantic associations is the musk rose of the poets. It has been hybridized by Reverend Joseph

Pemberton and is usually listed under Pemberton's hybrids. The original musk rose, *Rosa moschata*, was a fragrant white semi-climbing rose with shining foliage. From it Reverend Pemberton produced a group of roses less well known than they deserve. They grow five to eight feet tall and bloom more or less all through the growing season. They also have the old musk fragrance and are altogether one of the most delightful groups of roses in existence today.

Of all of them perhaps Pax, white, fragrant and ever blooming is my favorite. Others that are particularly effective are Clytemnestra, which has coppery buds and small deep pink and salmon flowers, and Thisbe with small pale yellow flowers. They are hardy and require only average garden soil to grow vigorously and produce a wealth of exquisite fragrance and beauty.

Less romantic in association and unfortunately much misused is the toughest of all the shrub roses, the rugosa rose. More than once I have had clients or friends almost visibly turn up their noses when I suggested using *Rosa rugosa* in the shrub planting or as a hedge. Part of their distaste for it comes from the most commonly seen type which has magenta flowers. As the rugosas bloom all summer it is even more objectionable than most magenta flowers because there is always something coming along to clash with it. This group of roses, however, does come in other colors through its hybrids. Many of them have kept the clean, disease-resistant dark foliage and constant bloom of the type and most of them have the large brilliant red hips that make it as beautiful in fruit as in flower.

The most desirable of the rugosas are possibly the white ones, either R. *blanc Double de Coubert,* or the single R. *rugosa alba,* or the hybrid Sir Thomas Lipton. Against the dark green of the rather rough foliage these white roses have a purity and effectiveness hardly equaled by any of the Hybrid Teas or Hybrid Perpetuals with which we are more familiar. The yellow-toned Agnes and Vanguard and Dr. Eckener are stunning six to eight foot plants. The pinks and reds in the rugosa hybrids unfortunately have the rather blue tone of their parent, particularly as their flowers fade, so that they are a little harder to blend in with other shrub bloom and not as clear and fine a subject generally.

The rugosas grow in the most difficult situations, even on the shore where salt spray hits them. The dryest summers and the hardest winters have very little effect on them. They can be used either as shrubs or as hedges. Even severe pruning to keep them fairly low does not discourage their bloom completely so that the hedge has bloom and rose hips on it at the same time all summer. They are excellent contrasted with the fine leaved shrub roses like Father Hugo's and the Sweet Briars.

Fortunately for those of us who like roses but have no time to grow the true garden roses, the hybridizers are working constantly on developing new shrub roses, with hardiness, disease-resistance and constant bloom. Some of the new hybrids like Lipstick, Skyrocket, Nevada and Eos are, we hope, only the forerunners of a big new group.

Even some of the modern floribunda roses can be used as shrubs. Both Donald and Betty Prior grow three to four feet tall and have bloom almost constantly during the growing season. Elsa Poulsen is another whose growth is so vigorous that it is hard to keep in bounds in the ordinary sized rose beds. Groups of them on the front of a shrub border or as facing down plants in a shrub rose border have great effectiveness and thrive very well. Some of the floribundas grow only one and a half to two feet, others grow four to five. Many of the catalogs unfortunately do not go into detail as to the habits of the variety. If the description says, "Vigorous grower" or "Growth to three feet," it usually means you will have trouble keeping it any lower than that and that it is therefore better used as a shrub rose than as a garden rose.

In the old group of the Hybrid Perpetuals some of them in temperate climates grow so vigorously that the ordinary rose bed is too small space. I have used Frau Karl Druschki in the front of a shrub border with excellent results and comparatively little work. Both the Floribundas and Hybrid Perpetuals do get black spot and mildew so that they do not have the quality of care-freeness so desirable in the rest of the shrub roses. They need to be well to the front or in a location where you can prune and spray them to keep them looking attractive.

In parts of the country where the Hybrid Teas do extremely well and a real rose garden is possible, how much more fun to make its enclosure of shrub roses rather than a miscellaneous lot of other shrubs! If you have no room or no inclination for a garden entirely of roses, a section of the shrub border, a special corner planting, or the enclosure for a flower garden may well be of shrub roses.

Where winters are too severe for tender climbing roses, certain of the heavy caned shrub roses can be used on posts or on trellises. The Pemberton roses are outstanding for this use in many areas, and our wild *Rosa setigera* and Japanese *Rosa multiflora* or *rugosa* hybrids can be trained flat on a wall or fence to excellent effect. On a low wall near the house the sweet briars, carefully trained, give fragrance that few vines can equal.

No matter how used the bush roses always give you the variations in texture of foliage, the persistent bloom and beautiful fruit that are the requirements of a good shrub. Properly combined and well used they can be the show planting of a property. There is no part of the country where it is not possible to use several of them in excellent combinations. If I were asked to make a list of the ten shrubs I would not do without, three out of the ten would probably be shrub roses.

CHAPTER XIII

Green Gardens

WHENEVER a friend asks me to look at her evergreen garden I find myself inclined to hope for the best and expect the worst. Of all the kinds of special garden, there is none that can be more funereal, duller and less rewarding than a garden of evergreens. On the other hand, the desire for the repose and quietness that green gives in hot weather, or the warmth it gives in the winter, can be satisfied completely by a well planned and well planted green garden.

In sections of this country and in England and France there are outstanding examples of really fine evergreen gardens. Some of the old box gardens of the south or the yew gardens of England have a dignity and richness that no one who has seen them can forget. The good ones are usually large, done in one kind of material, that is all box or all yew or all holly. They belong only in kindly climates, on large places and in formal surroundings.

In contrast to this there are all sorts of places where the small and more informal type of green garden is not only appropriate but most desirable. The term "Green Garden" seems to me much more appropriate than "Evergreen Garden" and indicates my conviction that a garden of only evergreens is much harder to do well and much less likely to be interesting than one in which there is room for some deciduous or half-evergreen plants, for lightness and variety.

It is a curious fact that people are less familiar with different types of evergreens than almost any kind of plant material. Time and again as you drive along the road you see some tourist camp or roadside stand firmly labelled, "Twin Spruces" or "Three Cedars." If you look carefully you will find that they are rarely named correctly. Twin Spruces is likely to have a fine pair of pines in front of it. The three cedars are likely to be spruces or firs. Checking up among your acquaintances you will find that most of them call all needled evergreens by one general name, that is, they are either all pines, all spruces, all cedars or perhaps just Christmas trees.

When it comes to the broad-leaved evergreens there is even less acquaintance. Most people lump them all as evergreens or occasionally call everything rhododendron or laurel. It is this very lack of observation and lack of familiarity with the characteristics that make so many green gardens monotonous and dull. In fabrics or in paint certainly all of us know that green can be anything from a pale chartreuse to an almost black bottle-green. When we get outdoors, however, green is green and there is little appreciation of the slightly gray-green of certain hollies, the almost black-green of others, the bronzy-green of andromedas or cherry laurels.

Quite aside from the leaf color there is even less observation of the over-all general darkness or value of the shrub whose evergreen leaves are heavy and set close together as contrasted with one with small leaves, set along fine branches, or the upright tightly grown mass of some of the evergreen privets of the south, as contrasted with the almost silver gray-green of *Rhodomyrtus*. Planting masses of solid color and solid tone are lacking in variety and in the play of light and shadow no matter what the material, whether deciduous or evergreen. But in the evergreens they take on an added disadvantage of somberness.

A collection of assorted evergreens does not make a green garden. It may make an arboretum—interesting only to the plant collector or horticultural student. Like a museum room of furniture it is something to look at, but not to live in.

Careful selection and arrangement counts for more in a green garden than in almost any other kind.

Nature plants evergreens to fine effect and gives us valuable hints on what to use, how and where to plant it, and how to combine it for full effectiveness. The first thing to take to heart is that in the wild we seldom find solid banks of green unrelieved by deciduous planting. Where rhododendron or laurel grow in profusion on north slopes of the hills and mountains, they are likely to have among them the bare trunks of oaks, the gray stems of azaleas, ironwood, *Viburnum acerifolium*—giving it lightness, and by contrast making the green richer and more effective.

On an open windy hillside cedars are exclamation points in a field of blueberry or a dark foil for the delicacy of shadblow or crabapples or hawthorns. Not apparent in the winter, but important later on, is the bloom of the deciduous material against a dark background, giving another season of beauty from the same planting. Translated into home use a planting of rhododendron or laurel on the shady side of the house is less gloomy with its pathetic drooping leaves on a cold day and more effective in spring if it has pink azaleas, *nudiflora* and *arborescens*, or orange azaleas, *calendulaceae* and *kaempferi* with it, and has a picturesque skyline of dogwoods rather than only dark cedars or hemlocks.

Even with these principles well in mind, making a good evergreen garden requires self-restraint. It is far better to restrict the planting in any but a tremendous garden, to four or five varieties of evergreens, which contrast well with each other but blend together, and of these four or five varieties to make one certain kind predominant. For example, if you are in the acid soil sections of the country you may want to make the garden mostly rhododendrons. Farther south you may choose the evergreen azaleas so famous in the gardens around Charleston. In the limestone sections of the country where neither of these will do, the yews or certain of the hollies may take first place. To use them well this one species should be used for about fifty per cent of the planting in the garden. It may go as high as seventy-five per cent but except in very formal locations it should not go more than that if the garden is to have variety.

When this main-stay is chosen the others to be used should be selected both for contrast of foliage, color and texture and for contrast of habit and growth with each other and with the main evergreen. The way in which they are combined depends, of course, on the general design of the garden. It may be a tiny space outside the living room windows in a northern climate, where bleakness is relieved by the dark green of holly and yew, with their bright red berries for contrast and the fat buds of deciduous azaleas on clean gray stems to give it lightness and delicacy of silhouette. When the summers are hot as they are in most parts of the country, the cool darkness of yew or holly may be contrasted with the arching sprays of cotoneaster, the shiny green of abelia, with the cool looking edge of *Pachistima canbyi.*

If the garden has a curving outline, fine-leaved and angular evergreens like *Ilex microphylla* left to grow loose with no shearing, may accent the points and the dark somber green of rhododendron give shadow and depth to the bays. For further contrast some of the evergreens may be trimmed to a tight hedge with the rest allowed to grow freely in their natural habit. A dense hedge of dark green like the small leaved hollies, the yews or boxwood is a fine foil for the loose growing andromedas, evergreen azaleas, cotoneasters behind it.

Reversing the picture, a tall tight hedge of hemlock or arborvitae is a substantial background for the delicacy of the smaller leaved rhododendrons like *carolinianum* and *minus* or mountain laurel, with occasional accent of flowering dogwood for lightness, and masses of the native azaleas for contrast of both leaf and flower. When it is possible the green garden should have certain sections in full sun and others in at least half shade. The contrast of sun and shadow brings out the highlights in the shiny leaved evergreens and makes the dull ones look deeper and darker by contrast.

XI. a. A small evergreen garden uses dwarf Japanese holly for its hedges, with accents of andromeda and clipped yew. Behind the garden are rhododendrons, azaleas, enkianthus, and inkberry.

b. The same garden six years later takes on greater formality from tightly sheared hedges and the larger mass of its accents.

Richard Averill Smith

Gottscho-Schleisner

XII. An informal green garden seen from the main rooms of the house has an air of seclusion and restfulness in a space 75 feet long by 35 feet wide.

Nature again is a good teacher, as she always plants her evergreens where the conditions of sun, soil, wind and moisture are most favorable to their growth. Hemlocks like shade, good rich woods soil, no wind. Cedars, the juniper family, grow in open, sunny, windy locations in comparatively poor soil. Pines, spruces, arborvitae, firs, grow in sun, good soil, not too heavy wind. None of them like constantly wet feet or boggy locations. They carry over their preferences to our own grounds and when cedars are planted in airless or shady places, or hemlocks on a windy corner, they may survive feebly but will never thrive.

Perhaps the most useful of all needled evergreens for the home grounds is the yew, *Taxus*. It stands either sun or shade, moderate winds, but likes rich soil. In the broad-leaved evergreens, the rhododendrons and laurels like at least semi-shade, preferably that of oak trees. The hollies, andromedas, boxwood and evergreen azaleas like sun, or very light shade, but all the broad-leaves dislike winter winds.

Part of the beauty of evergreens in the native landscape is that they are seen as dark green accents in a large landscape picture and from a distance often with a foreground of snow or rolling fields. These same plants seen close at hand might look decidedly rusty green or brown in the case of arborvitae or juniper or most unhappy with the mournful droop of their leaves if they are rhododendrons or laurels. On our own places we too often forget that in winter we are in the house looking out far more than we are outside looking at the house. This leads to the banking of the house itself with evergreens which we see only hastily in coming in and out, and which, on cold days particularly, are not objects of cheer or warmth with their bad color or habit seen close at hand. On the other hand, if a view from the living room window gives us a picture across a snow covered lawn to a dark green group of yews or pines or the red and green of American holly, the bleakness of the world is considerably relieved.

The arborvitae or cedars which fail to thrive and look forlorn pasted against a house, are most welcome sights in groups at the back of a green garden, where their narrow spire shapes give accent to the broader shapes of the other plants. Waking in the morning to see a tall pine, spruce, fir or hemlock across the lawn, its branches powdered with snow, makes man-made decorations seem very weak. Those same trees against the house would hardly be seen until either the snow had melted from the house warmth or the snow slide from the roof had broken the evergreens.

In the warmer parts of the country the biggest proportion of the shrubs are broad-leaved evergreens and the range in foliage color and texture and in bloom colors is so wide that almost any garden is an evergreen garden. For that reason it is all the more amazing to see so much planting where nothing is used except the rather large-leaved dark greens, like the evergreen privet and other shrubs of that same color and texture. In the first planting I ever planned in Florida I was so overwhelmed by the incredible wealth of beautiful shrubs of every size, texture, color and habit that I was like the little girl at Christmas who suddenly got everything on the Christmas tree that she could possibly ever have wanted. It took considerable firmness to combine and discriminate among the shrubs until I had the same effect with evergreen material that I was used to getting with deciduous material in the north. Where the world is green most of the year it is not a case of using a very restricted list and combining it so as to avoid monotony. Rather, it is a problem of selecting from too large a list in order to get exactly the same kind of combinations and arrangements that the deciduous lists of the northern parts of the country can give.

For example, if the entrance into a flower garden is framed by a pair of kumquat trees in Florida, rather than the crab-apples or hawthorns of the north, not only must we keep from repeating the same size and dark green color of the kumquat leaves, but we must remember that for many weeks during the winter the dominating color at that point is orange, from the fruit. For that reason the white of gardenias, the blue of plumbago and the yellow of allamanda or the yellow hibiscus and white of certain camellias give both the contrast in foliage that we need and also a color combination as fine as any perennial flower garden. If either you or your neighbor have the ubiquitous but very beautiful flame vine rioting over a fence or up a telephone pole, you need very little strong color near it to make a picture. The green of privet and the bronze of cherry laurel are excellent nearby. The yellow berries of *Duranta plumieri*, or the snowy white of the night-blooming jessamine, *Cestrum nocturnum*, or the orange jessamine, *Murraya paniculata*, add lightness and fragrance as well as delicate color.

The high points in the skyline in a southern garden can be of evergreen trees of beauty such as no northern garden can know. The banana shrub, *Michelia fuscata*, the *Franklinia alatamaha*, the silk tree, *Albizzia julibrissin*, can give the interest in a southern garden that the crabapples, hawthorns and dogwoods do farther north. The next highest planting in such a garden can be the gray-green leaves of the *Viburnum odoratissimum*, or *Eleagnus pungens*, or the wine colored foliage of *Photinia glabra*. Against these tall shrubs, groups of camellias or azaleas make a specialty garden almost incredible in loveliness.

Wherever the garden and whatever its size, the important thing to remember in the green garden is the need for contrast of color and texture, habit and growth. It is primarily a foliage garden in most parts of the country most of the year and fine gradations must be worked out to make it sparkle in some lights and look cool, green and inviting in the heat of the mid-day sun. Evergreens grow more slowly and are more easily affected by poor growing conditions than most deciduous shrubs, so should be chosen extra carefully and planted with attention to their likes and dislikes.

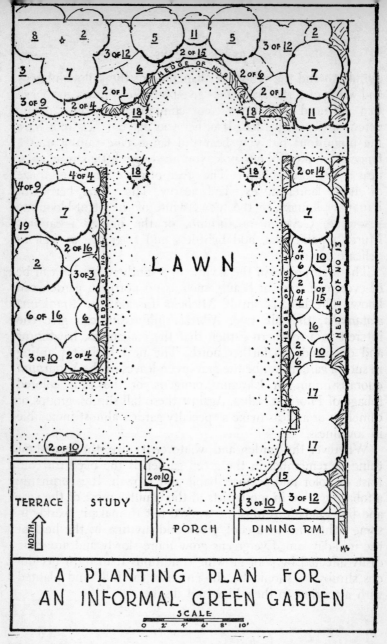

A PLANTING PLAN FOR AN INFORMAL GREEN GARDEN

This informal green garden is seen constantly from the windows of the house. It has variety of color and form, from a combination of evergreen and deciduous shrubs, with handsome flower masses of the azaleas and rhododendrons in late May, brilliant color in October from the hawthorns, dogwoods and cotoneasters.

PLANTING LIST FOR AN INFORMAL GREEN GARDEN

DRAWING NO. 4 (opposite Drawing No. 4)

The first number on the plan refers to the quantity of plants, the second, underlined, to the key number on the list below. Where only the key number is given, one specimen is used.

KEY NUMBER	LATIN NAME	COMMON NAME	TOTAL QUANTITY
1.	Abelia grandiflora	Glossy abelia	4
2.	Amelanchier canadensis	Shadblow	2
3.	Azalea obtusa Appleblossom	Pink Kurume azalea	4
4.	Azalea indica alba	White Indica azalea	8
5.	Cornus florida	Flowering dogwood	2
6.	Cotoneaster zabelli	Cherryberry cotoneaster	7
7.	Crataegus phaenopyrum	Washington hawthorn	4
8.	Halesia carolina	Silverbell	1
9.	Ilex crenata convexa	Convexleaf holly	19
10.	Ilex crenata	Japanese holly	7
11.	Ilex opaca	American holly	2
12.	Juniperus virginiana	Red cedar	10
13.	Ligustrum ovalifolium	California privet	25
14.	Pachistima canbyi	Canby pachistima	100
15.	Pieris japonica	Japanese andromeda	9
16.	Rhododendron carolinianum	Carolina rhododendron	9
17.	Styrax japonica	Japanese snowball	2
18.	Taxus cuspidata capitata	Upright Japanese yew	4
19.	Viburnum tomentosum	Doublefile viburnum	1

CHAPTER XIV

Fruit Gardens

PART of the fun of owning your own place is certainly being able to pick your own fruit fresh from the tree or the bush or the vine, at exactly the right stage of ripeness. If at the same time these fruits can be used as decoration on the home grounds, they give two-fold pleasure, both to the eye and to the palate. Almost all of them can be classed as shrubs or flowering trees and used in the same way that the purely decorative plants are.

Many of us remember with great pleasure the sight of apple or cherry or plum or peach orchards in bloom. Even the most carefully hybridized and ornamental varieties are if anything less beautiful than the kinds that are grown primarily for eating purposes. The finest specimen of Japanese flowering crabapple is no more exquisite in its pink and white bloom and its gnarling habit than a well grown specimen of Hyslop or Transcendent crabapples. When the relatively small trees are loaded with red fruit in August and early September the Hyslop is one of the most beautiful pictures in any landscape. In the same way Black Tartarian or any of the sweet cherries, Montmorency of the sour cherries are just as delicate and as much of a white cloud in the landscape as the horticultural varieties like subhirtella or Mt. Fuji, and again when they are in fruit, the red sour cherries particularly are an exquisite sight. This beauty can be put to use on even the smallest property, particularly if dwarf and semi-dwarf varieties are substituted for the full size.

The really dwarf apples are almost like bushes rather than trees and take up no more room than a good sized forsythia. The semi-dwarf varieties are a third to half as large as the older kind of standard height trees and are perhaps even more solidly covered with bloom and fruit. If there is room, the standard size varieties fit perfectly into the informal country type of place and can be used either as shade trees or as accents and specimens on the grounds.

If a neighbor's house or garage stares down on your property and seems too intrusive, the high head of a cherry or an apple will screen it as effectively as a small shade tree. On the place with shrub borders fairly near the house, a pear or plum or a cherry or a small apple will accent the ends of the planting with the year-round beauty such important spots must have. Near a flower garden or any other special area, a pair of fruiting trees will frame the view and give the emphasis needed at that point. An old apple or pear leaning over a pool gives the feeling of age and informality that is most effective in a garden. Where shade is needed on a terrace nothing is finer than a large, gnarled appletree.

Of the fruiting trees the pears, plums and peaches are medium sized even when full grown. The apple and the sweet cherries are taller and broader. In standard sizes they come closer to being true shade trees and should be used accordingly. One difficulty with the fruiting trees on small property has always been that most of them need two or three varieties to cross pollinate in order to bear good fruit and there has not been room for so many. This has been overcome in the last few years by grafting three or even five varieties on the same tree. It not only has the advantage of cross fertilizing but it also means that you have fruits at different seasons from the same tree.

These three-in-one and five-in-one trees come, unfortunately, only in small specimens at the present time, but they grow as rapidly as their parents do, and are not only practical but highly desirable, particularly for the small place. It is important to get them from a reliable fruit nursery so that the tree will be a nice shape. If varieties which grow differently or at different rates, are grafted on the same tree, one part of it will undoubtedly outgrow the other and give a queer lopsided effect. Reputable growers take care of this by grafting varieties whose habit and rate of growth is similar.

In the south certainly the fruit trees are among the finest ornamentals grown. The kumquats and the guavas are the comparatively small trees. The tangerines are middle size and the oranges, grapefruit and avocados are handsome big shade trees. Whether in flower or in fruit all of them are fine and have few competitors in sheer beauty among the purely ornamental flowering trees.

Next in size to the fruiting trees are the shrub fruits, usually called the bush fruits. Most of them are fairly easy to grow and come in the size where there are not too many good shrubs, the two to five foot height. Perhaps the two handsomest ones are the currant and the blueberry. A currant bush in heavy fruit is one of the gayest sights in the plant world. Even a large family needs very few currants for eating fresh or preserving. A pair of bushes on either side of the kitchen door, with proper pruning and spraying, can be just as effective as dwarf flowering quinces or spireas. Marking the entrance to the vegetable garden or used as a low hedge in front of it, they are highly decorative. Gooseberries can be used in much the same way and their interesting light textured leaves make a beautiful shrub.

Of all the bush fruits undoubtedly the handsomest, as well as the most delicious to a great many of us, is the blueberry. The native blueberries come in everything from the small ground cover ones to the tall highbush blueberry. Except in limestone regions of the country or very hot climates they grow well and with the range of sizes there is place for some of them on any property. Aside from the wild ones there are the hybridized varieties such as Jersey, Rancocas and Rubel. Like their wild ancestors they must have acid soil and in appearance are similar to the highbush, Vaccinium corymbosum. The fruit and leaf is larger and they are fairly slow growing. The different varieties differ greatly in habit and rate of growth and it is well to find out just what size the varieties you choose are likely to get. It is necessary to have two or three varieties for cross pollinization and a half dozen bushes is the minimum for even a small family.

The very low blueberry is beautiful as a ground cover in a sunny location. In Maine where they grow so prolifically as natives, I have seen them used as the cover for the center of an entrance court. Their shiny foliage and beautiful fall color are only an added dividend to the pleasure the family has in being able to pick their breakfast berries by just walking out the front door. A planting group of white birches and red cedars with the blueberries as a ground cover has color and interest all year long.

They can also be used as a hedge, either a very low one of the low variety, Vaccinium angustifolium, a middle sized one of Vaccinium vitis-idaea, or a tall one of the highbush blueberry, Vaccinium corymbosum. It is better to leave these hedges untrimmed if you wish fruit in quality from them but even trimmed you will get a certain amount. An untrimmed hedge of highbush blueberry will get seven or eight feet high and in June the creamy white flowers will give you one of the most enchanting fragrances of the entire summer.

The hybrid berries are also excellent as specimens or as accent plants. All the blueberries come very close to answering the description of the perfect shrub. Their habit is open and picturesque, their leaves are good color and disease-resistant, their flower is beautiful, their fall color is extraordinarily brilliant and in the winter their twig color is a lovely orange haze in the landscape. They are also outstanding for cutting arrangement in the house, either in fruit, in flower or in fall leaf.

Most of the other bush fruits are the half-vine, half-shrub class—the raspberries, the blackberries, dewberries, loganberries, boysenberries. Of all of them the blackberry is possibly the handsomest in foliage and in flower. Their color in the fall is winey red and persists long after the early frosts. They need no spraying and very little care except pruning out the old canes after blooming and pinching back the ends of the new canes and side branches. Trained flat against a white fence or on wires to form a fence of their own, they are highly decorative. The bloom of most of the bramble fruits is showy and in native planting some of them can be used to excellent effect for the sheer beauty of their blossoms. In this case, of course, they probably will not give the largest fruit but will be less trouble than when tame. The raspberries can be trained flat or used upon the fence much as the blackberries and its relatives can. Their leaf, for the most part, is not as attractive nor their flower as large. With the blackberries a dozen plants give plenty of berries for a small family. With the raspberries twenty-five plants is usually the minimum of all except the extremely vigorous varieties like Sodus.

The tall growing varieties of brambles and the ones that act more like vines, such as the boysenberry, can also be used as pillars. In such use they are spiraled around a post and then allowed to fan out at the top to form a head. They are interesting as accents but the production is less and the picking is harder than when they are spread out and pruned back to the proper height.

The Hansen bush cherry and the beach plums are also handsome and beautiful shrubs in places where they do well. The beach plum likes a sandy, seashore location best of all but recent hybridizing and propagating work on it will undoubtedly make it adaptable to more locations and with finer quality fruit. When it is in bloom on its native dunes the whole countryside is a feathery mass of white. Anyone who lives near the shore should certainly use it as an ornamental plant. It should be bought as a nursery-grown plant, not collected from the wild, whence the chances of survival of transplanting are very poor.

The other most commonly grown fruit, the grape, is really a vine but properly trained can classify as a fence or wall shrub. A boundary between the vegetable garden and the lawn or on the edge of the driveway can be utilized to grow three or four grapevines trained to the four-arm system. On an informal place a trellis behind the flower border may be used for grapes instead of roses or other purely ornamental flowers, with excellent effect. The tremendous spreading roots of the grapes may cause a little trouble in the flower border and your grapes may not be as perfect as they would if they were grown with no competition. But they are certainly effective and even better than that, accessible while you are working in the flower or vegetable garden. Grapes fresh off the vine when you are really thirsty and hot are an entirely different story from the ones shipped long distances and picked under-ripe.

The varieties of fruits to be used must always depend on the locality. The best source of information is the State Agricultural Department and the local fruit growers. If fruit is really a hobby with you (and I can think of no more delightful one) a garden entirely devoted to fruit can be beautiful without losing any of its practicality. As a matter of fact, concentrating all the fruits in one area really makes it easier to take care of them and to produce quality fruits. With or without such a special garden it is possible to have fresh fruit right at home from June to November in most of this country. In the colder climates, of course, the season will be shorter but in the warmer ones you should be able to pick fruit twelve months in the year without going off your own grounds.

CHAPTER XV

Flower Gardens

USUALLY when we speak of a flower garden we mean beds or borders of perennials and annuals and are likely to visualize it as a sheet of color. Nowadays, however, fewer people have time for the big elaborate gardens that require a great deal of care. Fortunately it is possible to have a completely satisfactory flower garden in which the shrubs play a major role in the bloom throughout the season and reduce the number of less sturdy herbaceous flowers. The important thing in planning such a garden is to realize that it is not the number of plants you have nor the number of square feet of bed or border that makes a garden. Sometimes a very tiny garden with a very few perennial or annual flowers in it can be as completely satisfying as the large formal gardens.

The success of a garden is always primarily in its design, the combinations of colors and the over-all effect of the color scheme as a whole. Quantity does not mean quality by a great deal. The extremely floriferous shrubs are the ones to use near the garden. The spireas, the lilacs, some of the bush roses, the beautybush, the doublefile viburnum, the dogwoods, hawthorns, crabapples and cherries are covered with blossoms. They are solid bouquets on bushes and make the mass color the garden needs. Many of them, unfortunately, are so twiggy that they are ugly in winter and have quite uninteresting foliage in the summer when they are not in bloom. The ones that are very poor in the winter can be used around the flower garden if it is far enough from the house that you do not see them staring you in the face when the leaves are off, or if they are at the back of the border with good-foliaged plants in front of them.

There are a number of shrubs that have particularly interesting or effective bloom, although not a solid mass of it. The gordonia, the stewartia, *Magnolia virginiana*, have distinguished looking blossoms and need to be seen close at hand to be appreciated. They also have characteristics that some of the more floriferous shrubs lack—clean tidy habit and beautiful foliage, so that they are essentially handsome shrubs at all times. They are good garden shrubs.

Plants like most of the viburnum family and most of the dogwood family, except the flowering dogwood, have few outstanding characteristics of either summer leaf or bloom, and while they may not be objectionable near the garden, they do not add anything to it, except a green mass. If space is limited every shrub around the garden should be part of the flower picture and contribute its full share to it. There is no room for undistinguished masses of leaves with no particular beauty at any period.

The shrubs that grow too rapidly and require constant pruning and training are usually a poor choice around a garden. This top growth is usually accompanied by a very hungry root system and no matter how few the annuals and perennials, they will not be improved by the roots of shrubs stealing all their food. These rank growers will also probably increase the problem of shade in the flower garden. Since most garden flowers demand at least a half day's sun and many of them a full day's sun, the problem of enclosure without cutting off sunlight has to be taken into account all the time. Any bush that has to be chopped and slashed back constantly to keep it in bounds is sure to be unpresentable most of the summer. The heaps of debris which have just been pruned off are no addition to the garden and friends always arrive just after drastic pruning operations.

There are two schools of thought about the shrubs that attract certain pests near the garden. One of my friends maintains that she might just as well have a smoketree near her flower garden because then all the rose chafers go to the smoketree and not so many of them get on the garden flowers. Others think that the beetles come from miles around just to find the smoketree and when it gets over-populated they take the flowers in their stride.

Whatever your opinion about this may be, the flower garden has enough troubles of its own without adding to it shrubs that you know beforehand will demand a great deal of spraying and care. The ills that shrubs are heir to differ in different parts of the country but it is well to find out whether any shrub on your list for flower garden use demands special conditions or special cultural handling that might make it difficult and more work than it is worth. In sections where root knot, for example, is prevalent, putting shrubs that are particularly subject to it in with the flowers means much more trouble than if you keep these shrubs in a special section where you can look after them constantly. In the same way, azaleas in the flower beds themselves are not too successful because they demand acid soil. Of course flowers tolerate a little acid but not the extreme acidity under which most azaleas flourish. There is nothing lovelier than azaleas and rhododendrons near a garden but they should be outside the beds, so that the flowers will not have the competition for proper soil conditions.

The very fact that you choose garden shrubs primarily for their bloom means that you must plan the garden so their color is the basis for the whole scheme. There are certain shrubs which are particularly effective in making combinations and others whose bloom color is so difficult that it is almost sure to clash with some of the flowers you may desire in the garden.

The largest plants of the garden are likely to be flowering trees. They may be at the entrance, or arching over a path, or strong accent in the pattern of the garden. Their size demands that their variety be chosen with greatest care. I have found generally that white or pale pink trees are better garden subjects than the stronger-colored varieties. Part of the pleasure of a garden is changing it from year to year as most of us do get tired of having the same color combinations year after year. If your cherries or crabapples or dogwoods are white, you can vary the early garden scheme to suit your fancy. If you particularly like the rose-colored varieties of these same trees, it is safer to put them somewhere else on the place where they will not restrict you so much. Even without any of the flowering trees, the shrubs themselves have to be chosen most carefully. If you are particularly fond of the breeder or bronze tones in tulips, all the shrubs around the garden must be white or yellow or blue at tulip season. This rules out all the pink lilacs, the pink weigelas, many of our most familiar and beloved garden shrubs.

If in midsummer you like only salmon pink phlox, such as E. I. Farrington and Salmon Glow, the rosy pinks of some of the Rose of Sharons and the pink buddleias, like Fascinating and Charming, do not belong in the same picture. Later in the fall if you prefer pink and lavender garden chrysanthemums all the bright fall-coloring shrubs must be left out of the immediate surroundings. Otherwise the chrysanthemums will only look dirty and faded. On the other hand, if you want a brilliant show in the fall you can intensify the colors of the copper, yellow and maroon chrysanthemums by adding brilliant foliage of blueberry and flowering dogwood and the scarlet berries of Viburnum dilatatum. The important thing is to know what colors you intend using in perennials and annuals and then to choose shrubs that enhance that color scheme. Of course if you have old specimen trees or shrubs that are the reason for the site of the garden and its chief interest, you have to make your garden color scheme at their period of bloom conform to them but there is no reason for choosing new shrubs of the wrong color from sheer thoughtlessness.

There are many ways in which shrubs can be used as part of

a flower garden picture. The perennial garden can be enlarged to all appearances by making the enclosures of flowering shrubs in careful combinations with the perennials in the garden itself. Where there are comparatively few early-blooming perennials, the show of the spring garden can be greatly enhanced by combinations of shrubs immediately behind them or in the same eyeful. Tulips in groups through an otherwise almost bare bed look a little spotty and are not nearly as fine as they are when reenforced by a heavy mass of nearby shrub bloom blended with them. Daffodils need not be used in such tremendous quantities for large spring effect, if the yellow of their trumpets is picked up by a single fine forsythia, or perhaps a combination of forsythias with a white early-flowering cherry. In midsummer, when it is too hot to make gardening very attractive, shrubs like buddleia, vitex, Rose of Sharon around the garden give enough blossoms to satisfy the desire for color without much care. The earlier blooming shrubs are cool green foliage background for midsummer flowers, softening the blaze of color and making the garden more restful.

Far too little use is made of shrubs directly in the flower beds themselves. Of course many of us have planted small trimmed hedges around the beds, particularly of dwarf box and dwarf barberry, but gone no further in the use of shrubs in the midst of flowers. There are certain ones which seem almost like perennials and can be used in much the same way. The fact that they freeze to the ground or almost to the ground every year in the latitude of New York, keeps them from getting too tremendous and out of proportion with the rest of the flowers. If the border or beds are large, six to ten feet wide, at least, there is room for the buddleias and the vitex either at the back of the border, at the end, or in the middle of the bed to fill the space where it is hard to reach in to cultivate. In order not to make their part of the bed too unattractive in the spring before they leaf out, the space which will later be covered by their leaves and branches can be filled

Richard Averill Smith

11. From early May to frost, this group has flower and is an excellent example of contrast of fine and medium texture foliage. White lilac, Father Hugo's rose, daphne, and abelia are background for phlox, lavender, day lily, and peony.

Richard Averill Smith

xiv. The picturesque old flowering plums were the reason for this garden. The shrubs that surround it and the flowers in the garden beds are planned to blend with the plums for a great May bouquet.

with the very early flowering bulbs and perennials—narcissus and tulips, bleeding heart, *Mertensia, Doronicum, Phlox divaricata*—so that this same spot of the garden is a sheet of color twice during the year.

In smaller beds or borders *Abelia grandiflora, Caryopteris* (particularly Blue Mist), *Hypericum, Potentilla, Daphne somerset,* and among the evergreens the andromedas and occasionally the almost-evergreen cotoneasters, can make more effective flower combinations than merely repeating the same mass of perennial or annual bloom over and over again. One difficulty with the midsummer garden is that most of the flowers are too similar in shape and general habit so that it is hard not to make it monotonous. The very contrast of larger leaf and substantial bulk of shrubs with the lighter foliage and the different habit of the perennials and annuals gives variety.

In the south the camellias and gardenias are far finer than most perennials and they can be used in the garden itself. They are sufficiently slow-growing that there is little danger of their overcrowding and growing out of bounds. All these uses of shrubs are assuming that there is actually a definite area which is a flower garden or flower border.

In contrast to this it is possible to give the illusion of a garden without actually having one, by the proper use of combinations. Again it is a matter of realizing that it is not the number of flowers that are in bloom but the beauty of the particular group and its location that makes a garden or suggests one, or that gives you the same satisfaction a real flower garden does. If, for example, you have not the room, the desire nor the budget to have hundreds or thousands of bulbs in the spring in a real flower garden, making color combinations of the various bulbs with your shrubs can give you the same enjoyment.

Starting off the season near the house an early-flowering spirea or forsythia, *Magnolia stellata* or *Magnolia soulangeana* is beautiful in itself. With the addition, however, of the early trumpet daffodils and short-cup narcissus and a succession starting with blue glory-of-the-snow, through scilla and on into grape hyacinths, you have a garden which is completely self-sufficient, takes no care and is near enough at hand that you can enjoy it without putting on your rubbers to go out into a muddy and otherwise bare flower garden. Following them a group of lilacs along the walk or at the corner of the house may have the white Poet's narcissus, with salmon pink tulips, Clara Butt, and blue phlox divaricata under it. Somewhere else a white lilac may have bleeding heart, rose-pink tulips Rosabella and Barronne de la Tonnaye, mertensia. A bright red flowering quince is a garden all in itself with the addition of scarlet tulip Kaufmanniana, white guinea hen flowers and blue grape hyacinths. The bulbs alone are hardly strong enough except in tremendous quantities or important enough to make much of a picture but intensified by the size and brilliance of the shrub bloom, it will be one of the high spots of the garden year.

Near my own kitchen porch I have a group where there is always some bloom from May through October and yet there are only eight plants in quite a large area. It consists of one white lilac Marie le Graye, *Rosa hugonis*, *Daphne somerset*, *Abelia grandiflora*, morning glory Heavenly Blue on the white porch post, a clump of pale pink phlox Ruth May, and a large plant of lavender *Hosta lancifolia*. There is a group of tulips under the abelia. Aside from planting the morning glories, this group takes absolutely no renewing from one year to the next. Occasionally when the *Rosa hugonis* gets too rampant I prune out some of the old canes. I cut the abelia to the ground every spring and for six months I have the pleasure of effective combination of bloom without any of the care that larger masses of flowers alone would take. As a matter of fact, more people comment admiringly on that particular group than on larger flower beds nearby where there are fifteen or twenty clumps of phlox in midsummer and many annuals and other perennials. The very contrast with the shrub leaves with their varied texture and rather light bloom of the abelia intensifying the phlox is more satisfactory than a blaze of color.

One warning, however, is important. In making these small garden pictures they should be placed where they are effective but few enough in number that the whole place is not spotted up with pseudo-gardens. If you have lived in your place long enough you know what part of it you are likely to be in or looking at certain seasons of the year. Therefore you can plan combinations of shrubs and bulbs, perennials and annuals for one picture at a certain season without ever getting into the hodge-podge of flowers everywhere you look, under all the shrubs, and usually weeds along with them because you have over-extended to the point where you cannot possibly take care of them. This does not mean that you can stick perennials indiscriminately under all the shrubs on the place. That improves neither the looks of the shrub borders nor the health of the perennials. Shrub roots will inevitably take most of the nourishment from the flowers, so that the only flowers you should select are the ones that will stand a certain amount of casual treatment and that look natural near the shrubs. This may mean eliminating some of your favorite perennials. With a little care, two or three groups of iris, or a half-dozen peonies, specially fed to counteract the effect of the shrub roots, or screened from them at the back by a piece of tin so the shrub roots cannot rob the perennials, can give you as much pleasure as twenty-five of each kind.

If you have room and desire for a specialty garden there are certain shrubs that can be used in infinite variety to make a flower garden of nothing but shrubs. The camellias, the azaleas —particularly the *kurumes* and *indicas*—are perhaps the two best. They will not be in bloom for the entire garden period as we think of it from May to October in the northern sections of the country, but they will be a beautiful mass of color for many weeks in the climate where they thrive. They can be worked out in a subtle gradation of color and interesting pattern that puts most perennial gardens to shame. Anyone who specializes in or is particularly fond of a certain group of shrubs that is low and neat in habit, slow growing enough that you can keep it in proportion but has variety in color of bloom, will do well to consider using it as a real flower garden on the place, designing the shape, the proportion of the beds, the general area, with the greatest care and making it the show garden of the community.

Whether they are used to make an entire garden, to strengthen and enhance the surroundings of a flower garden, to take the place of perennials in a garden, or as the backbone of certain individual garden pictures, shrubs have a very useful and very beautiful role to play for the person who, when he says "garden" thinks only in terms of flower bloom. The combinations suggested in the list are some of the ones which I have actually used myself with the greatest pleasure. Innumerable others are possible by selecting shrub combinations just as you do flowers and using a few flowers with the shrubs to get the mass effect which is the joy of any garden.

SHRUB AND FLOWER COMBINATIONS

(in order of seasonal effect)

SPRING (April first to May first in latitude of New York)

SHRUBS		FLOWERS	
NAME	COLOR	NAME	COLOR
Cornus mas	Yellow	*Narcissus, King Alfred*	Yellow
CORNELIAN CHERRY		*Narcissus, Emperor*	
Prunus tomentosum	White	*Yellow crocus*	Yellow
MANCHU CHERRY			
Forsythia intermedia spectabilis	Yellow	*Narcissus Glory of Sassenheim*	White and yellow
SHOWY FORSYTHIA		*Narcissus Spring Glory*	White and yellow
Magnolia stellata	White		
STAR MAGNOLIA		*Scilla sibirica*	Blue
Magnolia stellata	White	*Scilla sibirica*	Blue
STAR MAGNOLIA		*Muscari botryoides*	Blue
Chaenomeles japonica	Scarlet	*Fritillaria meleagris alba*	White
DWARF FLOWERING QUINCE			

List No. 26—Continued

SHRUBS		FLOWERS	
Name	Color	Name	Color
Pieris japonica JAPANESE ANDROMEDA	Cream	*Narcissus Diana Kasner*	Pale yellow and white
Jasminum nudiflorum WINTER JASMINE	Yellow	*Scilla sibirica*	Blue
Prunus subhirtella HIGAN CHERRY	Blush	*Narcissus John Evelyn*	Pale yellow
		Muscari botryoides	Blue
Chaenomeles wilsoni Appleblossom FLOWERING QUINCE	Pink	*Viola cucullata*	Purple
Magnolia soulangeana SAUCER MAGNOLIA	Pink and white	*Iberis sempervirens*	White
		Tulipa clusiana	Pink and white
Prunus yedoensis YOSHINO CHERRY	Pink	*Narcissus poeticus*	White

MAY (In order of bloom)

Amelanchier canadensis SHADBLOW	White	*Arabis albida*	White
		Tulipa Lord Carnarvon	Pink
Azalea vaseyi PINKSHELL AZALEA	Pink	*Tulipa Chicago*	Red

Plant	Color	Plant	Color
Exochorda racemosa PEARLBUSH	White	*Narcissus poeticus Actaea*	White
Prunus serrulata fugenzo ROSE FLOWERING CHERRY	Rose	*Dicentra spectabilis*	Rose
		Tulipa Magnolia	Rose and white
Spiraea thunbergi THUNBERG SPIREA	White	*Dicentra spectabilis*	Rose
Malus atrosanguinea CARMINE CRABAPPLE	Carmine	*Phlox divaricata canadensis*	Blue
		Tulipa Rosabella	Pink
Viburnum carlesi KOREANSPICE VIBURNUM	Blush	*Primula elatior*	Pale yellow
Daphne somerset GARLAND SHRUB	Pink	*Narcissus poeticus*	White
Daphne cneorum GARLAND FLOWER	Pink	*Tulipa Kathleen Parlow*	Pink
Cornus florida FLOWERING DOGWOOD	White	*Mertensia virginica*	Blue
Rhododendron carolinianum CAROLINA RHODODENDRON	Pink	*Narcissus poeticus ornatus*	White
Azalea vaseyi PINKSHELL AZALEA	Pink	*Tulipa Clara Butt*	Pink

| SHRUBS | | FLOWERS | |
NAME	COLOR	NAME	COLOR
Syringa persica PERSIAN LILAC	Lavender	*Tulipa Marjorie Bowen*	Salmon-pink
		Iberis sempervirens	White
Malus parkmani PARKMAN CRABAPPLE	Pink		
Syringa persica alba WHITE PERSIAN LILAC	White	*Geum chiloense*	Orange
		Tulipa Bronze Queen	Bronze
Rosa hugonis FATHER HUGO ROSE	Yellow	*Tulipa Louis XIV*	Brown
		Tulipa Garibaldi	Orange
Syringa Marie Legraye WHITE HYBRID LILAC	White	*Tulipa Pride of Haarlem*	Rose
		Tulipa Baronne de la Tonnaye	Pink
Syringa Ludwig Spaeth PURPLE LILAC	Purple		

LATE MAY AND EARLY JUNE

| SHRUBS | | FLOWERS | |
NAME	COLOR	NAME	COLOR
Cornus kousa CHINESE FLOWERING DOGWOOD	White	*Iris sibirica alba*	White
		Paeonia officinalis rubra	Red
Rhododendron catawbiense Charles Dickens RED HYBRID RHODODENDRON	Red		

Philadelphus coronarius SWEETSCENTED MOCKORANGE	White	*Lilium umbellatum* *Baptisia australis*	Orange Blue
Spiraea vanhouttei VANHOUTTE SPIREA	White	*Aquilegia coerulea* *Paeonia Therese*	Blue Pink
Kolkwitzia amabilis BEAUTYBUSH	Pink	*Hemerocallis flava*	Yellow
Philadelphus Virginal HYBRID MOCKORANGE	White	*Paeonia Martha Bulloch* *Lupinus polyphyllus* *Verbascum Pink Domino*	Pink Pink and blue Rose
Syringa villosa LATE LILAC	Lavender	*Digitalis gloxinoides* *Thalictrum aquilegifolium*	Rose Cream
Rhododendron catawbiense CATAWBA RHODODENDRON	Rosy purple		
Azalea viscosa SWAMP AZALEA	White	*Hemerocallis Modesty* *Thalictrum glaucum*	Yellow Yellow
Magnolia virginiana SWEETBAY MAGNOLIA	White		

MIDSUMMER

Buddleia davidi Ile de France BUTTERFLYBUSH	Purple	*Aconitum napellus Sparks* *Hemerocallis Hyperion* *Phlox Mrs. Jenkins*	Purple Yellow White

SHRUBS		FLOWERS	
NAME	COLOR	NAME	COLOR
Vitex agnuscastus latifolia HARDY CHASTETREE	Lavender	Echinops ritro	Purple
		Phlox E. I. Farrington	Salmon-pink
		Petunia First Lady	Pink
Buddleia davidi White Bouquet BUTTERFLYBUSH	White	Hemerocallis Ophir	Yellow
		Phlox Marie Louise	White
		Lilium henryi	Yellow
Abelia grandiflora GLOSSY ABELIA	Pink	Phlox Dolly	Pink
		Salvia farinaceae	Blue
Caryopteris incana Blue Mist BLUEBEARD	Blue	Petunia Elk's Pride	Purple
Caryopteris incana Blue Mist BLUEBEARD	Blue	Marigold Mayling	Yellow
		Monarda fistulosa	Lavender
Hypericum moserianum Sun Gold GOLDFLOWER	Yellow	Lilium tigrinum	Orange
		Petunia Snowstorm	White
Hibiscus syriacus ROSE OF SHARON	Flesh	Aconitum napellus Sparks	Purple
		Lilium speciosum rubrum	Pink
Buddleia davidi Fortune BUTTERFLY BUSH	Purple	Boltonia latisquama	Lavender

AUTUMN UNTIL FROST (Fruit and foliage color of shrubs)

Euonymus alatus WINGED EUONYMUS	Rose-red foliage	*Chrysanthemum Astrid* *Chrysanthemum Little Bob*	Pink Red-bronze
Cotinus coggygria SMOKETREE	Red-orange foliage	*Chrysanthemum Apricot Glow* *Chrysanthemum Mandalay*	Apricot Orange
Abelia grandiflora GLOSSY ABELIA	Bronze foliage	*Chrysanthemum Harbor Lights* *Chrysanthemum Fireglow*	Pale yellow Red
Cotoneaster apiculata CRANBERRY COTONEASTER	Red berries		
Cornus florida FLOWERING DOGWOOD	Red foliage	*Chrysanthemum nipponicum* *Chrysanthemum Red Velvet*	White Red
Azalea vaseyi PINKSHELL AZALEA	Bronze-red foliage	*Chrysanthemum Autumn Lights*	Copper
Rhododendron carolinianum CAROLINA RHODODENDRON	Dark green foliage		
Pieris japonica JAPANESE ANDROMEDA	Green foliage	*Anemone japonica alba* *Cimicifuga simplex*	White White
Tsuga canadensis CANADA HEMLOCK	Dark green foliage		
Symplocus paniculata SAPPHIREBERRY	Blue fruit	*Eupatorium coelestinum* *Anemone japonica alba*	Lavender White
Ilex crenata JAPANESE HOLLY	Dark green	*Chrysanthemum King Midas*	Yellow

SECTION FOUR

HOW TO STUDY SHRUBS

CHAPTER XVI

How to Learn from an Arboretum, Park or Botanical Garden

ONE GREAT trouble with learning or studying most subjects is that too much of the teaching is done in the lecture room, in long sleepy hours of class room instruction. When it comes to learning about trees and shrubs, however, most of the work is in the outdoor laboratory learning about them first hand as they grow and comparatively little of it hunched over a desk.

There are many sources from which first-hand knowledge can come. Of all of them the one which exists primarily for the purpose of studying and teaching people the ways of plants are the arboretums, parks, and botanical gardens of the country. In almost every state of the union there is at least one institution where the study and use of plants is of primary importance and is actually the reason for its existence. To too many people, however, the grounds of institutions exist only as pleasant places in which to rest or play. Little actual use is made for real information. They may teach imperceptibly by unconscious appreciation of their beauty but a more careful observation can make them really valuable.

Much of my own early knowledge of shrubs and trees was absorbed as a small girl in a college town where the superintendent of grounds was a fine horticulturist. He had brought in over a long period of time many rare and valuable shrubs and trees and used them to excellent effect on the grounds of the college. Each one was carefully labelled, both with the Latin name and the common name. I think I learned a certain amount through sheer curiosity in seeing some peculiar leaf or interesting flower or fruit and looking to see what its name was. As I recall it my family also offered a reward for being able to identify every tree on the campus. That may have had something to do with my desire for knowledge.

When I went back later I noticed that the planting in general all over the town showed the results of this fine horticultural background on the college campus. The grounds of many homes had unusual plants, well selected and arranged—doubtless influenced by the example of good planting on the college grounds and the willingness of the superintendent to give information to anyone who came asking for help. A mental picture of a plant you have actually known well for some time and the example of good planting is far greater help on your own grounds than any number of catalog descriptions or classroom lectures.

Many of the best parks of the country have fine horticulturists on the staff. The park department usually has a general plan of the grounds and frequently planting plans giving the names of the plants in every section. Some plantings are well labelled outdoors and others are not. Labelling is a problem for a park and other institutions just as it is for the nurseries and for the private individual. But if you see a mass planting that is particularly effective at a certain season it is almost always possible with a little determination to find someone in the park system who can identify all the material and give all the information you need about its ways.

There are, of course, famous park systems in this country with special collections like the lilacs in Rochester, New York, dogwood at Valley Forge, and the native planting along the stream banks in beautiful Cypress Gardens in Florida. Some of the smaller cities have a great opportunity to make their parks a source not only of recreation and beauty for the people, but fine horticultural teachers by both example and information centers. Many communities are taking advantage of it and while they may be only locally famous they have been of great help in their own region and in almost all cases, the town as a whole shows the result.

Most of the arboretums and botanical gardens are in or near the large cities. If you are fortunate enough to live nearby or can spare a few days on a visit to the city, they offer the best opportunity for learning the adult habit of shrubs when they are fully grown and properly cared for in their right place. These grounds differ greatly in the way the planting is arranged and some understanding of the possible combinations is of help.

You may be a little surprised to find roses, hawthorns, shadbush, cherries, apples, crabapples, cotoneasters, photinia and several other shrubs all in one group. They are all members of the rose family and therefore belong together in that kind of planting. To the botanist the reason they all belong together is easily determined but to the layman the only thing they seem to have in common is that they all like the sun and their fruits all have the little stem and blossom end like a miniature apple. The rose family is a large one with many relatives, but some of the families have only three or four members.

In the Tea family are three of the finest shrubs in existence —the camellia, the stewartia and the gordonia. To be sure, the blossoms of the gordonia and the stewartia look individually a great deal like single camellias, but the habit of the plants is quite different and their use is varied. The planting by families is perhaps more interesting to the botanist or the scientist than it is to the amateur who is seeking knowledge primarily for the sake of use and familiarity in terms of general over-all appearance, not scientific differences or likenesses.

Others of the arboretums or botanical gardens group by plant association. That is the shrubs and trees which naturally grow along a stream edge or in lowlands are all together. Somewhere else in the arboretum, on a north slope, are the hemlocks, laurels, rhododendrons, azaleas, that would naturally grow in such a place. Some of the parks and parkways have done beautiful work in this kind of native planting by association.

One disadvantage of this method is that it is much harder to label where the plants are in large and informally planted groups. But this is probably counterbalanced by the almost unconscious teaching of natural neighbors. It is far easier to remember that red maples, benzoin, elder, sweetgum, black alder, grow wild together and make an effective planting group, because you have a picture in your mind of seeing that group repeatedly, than it is to learn it from a book or from some list. When you know your shrubs in such a location and afterwards want either to use some of those shrubs or plant that kind of location you will probably find that you instinctively think of laurel and rhododendron in filtered shade, and of sumac, crabapples, cherries, little gray dogwood in full sun.

Most of the institutions combine the two methods to a greater or less extent so that there is very little danger of finding the things that like wet, swampy soil high on top of a windy hill, or the dry land plants down in the low part of the botanical garden. When it comes to the purely non-native, hybridized and horticultural kinds of shrubs like the forsythia, beautybush, camellias and hibiscus, they are usually planted in very excellent arrangements, both as to color and season of bloom. If it is a shrub which has a great many varieties in interesting colors, they are often in collections, close enough together that you can make your own combinations by looking from one to another. Anyone who has tried to make combinations by remembering the color of his own lilac until he could get to a friend's place to see the color of another one, knows how next to impossible it is to carry flower color mentally. It is equivalent to matching ribbon or dress material without actually having the sample along.

Almost all the gardens have an excellent information service, so that it is possible when you have seen or read about a shrub that sounds likeable, to go to the garden office and ask if they have a large specimen of it. They can tell you exactly where it is or often send a guide to show it to you. Thus you can get a much better idea of what you can expect to have some years hence. From the same information service you can have plants identified that you have seen somewhere, by furnishing the office with either a very accurate and careful description or samples of the leaf and flower. If you see plants in the arboretums which particularly appeal to you but whose labels are not immediately visible, a description of where the plant is will usually promptly produce the name and any other information about it you may need.

If you live close enough and can make weekly trips to such a garden, the lessons you will learn about actual succession of bloom or of leaf or of fall color are invaluable. The catalogs and lists may do a little classification by saying that such shrubs bloom in April, others in May, and others in June, and occasionally will mark things "early, mid-season, and late" in varieties of the same shrubs. If, however, you can have first a mental picture and can note just what date the flowering crabapples bloomed and which of the flowering cherries were still in bloom with it, when the latest of the flowering crabapples bloomed and what came along with it, you will do a far better job in making combinations and successions on your own place than if you have to trust to catalog or book descriptions. I have such notes taken at the Arnold Arboretum many years ago and that notebook is probably one of the best thumbed volumes in my office. An almost illegible note that on May fourth of a certain year the white *Malus baccata* and *robusta* were both passing out of bloom while *theifera* and *sargenti* were at their height, and *sieboldi* and *ioensis plena* were in bud, is not just words. I have a mental picture of what that group looked like at that moment so that I remember it was better than having them all in full bloom at the same time.

In addition to all the knowledge you can gain almost entirely by yourself from personal observation, careful study at first hand, and asking questions, most of the gardens and arboretums have courses of lectures or classroom courses with laboratory training in various kinds of work. These are given primarily for the amateur and are either free or at a very nominal charge. They have the advantage over other school courses of having the illustrations of the subjects of the lectures close at hand so that the eye as well as the ear gets the knowledge.

The gardens and arboretums also have a great many publications. Some of them, to be sure, are highly technical and are primarily for the scientist or the professional horticulturist, but others are in very simple language, written for the amateur by an authority on the particular subject and illustrated from the grounds immediately at hand.

The growing interest on the part of the public in plants and plant material is being evidenced more every year in the crowds that come to see particular displays at botanical gardens or arboretums and the number of questions that come into their information desks. They are carrying on all the time interesting studies and experiments of great value in the scientific world as a whole but often particularly applicable to your own part of the country. Their service to the community is dependent largely on the local interest and support so that your appreciation and use of their value and facilities enables them to extend their field of service. A good botanical garden, arboretum or park system is certainly the most valuable source of accurate and scientific information on horticultural subjects and often the only place in which you can learn plants at first hand in their ultimate sizes and natural way of growing.

CHAPTER XVII

How to Visit a Nursery

A NURSERY is a business, not an educational institution. Unlike most businesses, however, it not only sells but it also produces most of its own merchandise. While it is unusual for a butcher actually to raise his own livestock, the nursery starts the products they sell, from the seed or seedling state and brings them through to selling age. For this very reason there is a great temptation to go to the nursery for all sorts of information on the care, the growth, and the habits of plant material.

Though we would not think of going to the butcher and asking him exactly how to feed the chickens or the pigs on our own place or how they were butchered and dressed, or how to cook them, we often expect the nursery to tell us every detail, not only of growth and care but even of use. Quite often we do not take care of the plant material properly and then go back to the nursery with a complaint. It is much as if we bought the meat, cooked it badly and then complained to the butcher because the recipe we used was no good, or the stove wasn't working properly.

The chief business of any nursery is to sell first class plant material, with good tops and good root systems, true to name, and to deliver it in good condition. The nurseryman is not primarily a designer, a caretaker nor a plant nurse, except in his own establishment. Neither is he primarily a teacher. While it is true that many of the nurseries have done and are doing a fine job in improving public knowledge of their field, this is done largely because it does help sell good plant material. The educated customer is the best customer.

There is no business with which I am familiar that has as many handicaps, it seems to me, as that of the nurseryman. He has heavy overhead for six months in his business, with labor, unusually wet or dry weather, cold winters or hot summers, very heavy and unpredictable factors in his success. To be in the nursery business a man must really like plants and appreciate their value. Dealing with any sort of growing thing, whether animal or vegetable, takes a certain kind of patience and philosophy that a good farmer or a good nurseryman always has. Perhaps kindly, patient, honest men are attracted to the nursery business or perhaps the nursery business makes a man into that kind of person. Whichever it is, some of the finest, most upright and honorable men I have ever known or done business with have been nurserymen.

During the week of the International Flower Show I look forward to visits from the nurserymen, in town for the show. They come in not to sell anything but just to talk over the state of plants in general, what kind of a winter we have had, what is new in the plant world and what the spring promises. The enthusiasm, interest and integrity of the owners and men engaged in the nursery trade is of vital importance. There is perhaps no business in which the actual value of the material depends so much on the individual word of the man who is growing it. He knows far better than anyone else what kind of a root system is under the plant. He knows which things will grow in his climate and which have proven unsuccessful and his word is the only actual guarantee on the material.

There are no trade-mark products in the nursery business. There are, to be sure, patented plants but that insures only that a plant is true to its name. It does not insure at all that it is a well-grown plant of that variety. It is this personal standard that makes catalog prices mean little in shrubs. A bush listed as 5'-6' may have two feeble shoots five feet high and some straggly roots. It is priced at fifty cents. Another will have plants with six or eight sturdy shoots, five feet high, a mass of fiber roots and listed at a dollar and fifty cents. Both are literally 5'-6' material but are not comparable, either now or five years after transplanting. If three equally good nurseries quote similar prices and another quotes an apparent bargain, only personal inspection can convince me that the cheap one is worth the labor of planting. Occasionally the need of thinning certain rows or clearing a certain section, enables a nursery to offer fine material at a lower price, but this is rare. Over-cheap plant lists are a danger signal, nine times out of ten.

It is certainly advisable to deal with the local nurseryman when a good one is available. For one thing, his plants are adapted to your locality and he has had experience in which ones thrive and which ones do not. If, however, there is no nursery close at hand of established reputation, it is better to go a little farther afield and get well-grown plants from a reputable firm. There is no well-known nursery that will risk its reputation by intentionally sending out poorly grown or poorly adapted plants. Mistakes may occur but it is certainly always worth while to give the nursery the benefit of the doubt and realize that they are dealing with living things and that in a rush season they may send out plants which are not up to their own standards.

They are much more likely, however, to say that they cannot supply a certain variety or a certain type because they know theirs are not good enough, than they are to send out second- or third-rate material. For their own protection as well as yours, it is much better to report unsatisfactory or below standard material at the time it is received than it is to wait until it dies, three or four months later and then tell them it was no good. If you buy a chair from a furniture store and find the webbing poorly tacked or the strings badly tied when you get it, you can hardly expect the store to do anything about it if you wait for six months when the whole bottom falls out of the chair.

In a nursery you see plants from two to ten years old. This

means it is a poor place really to study plants for characteristic appearance. A large nursery may have a few specimen plants of certain varieties at full size and full age, but the bulk of their material is in small sizes and gives you a very poor idea of what the habit and shape of the plant is when it really is old enough to have some character. It may be valuable to know what the plant looks like when it is young, so that you know what you are getting when you order it, but it is much more useful to know what it looks like at its full size so that you have a better idea of how many of them to plant in a certain place and what you can expect as they mature. For that reason, familiarity with mature plants comes primarily from other sources than from a nursery.

Labels are rather a sore subject with most nurserymen. All of the good ones make a real effort to keep their plants labelled at least in rows, but the same pixies that pull up stakes in your flower garden work overtime in a nursery. The most careful, thorough and painstaking labelling, with labels at the ends of the rows that seem indubitably permanent, results all too often in a row of forsythia being firmly labelled "crabapple" and a row of flowering dogwood being called hybrid lilacs. The cultivating in a nursery is usually done by men whose job it is to cultivate, not to know plants. Therefore if labels come out in the process, they are stuck back wherever seems handiest, with very amazing results. Children have the most surprising way of pulling up heavy labels deep in the ground, and then with a tremendous amount of work, putting them in somewhere else. Every nursery is a playground for the children in the neighborhood after hours. It is a wonderful site for hide-and-go-seek and all sorts of games and no amount of effort ever seems to check the innocent damage they do.

For all these reasons, the best way to visit a nursery is to visit it when you are ready to buy and have some idea of what you want to buy—at least what it looks like, or where it is to go and how many of it you need. Far too many people waste the nurseryman's time and their own by turning up at the nursery

with the vague idea that they need fifty feet of planting on a
property line and have no further suggestions than that. Those
same people would not go to a department store and say, "I
want four dresses," and give no details of what purpose the
dresses were to serve, where they were to be worn, what color,
what material, or anything else they were to be. Even though
your education in shrubs may not be complete, it is far better
to go to a nursery and say, "I have a place in my yard in which
I need a shrub that will be eventually ten feet wide and fifteen
feet high. I see it every day from my living room window, so
that it ought to look well at all times in the year." The nurseryman will then have some idea of what to recommend and
can give you a far better choice in material.

If you are planning an entire place, it is wise, after considerable study of books, articles, botanic gardens or parks,
observation in all sorts of places, to have a list of the things
you think you want for the property and to go to the nursery
with the list in hand. They will then be able to help you and
to guide you in knowing that certain things will not stand the
locations you have in mind, or that they will be too slow-growing to purchase in the size you thought you wanted. In the
long run you will have a better planting with the expert help
that the nurseryman can give you. He can make suggestions
for substitutions in your original list without changing your
basic idea.

For example, if you want a pair of picturesque-shaped trees
to frame a garden entrance, you may have hawthorns in mind
because of their vase-shaped head and picturesque outline. He
may have available a pair of dogwoods, tree hollies, tree box,
that have the shape you want and are good substitutes, unless
the particular flower color of hawthorns is important. Unless
you can give him some idea of the effect you are after he cannot tell whether tall, slender poplars, slender yews or any other
matched pair of plants will do just as well. I frequently go to a
nursery and say, "I want a plant this shape," and draw a rough
outline sketch of the head and form that I want. In combing

the nursery I often find that shape in an odd specimen of a plant that I would never think of as taking that shape. In other words, it is the effect I am seeking and not the name of the plant.

One warning that seems to me important in visiting a nursery is not to go with the idea of buying, at the time the plants are in bloom. It is all too easy to buy a plant simply because it is a lovely color for ten days in the year, without in the least noticing what it looks like underneath the bloom, or knowing anything about what it is going to be as it gets bigger. A nurseryman friend of mine tells me that they can sell anything that has a red flower on it, and it makes no difference what the plant is as long as it has red flowers. In the fall they can usually sell anything that has beautiful fall colors in either foliage or berries. It may have looked like nothing at all the other eleven months in the year, but if people come to buy in the season of autumn color they will buy the plant that is most brilliant, regardless of its health, habit or looks the rest of the year.

As a matter of fact if you are buying plants for a permanent effect, it is wiser not to buy those that are too heavy in bloom or in fruit. The plants will actually come along and do better after transplanting if they do not exhaust themselves too much in bearing flower and fruit. If you are picking out a flowering dogwood it is perhaps surer to live if you choose one with few buds on it rather than one that will blossom in a great burst the following spring and then take some time recovering from the effort. Frequently plants, in order to perpetuate themselves, throw out a very heavy flower and fruit effect when their vitality is low, so that actually you are getting a poorer plant as far as general condition and chances of success are concerned, than if you buy one whose leaf is good but whose flower or fruit is rather light. It may be wise to visit a nursery on a casual trip of observation during its season of most brilliant flower or fall colors, but it is not the best time to visit it with a definite buying order in mind, unless you are sure that you know those plants in other habits and at other times.

The best time to visit a nursery is certainly in their not-busy months. There is no business that has a worse rush season, with twenty-four hours a day all too few. It is not only human beings that are pushing the nurserymen then, it is the weather. It is the knowledge that no matter whether they can or not, a certain amount of work has to be done by the end of a certain period, so that their peaks are sharp and unavoidable. You cannot possibly get the attention and the help that you may need, no matter how willing they are, if you are taking time when every minute is worth its weight in gold.

If you know you are going to have a planting job to do in the fall by all means go to the nursery during the summer and give the order. Similarly, if you know you want to plant in the spring, do not wait until the first warm days come along in March and then start haunting the nursery. The buds are starting to swell and the nurserymen are beginning to go mad. There is far too much work to do, far too little time and too few men to do it. It may be a little chilly in January or February, if you live in the cold parts of the country, to go out and tag material in a nursery but that is the time when the nurserymen have time to help you and to appreciate your difficulties. Such foresight will get your planting done early and well in the spring. Rush hour shopping in the nursery is no more satisfactory than in any other store.

All this does not mean, of course, that the nurseries do not welcome visitors. They certainly do and many of them have separate little show places, with big specimens of their finest material, labelled and showing to its full advantage. Many of them have a large staff of men whose chief business is to act as guides, and indirectly salesmen, through the nurseries. It is a great help to even these well-staffed nurseries if you know what you want. If you see a shrub you cannot identify, the office or one of the salesmen can and will help very willingly. They usually have a catalog or list by arrangement or by location in the nursery, and with a fairly accurate description in the most familiar language, they can identify the plant for you, probably tell you how old it is and what you can expect it to do when it gets older. They are eager to help increase the knowledge of plant material because the greater the knowledge, the greater their audience is and their selling public. It has been most gratifying in the last twenty years to find the public appreciation of really fine material increasing. It benefits the looks of the country at large but it also benefits the nurseries and they will do everything in their power to increase it.

CHAPTER XVIII

How to Learn from Nature

NATURE is the world's best plant arranger. Like all good gardeners she knows what plants to use, where to put them and how to grow them so that they look right and do well. She does over-crowd her plantings rather badly but the effects are amazingly beautiful. An appreciation of her schemes through study and analysis helps all of us to do better work.

The best way, perhaps, really to understand what a good job Nature does is to take a barren piece of land and try to create a natural planting that looks as if man had nothing to do with it. After a man-destroyed or damaged woodland field has been replanted with native material, there is no greater joy possible than having someone say two or three years later, "Oh, well of course you didn't have to do anything here, this is wild planting." Then you know you have really played Nature's own game to very good effect and been successful in your imitation of her ways. Even if the piece of planting is very small and not in the location where completely native planting would belong, the principles Nature uses are sound and should be observed.

The most important thing about native planting is that it always consists of the plants best suited to existing conditions of sun, soil, and moisture. The fascinating subject of ecology deals entirely with plants as adapted to their environment. It is a study of Nature's planting arrangement. If an open, sunny field has been ploughed and cultivated for years and then

allowed to go back to the wild, every farmer knows that the
first place where shrubs will appear is along the outer edges,
near the fences or the walls, or in spots where the plough
could not reach. There the leaves and debris have piled up and
rotted, making the soil perhaps a little richer and allowing
seedlings to lie undisturbed by man's cultivation. Certain
kinds of plants will spring up and make a thick hedgerow
which gradually spreads from the edges out into the rest of the
field. All these plants are sun lovers and grow in not too
rich soil.

There are usually several kinds of plants in such a hedgerow,
as Nature rarely sticks to one kind of seedling. Here and there
in June, if the place is a little damp, will be the wild elder
blooming in masses of white. In the fall, sumac in brilliant
colors may decorate the planting. In the prairie states the
lovely wild crabapples and wild hawthorns are almost sure to
spring at intervals through the hedgerows. Near the seashore
the wild cherry will take over in great profusion or the beach
plum and bayberry cover the field.

If an open, sunny property line exists on our own places,
there is no better way in which to learn how to plant it than
to take a walk in the country and really consider the places
where man has done no planting. We can find beautiful
native material, with some study identify it, and order it from
the nursery for home planting.

Since our planting will probably have some care and help
from the pruning shears and fertilizers, we need not crowd so
thickly as Nature does. We can also introduce some species
or varieties which are not a part of her planting scheme. If the
property line or location for shrub border is in the shade of
big trees or we would like to recreate a woodland feeling, an
exploration of the edges of some of the neighboring woods
will show how skillfully Nature faces down her woodlands.
The flowering dogwood and the redbud tree are native all up
and down the eastern seaboard and in many other parts of the
country. Used with the tall shady background of big trees,

they show to far greater beauty and advantage than they usually do when set out in the middle of a sunny lawn as specimens.

In sunny locations and in good soil, the white pine will take over the land. In filtered half-shade in the non-limestone parts of the country, are the azaleas, rhododendrons and laurel in large masses, usually interrupted by deciduous shrubs, like ironwood or dogwood, or with hemlock interspersed among them. They make our mountainsides and hillsides worth a trip to see, whether in flowering season or in the fall when the azaleas turn color and are a fine contrast against the darkness of the evergreens.

The reason for the association of plants in special locations is not deliberate artistic intention on the part of Nature. It is because each kind in the group is well adapted to the local condition. The ones that are best adapted to full sun and rich soil crowd out those that like sun but poor soil, as the fallen leaves make the soil better. Then as the trees get larger and the shade gets heavier the sun lovers die out and the shade-enduring plants come in. Nature's process takes hundreds of years but we can learn from it how to do the same thing in a very short space of time. Our man-made plantings have a much better chance for survival and success if we follow the natural process of putting plants where they have the least handicap from their environment.

Another important factor in Nature's successful pattern is that she rarely uses one kind of plant exclusively, so there is no monotonous sameness of both skyline and leaf texture. In the fall, a distant woodland may look as if it is all evergreen because the hemlocks or the pines or the cedars stand out dark green in a leafless world. In midsummer this same woodland looks as if it had no evergreen in it, because the trees and shrubs have all come out in leaf and the evergreen color is lost. This mingling of evergreen and deciduous material is one of the things that gives the all-round, all-year effect that is so important in good shrub planting.

There is almost no part of the country where some evergreen is not native. In southern climates, of course, almost all
of the material is evergreen, whether needled or broad-leaved,
so that the leafless season hardly need be considered. In others,
evergreens are scarce enough that they are really outstanding
accents in certain seasons of the year. In the very cold climates
of Maine or Minnesota, the bare branches of many shrubs
cast interesting shadows on the snow but the white snow glare,
unrelieved by any other color for weeks and months, makes
the dark green accent of the spruces, the hemlocks, the cedars,
more welcome than perhaps anywhere else in the country. In
the hot climates the very fact that most of the material is evergreen makes the heat more endurable because of the dark
green, and the shady quality that lasts twelve months in the
year. In contrast to this, however, a northern world made up
entirely of needled evergreens is likely to be somber, dull and
monotonous. A grove of virgin pine or hemlock has a cathedral quality that is inspiring but no one wants to live in a
cathedral all the time.

Nature's use of evergreens at a distance should give us ideas
on how to use them. Too many people have a mistaken idea
that since evergreens are noticeable most in the winter, they
should be tight up against the house. As a matter of fact, you
will probably enjoy them more often if in winter you can look
out of your house windows and see them in a distant border.
Since they are most conspicuous for seven months of the year,
it is vitally important that we place them strategically, so that
they form a nice pattern in the winter landscape. You lose
sight of them entirely for spring, summer and early fall months
of the year but when the leaves fall they can stick up like sore
thumbs if they are in the wrong place, or they can give great
delight if they are placed where you see them bringing out the
whole pattern of your property.

Most of the needled evergreens (pines, firs, spruces, hemlocks, cedars) are not really shrubs, but since we usually plant
them in fairly small sizes as part of the shrub border, they

should be considered in the shrub planting scheme. The broad leaved evergreens are for the most part true shrubs, and their effect is most important for the months of the year when they are conspicuous. Rhododendrons and laurels may be outstandingly beautiful during their bloom season but are perhaps more noticeable when the neighboring shrubs are all bare. The former particularly are a poor choice for an evergreen to be seen close at hand. Anything more mournful than their drooping, blackish-green leaves in a cold snap is hard to imagine. At a distance they are merely green and the droop of the leaves is not too apparent, but under closer inspection they are a depressing sight.

All the evergreen hollies, of which there are many varieties in this country, are excellent choices for evergreen effect in the shrub border. You can get almost any shape and any habit in them and one or more is adaptable in most parts of the country. Their flower is inconspicuous and some of them have no fruit that is worth mentioning. The Christmas holly, *Ilex opaca*, is familiar either in cut branches or in native plants, all over the country and is an excellent choice for tall growing shrubs, really small trees, where it does well. In the south it grows to be a large tree but as far north as New York City it can be used as a shrub. When Nature plants these broadleaved evergreens she almost always interrupts her dark greens with another evergreen which has different color in its leaf. There are gray-green evergreens, there are bronze-leaved ones so that there is no reason for an evergreen planting being nothing but monotonous dark green foliage. I was amazed the first time I saw the man-made plantings in the south, to see how little variation there was in the use of a very rich field of plant material. Nature, with her broad leaves in dark green, gray, bronze, of all size from the tiny hollies to the big magnolia leaves, had done so much better job than man had done. He had not tried to copy her choice of material and ways of planting and had used too exclusively the dark, coarse greens only.

The lighter effect of deciduous shrubs, mingled with the

dark heaviness of evergreens, gives a charm and gaiety to the wild planting that even the best of solid evergreen planting cannot have. Many of the broad-leaved evergreens with which we are familiar are somber and heavy if planted in too large masses. Nature, with an instinctive regard for this, always interrupts it with light tracery of branches in winter, with the delicacy of unfolding buds and young yellow-green leaves in the spring, and with a brighter green foliage in the summer.

Even when almost entirely deciduous you will rarely see Nature's planting consisting of one variety for many feet. There will probably be one shrub that is predominant. It may be one of the dogwood family. It may be sumac. It may be some of the viburnums that will be in a planting by the hundreds but here and there mixed in with it will be groups of other plants of a different leaf texture, of different height, and different color.

If the predominant plant is tall there are sure to be facing down shrubs of lower growth and different habit. On a sunny country road sometimes the wild blackberry, the wild raspberry or the wild roses come down a bank in front of tall, upright-growing shrubs and it is their arching grace that gives the planting the finish that it badly needs. Here and there through almost any planting, a seedling tree has come up so that it raises the skyline and makes the whole group more interesting.

The very fact that Nature usually uses one or two or three predominant things in a planting has suggestions for us. She never tries to put all the plants that might grow in that location into one shrub border. The seeds have been sown by various natural agents. Whether scattered by the birds or dropped from a parent plant, or carried by the winds or water, they will be restricted in the number of species or variety to those fairly close at hand. There is a certain homogeneity about such hedgerows, a certain predominance of effect from one kind of plant at a certain season that is far better than our polka-dot theme of one of everything known to the nursery trade, that might grow in a certain border.

Another important suggestion from wild planting is that its only fertilizers are natural ones. The leaves from the plants fall and rot in the hedgerow, field or woods, building up more and more humus and feeding the plants that best of all fertilizers, leaf mould. This same kind of treatment is important on our own places. I know of one beech and oak woodland in which all the undergrowth was cut out and the leaves raked up in a mad effort for tidiness. In the course of eight or ten years, all the big trees started to die at the tops. The owner was distressed but reluctant to let the woodland come back in for the sake of saving the trees. After spending hundreds of dollars on tree food and fertilizer we finally replanted the woodland with undergrowth of native shrubs. In a very few years the big trees started to recover, young trees by the thousands sprang up in the woodland, and the whole place was brought back to its natural balance.

With many shrubs no amount of fertilizing can take the place of the leaf mulch over their roots. This is particularly true of most of the broad-leaved evergreens, the rhododendrons, azaleas, laurels and hollies. If leaves blowing around on the rest of the place are too unsightly, they can be held down by a top mulch of leaf mould or peat moss over the leaves in the fall or even by evergreen branches laid over them until they start to rot enough to stay in place. Too many gardeners put themselves to a tremendous amount of work tidying up and raking all the leaves when it would be much better to let them blow into the shrub borders and stay there, or even to rake the ones off the lawn and leave them in the shrub borders to rot and form mulch. There is no particular reason for going to the tremendous labor of making compost in neat and tidy piles and then putting it on the shrubs when all you need to do is rake the leaves in under the shrubs and let them rot by themselves, making their own leaf mould without any further handling.

If you have lived in one community for many years, the chances are the planting in the fields and woodlands and along the roadsides of the neighborhood has been taken for granted. If you are thinking of doing some planting on your own place you may very well spend considerable time walking around the parts of the country where man has not disturbed the native planting, finding out how it is done and what you can imitate about it. If you have moved to a different part of the country from the familiar one, there is no better way to start a garden than to study the things native to the region and therefore well adapted to take hold on your own place.

Even a small suburban lot will frequently be much more charming by imitating along one property line an edge-of-the-woods border, or along a sunny open line, the hedgerow and meadow kind of planting seen along a country lane. Some of the finest plant material in this country is native to our fields and woods. While we would probably not want to do without the discoveries made in foreign lands and introduced to our gardens here, most places would be better off for using more native plants.

Although this material does grow locally, that does not mean that it should be dug up from the wild and transplanted. The chances of its living are rather poor since the root systems are not thick and heavy from frequent transplantings, as with nursery-grown stock. The labor involved in digging it and nursing it along for two or three years, is probably greater than the amount of money spent to buy it from a nursery. The collecting of native material is also responsible for a great deal of the damage that has been done to our landscape. Great acres, in certain sections of the country, have been completely denuded of all their fine laurel, of their dogwood, of azaleas, by collectors who came in and transplanted things from the wild. Using native material and using it properly is all-important but digging it up out of nature and putting it on your own place is both unwise and inconsiderate. Our countryside gives us the suggestions for ways of planting and should not be asked to supply the plants, too.

CHAPTER XIX

How to Learn from Friends

THE NEAREST-AT-HAND school in which to study shrubs is your own neighborhood—the grounds of your acquaintances and friends. A leisurely walk through a village or town street or a stroll through the country is a fine chance to compare and diagnose pieces of planting on other people's grounds. If you walk along a certain block and see one house whose foundation planting or boundary planting is particularly effective in comparison with the others in the block, you can start analyzing to see what gives the effect. It may be the choice of material as a whole, it may be the contrast of different textures and colors in the planting, it may be the arrangement or it may be the spacing. In order to decide whether it is the material itself a comparison with neighboring properties to see whether or not they have actually the same material will soon rule out the material itself, if all of them are identical.

The next thing is to find out what it is in the arrangement of the material that makes the difference. The easiest thing to determine is the general skyline and ground line of the planting. For example, if two adjoining places both have forsythias, spireas, lilacs, weigelas, dogwoods, cedars and flowering crabapples, one garden may have all the middle-sized shrubs in a mixed border with the dogwoods and crabapples as specimens in the lawn, unrelated to the border. The other one may have the dogwood and the crabapple to make an accent in the foreground of the border and a high mass in the skyline at the same time. The cedars may be used as exclamation point accents in the border or they may be sore thumbs sticking up at the end of it. One border may have so many of the flowering shrubs jammed in together that it looks more like a jungle than a shrub border, while the good border has half as many shrubs, well placed to give them room to grow healthy and beautiful and to assume their natural shape.

In foundation planting comparison is invaluable. If a small house looks as if it is about to be swallowed up by the green mass under the windows, try visualizing that house without the shrub mass—nothing but green lawn coming up to the foundations with individual specimens at the door and the corners. If no one is looking, you might even hold up a sheet of paper in front of your line of vision to see what removing all the green feather bed will do.

This kind of learning by comparison is probably better done on strangers' places really than on friends', since the friendship might be a little strained by having to compare certain parts unfavorably or seem to be looking at them with a critical eye as compared to the neighbors'. But it is very good practice to look at various places with an analytical eye rather than saying, "I don't like that" or "I do like this," without knowing just what it is you like or do not like.

When it comes to learning from friends directly, a certain amount of diplomacy and discretion is probably needed and very frequently a great deal of persistence. If you go to a friend's house and are charmed by a certain plant in leaf, fruit, or flower, of course you will want to know what it is and certain facts about it, from your host or hostess. First, how long has it been planted; how big was it when they got it; what kind of care in the way of pruning or spraying does it have to have; and finally, what is its full name. This last question is all too often the stumbling block. You are very likely to get the same kind of helpful information volunteered at the Flower Show one year. Two of us were looking at an exhibit and saw a particularly lovely salmon flower. One of us said,

"I wonder what that is," meaning, of course, what variety it was. A lady standing behind us replied in most superior tones, "Why, don't you know, that is a tulip?" To be told that a certain shrub is a crabapple or a viburnum or a magnolia is very little help. There are so many species or varieties in each genus of shrubs that the one you particularly admire needs to have its second name, so that you can go to a nursery and ask for that particular member of the family.

Of course, your friends will probably be sufficiently flattered by your admiration or worn down by your determination that they will go to their old bills or plant lists and after considerable search, unearth two or three names which might belong to that shrub. From then on you are likely to be on your own and have to seek further help in identification from the nurserymen, a botanical garden, an editor. If it is not convenient to take a sample of the leaf and flower or fruit in person, you will need to take down such data as the exact date on which it was in bloom or fruit and such details as the color of the bark, the size of the leaf, the number and size of the flower petals, and an accurate description of their color. The common name is not much help if you want to order the shrub as there are too many common names which are purely local or fit several shrubs. Nurserymen identify shrubs by their Latin names only. There are also in many cases several members of a family which have the same common name. For example, one of our finest native shrubs is known as shadblow, shadbush, juneberry and maywood and serviceberry, in different parts of the country. And all the members of the family are sometimes known by the same name, from the low one, *Amelanchier stolonifera*, to the very tall, *Amelanchier canadensis*. So asking the nursery for shadbush may get you almost nowhere.

After you have identified or at least partially identified the shrub on a friend's place, it will be helpful to look at its placing carefully to see whether it is the shrub itself which is attractive or whether it is the combination of that shrub with its surroundings and its background. In some cases you are likely to find that you see only the particular specimen itself and with a little thought can work out a better place to use it on your own grounds, or a more interesting combination. This is, of course, where discretion plays a major part because this kind of mental rearranging can quickly counteract the effect of admiration if you think out loud. They probably like it where it is and as they have used it.

Sometimes if they are very good friends they will allow the use of the pruning shears. You may seem to just be picking a bouquet but if you can get a twig or two of this new plant and try it in the hand with other branches from your own place or your friend's, you can get a new arrangement that is outstanding. For example, an orange azalea, Louise Honeywell, looked beautiful in itself the first year it was shown at the Boston Flower Show as a specimen. A little study of its color and texture in a bouquet resulted in a group of them planted against the almost black green of hemlocks with a white flowering dogwood nearby, and made the turn of a certain path some years later a place of pilgrimage every spring for all our friends.

Another thing you may learn from other people's places is that you need to consider your own planting from all directions. I know of one place where there is a beautiful rose-colored flowering cherry. The owner sees it out of her living room window, against a background of soft green spring leaves and dark evergreens and is completely enchanted with it. Several of the neighbors at the far end of the street, on the other hand, have been considering a dark night and a handful of salt on its roots, because the only way they see it is against the rather raw red brick of the owner's house and during the two or three weeks it is in bloom their teeth are set on edge constantly. The remedy here, of course, would have been a white or blush flowering cherry which would not have offended the neighbors.

The important point in seeing something beautiful in a

friend's place is to determine whether it fits into your entire color scheme, looking first from the street toward the house and from your house toward the garden or the street or the neighbors. If you have a very bright red flowering quince, then however much you admire your neighbor's rose-colored cherry, you do not want to introduce one on your own place in anything like close proximity to the existing shrub. Similarly, if your next door neighbor has a great mass of yellow forsythia on the property line, your red flowering quince or a new variety of rose-colored cherry will not belong. Also, if you like salmon-pink tulips you will not want rose-pink shrubs or trees in the picture.

One very valuable thing to observe on friends' places is the growth-habit of the different shrubs and small flowering trees. Even if there is no arboretum or botanical garden in which to see mature specimens, most communities have older houses where a little investigation and a few questions will tell you much more about the actual look of shrubs as they get old, than any amount of descriptions in books, magazines or catalogs.

If you notice that one neighbor seems to spend a great deal of time with the pruning shears on a certain shrub, it may be well to find out what that shrub is that is growing at too great a rate, so that you will not make the mistake of using it unless there are large spaces to fill quickly. I well remember an unfamiliar honeysuckle which was described as a slow growing and rare variety. It turned out to be much like the common one, Lonicera tatarica, and after four years' struggle with pruning shears and saws to keep it from completely swamping both a flower bed and a driveway, we gave up in despair and yanked it out bodily.

Friends in the neighborhood can also give information about the likes and dislikes of shrubs in your own locality. One of them may tell you that there is no use trying to grow rhododendrons. The man down the street, however, has beautiful rhododendrons. The difference is that the good rhododendrons are growing in half shade with a thick leaf mulch over their roots to keep them cool in the summer, while your unsuccessful friend's plants are plastered up against the hot south wall and have been vigorously cultivated in a mistaken attempt to make them grow. If some of your own plants are not doing well and some one else's are, comparison of the soil around them, of the relation of sun and shade, of the fertilizing program, and the amount of wind to which they are exposed will give you the reason for the difference in vigor.

Of course you are almost sure to have some friends for whom anything seems to grow and others whose plants all look rather down-at-the-heel and unprepossessing. This in itself can teach you a great deal. It is probably not a matter of luck, nor of climate, but primarily of care in selection of plant material, careful placing and planting, careful watering and feeding that makes one planting flourish and the other one stand still or go backwards. There is undoubtedly such a thing as "a green thumb" but all the green thumbs I have ever known have been very hard working ones. Even plants as nearly care-free as shrubs respond to good care and show the effects of neglect as any other living thing does. Your most valuable friends, horticulturally speaking, are the good gardeners who know what they have and how to take care of it. And a good gardener is always eager to share his knowledge.

SECTION FIVE

HOW TO SELECT AND GROW
SHRUBS

CHAPTER XX

How to Plan, Select and Order Shrubs

LEARNING TO KNOW shrubs may be in itself a fascinating hobby but like most hobbies the greatest pleasure is in acquiring some of the objects for yourself. The selection of exactly the right shrub for the right place not only puts your present knowledge to use but always increases it in the process of selection. If there is only one shrub needed on your place the course of determining what it should be will sometimes lead you into explorations of an entirely new part of the plant world, with a much richer understanding of the whole field.

Finding out whether you can put your knowledge to use means planning the over-all picture of your grounds, to assess what you have and what you need. The first thing to do is to determine exactly where on the property planting should be, reckon how much area it must cover, and what it is to accomplish. The easiest way to do it is on paper. With the title of the property you probably got a survey, usually a blueprint showing the house placed on the property and the property lines themselves. On the survey there will be a note giving the scale or how many feet equals one inch (usually twenty feet to the inch).

If no such survey is available it is reasonably easy to make one for yourself. With a tape and a rule the first thing is to measure the house, which is the one fixed object. When it is drawn on a piece of paper to scale, the property lines can be determined by extending the lines of the house till they run into the property line. This distance, measured from each side of the house, gives you the direction of the boundary lines in case they are not parallel to the house, and it is put down on the same sheet of paper with the house so that you have the total area of your grounds. The inexperienced surveyor of his own grounds will probably find it easier to use the big squared paper available in stationery stores, either one square to the foot or to two feet as convenience dictates. It is usually better not to make this plan too large as it is easier for even a professional to design at a size where the whole thing is apparent as one picture. With a very large painting you must get across a large room in order to see it properly and take it all in, while with a small one you can see it as a design at close range. Similarly, a large plan is too spread out to see the whole effect on the table where you are working. A plan of thirty by thirty-six inches is a comfortable working size.

With this surveyor's or home-made survey in front of you, the first thing to mark by arrows or notes is the objects that need to be shut out from your house or its terraces, or views that need to be emphasized. In other words, put down on the paper the most obvious things. Study outdoors will tell you about how much ground room you can afford to take up with groups of planting and translating that onto paper will give you the general rough shape and size of the area. You will also want to mark utilitarian areas, such as the drying yard or the vegetable garden, the site of a possible flower garden and the room it will take up, so you know where the enclosure for it needs to be. If all these general ideas are put on a piece of tracing paper or on one sheet of a tracing pad, another sheet can then be put over it and the actual outline of the shrub borders or beds worked over on repeated trial sheets so that the whole place has pleasant lines, well shaped lawns and satisfies all the important space requirements of the family. It may take a good many sheets of tracing paper before you are satisfied with the shape and the size of everything, but it is better than erasing on the first sheet each time you want a change. The trouble is that you are very likely to erase what afterwards proves to have been a good idea and then it has gone entirely from the paper and partly from your mind. If it is on a piece of tracing paper farther back in the pad, you can haul it out again and revise it to put in your final plan. The landscape architect usually calls this final layout plan the sketch plan or sometimes the preliminary plan. It is all-important as it is the one from which all the work will be planned in further detail. When it is once right in general feeling and proportion, many costly mistakes will be saved by knowing exactly where you want to work and how much area you are going to undertake.

With this initial plan as nearly perfect in proportion and line as you can get it, no matter how roughly drawn, the next step is to decide for yourself which piece of planting is the most important in the general looks of the place, in your enjoyment of it, and in the family budget. In planning work I like to make what is really a three to five year schedule with the client, so that each season what is done is exactly right and is complete in itself. Trying to compromise and doing a little here, there and everywhere only results in spreading one's self so thin that none of the place looks finished. For example, such a calendar on a small suburban place might read: First year—Foundation planting and trees; second year—Planting on side property lines; third year—Planting along street; fourth year—Flower garden enclosure.

With the plan and the order of business in mind, we can then proceed to select and order the particular plants for the unit which we are going to do first. Taking the place where most people want planting immediately, that is, around the house, the first step is to determine exactly where each important plant needs to go, in terms of the architecture of the house, the family's personal taste and the requirements of the neighborhood in general. It is almost a safe rule to say that you usually need about half as many plants as you first intend putting in and it is much easier to add planting later than it is to remove it.

Planning the planting carefully probably means a combination of paper work and work outdoors. A handful of stakes is a great help, as it is easier to visualize on the ground than it is on paper, for most people. If small stakes are put into the ground at the points where you think you want the essential plants, they can be moved around until their location seems right as far as distance from other plants or foundations is determined. If the short stake which marks the location is not enough, a yard-stick or a tall stake can be put in place beside it, so that you can look at it against the house or in the general location, to decide how high the plant wants to be eventually. It is a good idea actually to measure outdoors, so that you know how much room you are allowing for plants, if you are not too familiar with the way they grow. For instance, the impulse is always to put plants too close to the front entrance. They may look right when you first put them in but after four or five years you find your front door is getting closed up so that the feeling of welcome is destroyed by crowding, and on a wet day you are likely to get a shower as you go past.

Measurements are very deceiving outdoors so that until you have a good idea of how high ten feet is or how wide six feet is outdoors instead of indoors, it is helpful to know the actual height of certain outdoor objects for reference. For example, if you measure from the ground to the top of the first floor windows and find it is ten feet and then look at a plant which is listed as from ten to twelve, you can see in your mind's eye just where that plant will come on the house. For some reason six feet on the floor inside is quite a wide space but six feet between the house and the front driveway seems to shrink when plants get in it. It is all too easy to try to put too many plants in that space.

I have one friend who found that she was unable to visualize outdoor size, so that she made a collection of stakes of different heights, with other pieces of lath nailed across them, which gave her the ultimate height and the ultimate spread of various sized shrubs. The looks of her place one day when I drove up and found umbrellas tied to long poles, representing the proposed trees, and wooden laths in the form of crosses, all around the house, was something I shall never forget. But the result of it was that she put her planting in the right place and has not had to move it around since. She did her work on paper and on the ground, inexpensively and easily, instead of hiring a gang to correct mistakes five years later.

After you have decided about how big the plant should be when it is full grown, you need to determine what its general appearance should be. The color of both leaf and bloom, the seasons when it must be attractive, the amount of sun or shade it will get, and any special soil conditions like extreme dryness or extreme wetness should be noted. It is a help to have a little chart with columns for these various things so that you can write down all the things you have to take into account and then start trying to find the shrub or shrubs that fit that description. As you get more familiar with shrubs and have done more planting, such meticulous work will be easier, but while you are learning, or if you have some particularly important problem, orderly notes of what you are looking for will save mistakes. With such a list you can run through in your mind the shrubs you know, go through nursery catalogs to add to the list that fits this description, and when you have found one or more that you think answer it, go to look at them in person to see if they are right. After you are sure you have made the right choice the next step is to fill in the Latin name and the quantity of the plant you want on your chart.

Then it is a question of deciding how large a size the budget will stand on the initial purchase. There are certain factors in planting that are important in knowing how to allocate the budget for each plant or group of plants. In the first place there are certain plants which are slow-growing and will not give any effect for a long time if they are bought too small. In all but the warm climates this is true of most of the evergreens whether broad-leaved or needle-leaved and of certain deciduous shrubs like some of the azaleas and enkianthus. It is well, therefore, to buy the slow-growing evergreens in as large sizes as you can possibly afford.

Another thing determining the size is the importance of the location in the whole design of the place. Plants around the house should usually be fairly good size so the house immediately takes on permanence. Trees to frame a view, or shrubs at the entrance to the garden, or specimens for accent are at the most strategic points on the place and should be big enough to look important.

In planting groups it is better from the first to keep the feeling of relative size, if possible. That is, if you are using flowering trees and tall flowering shrubs, evergreens like the pines and hemlocks, and other evergreens like laurels or low hollies, the immediate effect will be much better if the pines are the tallest things in the planting, the flowering trees next, the shrubs next and the laurels the smallest, right from the beginning. If you can afford only eight foot white pine, it is better to use five to six foot dogwood, two to three foot deciduous shrubs and eighteen to twenty-four inch laurel or holly, than to get all of the same size, three or four feet, so that the planting has none of the skyline and variation of height that it will have later. Aside from immediate effect it is much easier to place the plants if they suggest to you what they will look like later, in proportion to each other. One of the funniest pieces of planting I can remember was a long screen planting along a subdivision road where the spruces were four feet high, undergrowth for twelve foot dogwoods. It obviously disturbed the new owner of the property, too, because the next time I came along I saw that the thirty or forty small spruces had been taken out and low laurel and rhododendrons used as the undergrowth, with three or four big pines planted at important points to give the skyline which the spruces would never have attained.

I carry this planting of relative sizes even to the point where if I am planting six witchhazels, which get to be twelve to fourteen feet in height, and six *Clethra* (summersweets) which get only six to seven, I try to get my witchhazels in five to six foot size to start with and reduce the clethras to two to three feet or even smaller. If you plant in relative sizes it is much easier to leave proportionately the right amount of room if a quick look at the shrub you have just planted shows that it is twice as high so it will probably need twice as much room as the plant next to it.

Sometimes this keeping of relative size is not possible. One place in central Florida where most of the plants were grown by the nurseries in tin cans, only the camellias, gardenias, the guavas and the fruits were available balled and burlapped in fairly good sizes, four to six or seven feet high. Next to them, in the finished planting, were tiny little sprigs of things, like pepper, hibiscus, some of the allamandas, which grow with astonishing rapidity in the warm climate. On first planting these small plants had to be marked by a tall stake beside them so no wandering gardener would mistake them for weeds. Such planting is much harder to visualize and do properly in the first place, and looks distinctly queer the first summer. It is hard to believe that a little plant, six to eight inches high, will be twelve to fourteen feet high and ten feet across within a season or two. Not enough room is allowed for future growth, and a jungle in very short order is the result.

In making up the list from which to order, the nursery catalogs will undoubtedly mark a great many materials "B & B" meaning "Balled and Burlapped," or dug with a ball of earth held in place with coarse burlap. Any plant so marked is sure to be one which the nursery either will not sell, or at least prefers not to sell, with bare roots. In such cases it is always wise to take the nursery's recommendation because they know the habit of that plant and how well it stands transplanting. If you are looking for quick results on planting, so that the plants take as little shock as possible, buying everything balled and burlapped is worthwhile. The nurseries usually have a standard small balling and burlapping charge, according to the size and variety of the plant, and you can determine from your own budget and from your own desires on the place whether it is worth the additional expense on everything. The commoner deciduous shrubs or the ones with many fiber roots move well bare root, in small sizes and at the proper time of year. Any large specimen material takes considerable setback from transplanting. It is far better, if you want four dogwoods of ten to twelve foot specimen size, to buy only two of them one year, well balled and burlapped and possibly even platformed, if necessary, and get the other pair the following season, than to get all four bare root and have them look sickly with perhaps eventual loss of one or two, just in order to get them in one year's budget. It is a fairly safe rule that all evergreens should be balled and burlapped, all specimen material, all flowering trees above ten foot height or one inch caliper on the trunk, and all shrubs over six feet. Late in spring or when leaves are out in summer, all material should be balled and burlapped.

With the list at least reasonably complete so far as your knowledge allows, it is time to go to the nursery actually to select and order the material. It is not necessary in most planting to hand-select every plant on the order, if you are dealing with a reputable nursery. Of course things that have to be of special shape to fit in odd spots or for special effects, specimens and matched pairs should probably be personally selected and tagged at the nursery. As special plants, they may not be at catalog prices and this should be verified at the time of tagging. If you are uncertain just what the size means, you can look at a row of them in the nursery, put a tag on one which shows the quality and size plant you want and leave it to the nursery to fill the rest of the order accordingly.

Sometimes where a very large quantity of a certain plant is needed it is possible to save money with no damage to the results by taking every other plant in a certain nursery row. If the whole row is four to five foot size the nursery is saved a certain amount of work in having to transplant, if it is beginning to crowd, so that they may make a special price by taking alternate plants in the row. In this way you will get some that are a little above and some that are a little below standard quality. This is possible only when you are using from twenty-five to fifty plants in a certain variety and where the nursery has a row that may need transplanting in order to grow well within the next season. This kind of material is excellent for naturalistic planting or for borders at a distance where it gives a better effect to have some plants tall and some short in the same group. It is never advisable where the plants are to be used for a hedge. A hedge, either trimmed or untrimmed, must be uniform and it will take too long for the poorer plants to catch up with the best ones.

If you are ordering in person at the nursery they will supply a copy of the order with the Latin name and size of the shrub on it, prices and the charge for delivery. Those are the things that must be on every order, both for your protection and for the nursery, so there is no possible cause for misunderstanding when the material is delivered. In ordering by mail a copy of the order should be kept, checked very carefully to be sure that the items are exactly as desired, and the shipping date given, if possible.

The farther ahead of planting time you can give the order and set the date, the surer you are of prompt delivery. Most of the nurseries schedule their deliveries in the sequence in which the orders come in. If you wait until the weather is really warm in spring or the leaves have fallen in autumn, rush season is at hand and it is all too probable that the nursery cannot possibly dig and deliver, much less plant for you, for two or three weeks. If the order is very small and they are delivering only, not planting, they will probably make it part of a load going to your general vicinity. If your order is in early, the date you want will be the one on which they will schedule latecomers for your neighborhood, so that your date will be the determining one.

If they are planting your order it is important to have this understood at the time the order is given, so that there is a notation on the order for delivery and planting, with the charge for, or the agreement on the rate of charge plainly stated. If you are going to do the planting yourself or with labor by the day, be sure you know beforehand how many men you need so plants can be handled carefully and get into the ground quickly. If some of the material is large and therefore heavy, or if there is considerable amount of planting to do, three or four men can accomplish in two days more and better planting than two can in five. Ordering the right plants is of minor value unless you estimate in the budget of both time and money, the work necessary to plant them well and provide for it in advance.

CHAPTER XXI

How to Plant Shrubs

THE PAPER WORK of planning and ordering properly goes a long way toward insuring that your planting of shrubs will be right so far as choice of material is concerned. Complete success both now and afterwards depends on the actual process of planting. Here again foresight and careful preparation before the actual day of planting is worth a tremendous amount, both to your own peace of mind and to the health of the plants. When you order a piece of furniture all you have to do is be sure someone is home to receive it and that the space where it is to go is cleared. It makes no difference in the wearing qualities of a big easy chair whether the floor under it is waxed or covered with broadloom carpet, or whether the table next to it is round or oblong. Since plants are living things, their success or failure can depend entirely on what is under and around them, and how they are set into their new place.

The important thing to remember is that plant roots must have something in which to grow and grow quickly in order to counterbalance the shock of moving. Sticking shrubs in just any old way, with their roots curled up in too small a hole, or with rocks thrown back in around them, means either that they will not start any growth at all or that they will have such a struggle for survival that the planting will look sickly for three or four years. If labor is scarce or the budget is limited it is far better to plant five plants well and carefully, allowing enough time and money for proper preparation, than it is to plant twenty shrubs and spend all the money on the plant material itself. If you are doing a considerable amount of planting it usually pays to have a nursery do it. They have trained men under a trained foreman and can not only do the work more carefully than untrained laborers but will get considerably more done in a day and will usually stand back of their material more cheerfully if they have done the planting themselves so they know it was done properly.

If planting is to be done on several parts of the property on the same day, it will help to give the nursery the list of material that goes together. Then in unloading the truck they can take out that particular material at the point nearest to the planting site, drive a little further along and unload the next batch, and so on until the truck is empty. The less carrying by hand or by wheelbarrow that has to be done the more time is saved and the cost of planting depends on time spent.

Whether you are planting three or three hundred plants, certain preparations need to be made before the plants arrive. Unless you are one of the lucky individuals that lives in country where the topsoil is deep and rich—two or three feet deep all over the land—you will probably need additional soil and fertilizers at the time of planting. It is a great deal easier to give plants the material they need around their roots at that time, than to try to feed them from the top and keep nursing them along for years afterwards just because you were too busy or thoughtless at the time they were planted.

Whether the plants are bare root or balled and burlapped, the holes for them will need to be considerably larger than the original root system of the plant. Any poor soil in this area will want to be taken away and replaced by good soil. The new soil should be close at hand on the day of planting so that you will not have to leave plants out in the air or hold up the work while soil is carted in.

In addition to the topsoil there is usually some need for additional humus-forming material either humus, compost, or well-rotted manure to put in near the feeding roots and under the plant. The kind of shrub determines whether manure is advisable but in general it is safe to say that well-rotted cow or stable manure is good for everything except the acid loving plants, like the rhododendrons, azaleas, blueberries and ericaceous things. I am old-fashioned enough to believe that well-rotted manure is the finest fertilizer anyone has ever found and almost all deciduous things and most of the needled evergreens respond to it. Manure that is too fresh will burn the soft roots of the plants and it has to be used with great care unless you are able to judge how completely rotted it is. If you cannot get manure locally in bulk, the dried shredded cow manure in bags is invaluable. It has the advantage of being lighter and easier to handle, free from weed seed and with no danger whatsoever of burning the roots.

Humus and peat moss come in bags or bales, or in bulk and are valuable for their humus-giving qualities in the soil. They enable the young fresh roots to make quicker growth and so establish the plant faster after the shock of moving. For plants which grow naturally in deep woods' loam like the azaleas, hemlocks, laurel and dogwood, humus or compost come the closest to reproducing their natural soil conditions and make them feel at home very promptly. If you have your own compost pile, the half rotted compost unscreened is more satisfactory for shrub planting than the finely screened compost used in your flower garden beds or as top dressing for lawns. It should be rotted enough so that it is crumbly but need not be completely pulverized.

The amount of any of these materials to use depends on existing soil conditions. If the soil is extremely sandy or very heavy clay, humus, peat moss, compost, or well-rotted manure are needed in considerable quantities to give the soil a better texture and enable it to hold moisture. If the topsoil is good garden loam, which means that it already has considerable humus-forming materials in it, less of these particular things will be needed. Enough of any of them or all of them to do the planting thoroughly should be ordered in advance and be at hand near the planting site.

The soil in many parts of the country also needs the addition of phosphates. This can be in the form of either superphosphate or bonemeal, whichever is the most easily available locally. It should be estimated at about a half pound for each four to five foot shrub, or a pound for flowering trees. The broad-leaved evergreens that like acid soil should never have bonemeal around them but it is safe to use superphosphate.

Chemical fertilizers are not necessary and usually definitely inadvisable at the time of planting. Most of them are stimulants both to leaf and root and the chief object when transplanting is to get a good root system established before forcing too much leaf growth. A reasonable amount of a general garden fertilizer like 5-10-5 with which many of us are familiar from vegetable gardens or flower gardens may not hurt anything but it will probably not be of any great help. Fertilizing a year or two later with a special shrub fertilizer will give better results and avoid the danger of forcing too much growth on a newly planted shrub.

If the planting is to go near established lawns it is well to make provision for protecting the lawn around the hole by having a burlap or canvas on hand on which the soil can be piled. It saves time in the long run as it is much easier to get the soil up again from the canvas or burlap than to have to rake and scratch it out of the grass, inevitably tearing out some of the grass in the process.

Sharp digging tools, hose, and a good, steady wheelbarrow are the other tools that should be convenient. A tamper (perhaps a child's baseball bat whose blunt end is perfect for tamping) will help, particularly if large material with heavy balls is to be planted.

I cannot emphasize too strongly the necessity for having everything ready for shrub planting in advance. As with any other kind of plant the less time it spends out of the ground the better its chances for survival. Shrub planting takes long enough anyway without having to stop to get needed tools or bring the wheelbarrow and hose from the vegetable garden or run down town to get the fertilizer or transfer compost from the compost pile. Quite aside from the health of the plants it also makes considerable difference in the expense of the planting operation. If you have extra men their time is charged by the hour and you save by having things ready for them. If a nursery is planting they should be advised of the specific tools or fertilizers they need to bring with them.

Preparation is particularly important if some of the material is large and heavy. The less it is handled the better both for the plants themselves and for your pocketbook. Sometimes you will have to decide whether it will be less expensive to let the nursery truck drive across your lawn and unload heavy plants right beside the hole where they are going, than it will be to lay down planks and roll the plants across the lawn. This will depend primarily on the condition of the ground which determines how much damage the truck tires will do. If it is dry and hard it is surprising how little permanent harm is done, but if it is spongy or if it is newly seeded, repairing the wreck may cost you more than having the men plank it across.

If you know heavy material is going to have to be carried or planked, by all means tell the nursery in advance that they cannot reach the site of the planting by truck so that they will be sure to have plank and rollers or carriers along with them. Similarly if you have very fine new grass and do not have burlap or canvas on your own place, warn them about the grass so they can bring along something with which to protect it. The more information they have about conditions under which they are to work, the better job they can do.

After the material has been unloaded there are two ways of starting to plant. If the individual plants are not too big to handle comfortably it may be well to actually set each one into the place where it is going, particularly if it is balled and burlapped, to look at it and see that it is exactly right. This is particularly important for specimen or accent plants which are the first things to be placed. If it is too heavy to haul around any more than is absolutely necessary at least get the plant near where it is going so you know what part of the property it belongs to. Then put in a stake to indicate to the foreman the center of the hole where that plant is to go. If you are your own foreman mark the center, then, either by eye or with a string, mark on the ground the circle inside which the digging is to be done.

The hole for balled and burlapped plants should be from six inches to a foot broader on all sides than the ball of the plant. For bare root plants they should be big enough so that the roots can be spread out into proper position and still have six inches around the outside of them. The depth of the hole should also be greater than the actual ball or roots of the plant, so that some fertilizer like manure or humus can be dug in under it. If there is hard pan or very poor soil below the plants will get to it and then stop growing vigorously.

Unless you are sure you have really good topsoil below the planting, it is best to go at least six inches deeper than the roots of the plant itself in digging the hole. If the soil even below that is extremely hard so that it will act like an impervious flower pot later, breaking it up with a pick will give the plant a better chance. When the hole is dug, it should be refilled so that the depth of the ball of the plant and the depth of the hole are the same. This material in the bottom, of topsoil and humus or manure, should be well tamped or trod down so that it will not settle after the plant gets in.

The heavier the ball, of course, the more weight and there is a definite inclination to settle, making the planting later sink down too deep. A folding rule will save a great deal of heaving and hauling later by actually measuring the depth of the ball or the depth of the root and the depth of the hole so that the plant when finished is at the same depth it was in the nursery. If it is too high the roots will dry out and if it is too low, they will smother. In either case the plant will not grow well. After the plant is set into the hole and before any filling is done the top should be untied and the best face of the plant put toward the side from which it will be most often seen. It is amazing what a little care in this particular can do in the looks of planting. Almost no plants are perfect all the way around and I have wondered many times why it is that untrained men and some trained ones, will invariably turn the worst side toward you.

A good nursery foreman will usually see to the facing himself, as that is part of his training, but if some special effect is being sought, you will need to do it yourself. Be sure that you are actually looking at the plant from the direction in which it is most frequently visible. If it is seen from two directions you may have to compromise so that it looks well from both ways, although possibly not perfect from either one. I have had the experience several times of having someone say, "But that looks bad from here," not realizing that the place they are standing is in the middle of the shrub border or at an angle from which no one will ever look at the plant. Ideally, of course, it looks well from any direction but probably there are one or two directions in which it looks particularly effective and they should of course be the ones from which you most often see it.

After the shrub is placed to your satisfaction the work of filling should be done most carefully. The place for the good soil and growing material is near the roots of the plants. If soil is of two different qualities by all means put the best of it in around the plant and save the poor for the top where there are no feeding roots. When the hole is filled about two thirds so that the roots are well covered, if they are bare root plants or the ball is protected and held firmly in place, the soil should be tamped either with feet or with the tamper. I prefer the tamper for balled and burlapped plants but not for bare root as I find there is too much danger of bruising or jamming roots with the tamper and that feet seem to do less damage. This should not be a hard packing but just enough to settle the soil firmly. Then the water should be put in with a very fine, gentle stream until it comes to the top of the hole.

It is usually better to set a number of plants before you start watering, then do a thorough job of filling all the holes with water. The water should be allowed to settle the soil firmly around the roots and often will settle it so much that the roots are exposed again. In that case more soil should be put in and watered again to be sure that there are no air pockets and no holes around the plant. When the water has disappeared and the soil is packed in thoroughly around the roots, the holes can be filled up the rest of the way and left slightly below the level of the ground. A certain amount of settling of the fresh soil will take place so it is helpful to leave a rim of soil outside the ball to form the rim of the saucer. This has two advantages in that it allows thorough watering for succeeding weeks while the plant is getting established without the water running away, and also gives extra soil close at hand in case the hole needs filling a little bit more.

If the planting is on a slight down hill grade the saucer should be omitted on the upper side so that any rain water that falls can run into the plant and not be diverted by the dam all around the ball. A practice which fortunately is getting less common is that of hilling-up the plants instead of leaving saucers around them. The inverted saucer formed by this hilling-up only insures that any water that comes along will run away from the plant instead of to its roots and also may encourage small roots in the hill which the first hot dry weather will burn out.

If there is a large amount of planting to be done it is far better to get all the plants into holes, partly filled and watered as rapidly as possible and leave the final filling of the holes until later in the day or the next day. As long as the soil and water are covering the roots the plants are safe and will not be harmed by the delay in filling the hole completely to the top.

If the weather is unusually hot or windy and there are more plants than you can get in quickly, the root systems of all plants should be protected from the moment of delivery. If the plants are all balled and burlapped, they may be set somewhere out of the wind and in the shade if possible, with the balls touching. If their planting is delayed two or three days sprinkling them lightly once or twice with the hose will keep them from drying out. If they are bare root they must not be exposed to the air. Where there is any quantity of them it will save your own peace of mind and take away the sense of hurry if you take the time to dig a trench somewhere out of the way and lay the roots of all of them in it, throwing enough loose soil over the top so that the air and sun cannot hit the fine fiber roots. Once those roots have dried out the damage is done. If they are going to be out of the ground only an hour or two they can be laid on the top of the ground and wet straw and burlap kept over them.

After the planting is done certain of the plants may have to be staked or guyed to keep them from tipping or from loosening in the wind. It is usually advisable to guy all flowering trees or all shrubs that have high heads, as they will be inclined to be topheavy. In very large specimen material I have frequently found it necessary to guy even regular shrubs of the common oval shape, so that there is no danger of their roots getting torn loose by rocking from side to side in a high wind. If the wind is always from one direction it may be possible to fasten the plant by driving a tall stake alongside it and tying the plant to this stake. This has one great disadvantage in that the stake has to be close to the trunk of the plant and there is considerable danger of damaging the root in driving the stake. With this method it is better to put the stake in at the time the plant goes in the ground, so that you can see what you are doing and avoid the big roots.

A better method is to put three short stakes outside the planting hole, driven well down to the ground, and fasten wires from the trunk of the tree to these stakes. Where the wires go around the trunk it must be protected by pieces of old rubber hose, or if that is not available, by burlap, so that the wire does not bruise or cut into the trunk. The wires should be tightened one after another until they are perfectly taut and at about a 45° angle from the trunk to the guying stake. The wires should be double unless the material is very small so that as they loosen from stretching or from the plant settling, they can be twisted and made taut again.

A loose guy wire does more harm than good. If one is loose and the other two are tight the tree will inevitably be pulled in the direction of the tight ones and the whole purpose of the guying destroyed. These guy wires should be left on until the plant is firmly established in the ground, usually two years after planting. If they are where there is traffic across the lawn or into the garden you will save the family a number of falls by tying a piece of white cloth or some kind of marker on the guys so that they are visible. There have been some nasty accidents on home grounds where invisible guy wires caught the unwary passerby.

Unless the season is unusually wet new planting should be soaked about once a week or every ten days during its entire first season. Anything less than a half day's steady rain will not count as far as watering is concerned and the new rootlets must have water in order to make the necessary growth. This is vital to the success of any new planting. Occasional hosing off of the foliage in case the weather turns hot and windy soon after planting will help considerably to freshen the plant and give it a chance.

You will need to keep an eye on newly planted material for several weeks after planting to make sure that it does not settle too much, that it does not tip out of position and that it is getting off to the right kind of start with no unnecessary handicaps. If you find some certain plant has settled much too deeply, it is better to lift it before it starts to make its new roots than to wait for a year and then disturb all the fine set of new roots and haul it up again. If it has tilted badly out of position you may have to re-dig the hole and replant it straight. If it is only a slight tilt you may be able to pull it back into position with a guy wire in the direction of the tilt. This is advisable only in the case that it is big or dangerous material to disturb or the tilt is so slight that it just needs a little pressure in the other direction to counteract it.

When you are doing new planting a little late in the season —when there is danger of hot weather coming in the spring or cold weather coming in the fall too soon for the good of the plants—a mulch over the root system will help the plant to establish without damage from inclement weather. This mulch can be hay, straw, compost, or half-rotted manure and should be thick enough so that the soil does not dry out in the heat or freeze too soon in the winter before the plant gets a chance to make itself at home in its new location. When the material is available and the budget allows, I like to put a mulch over all new planting, particularly on all the evergreens. Most of their feeding roots are close to the surface so that cultivation is unwise and the mulch keeps down the weeds and keeps in the moisture that the plant needs. After a little time it starts to rot and make part of the humus material for later feeding of the plant.

If you have selected the right plant and then given it the proper home, your worries about your shrubs from now on are over. They will continue to increase in size and in beauty with practically no further attention. On the other hand, if they get off to a bad start by careless work at the time of planting, it will take five times as much labor later to make them thrive or even survive in their new home.

CHAPTER XXII

Face-lifting the Shrub Borders

REARRANGING existing planting is often harder than planting new shrub borders. After you have bought someone else's house you are likely to find that instead of starting from scratch and fitting in new planting, your first problem is to sort out the conglomeration of miscellaneous planting left by the previous owner. It is less a question of what new shrubs to get than what to do with the ones already there. His taste or way of living may have been different from yours or the house may have been empty for some time with no one to care for the plants. Or he may have liked thick planting without much discrimination as to its composition or content.

The first step is to take a look at the general masses of planting on the place as a whole, judging them for size, shape and effectiveness, without bothering with the identification of the material. The first place to look at is the immediate vicinity of the house. See if any windows are blocked from light and air, or if the house looks as if it is being swallowed by the green masses around it, or if it looks bare and unfinished.

It may be well to look at the individual shrubs to see how much pruning seems to have been necessary to keep them in bounds. If they show many stubby ends, they probably are in the wrong place for their habit of growth.

After you have looked at the house from all sides and have at least a fairly good idea of where the general effect is right and where it is wrong, stand at the windows or doors where you most frequently look out and appraise the views with critical eyes. If you try to visualize what the scene looks like at all times of the year, you will get a better idea of your general approach. When you have looked in every possible direction from the house and perhaps have gone out on the street or near the various property lines to see the effect from there, you are ready for a more detailed study of the planting groups.

Your inspection from the house windows may have shown you that some group or planting is so thick and wide that it seems to be encroaching on the lawn. It may look like a dull, monotonous mass, with no skyline variety and nothing but the ugly legs of shrubs at the front of it. Closer examination may show you that it consists of only two or three kinds of shrubs, put in years ago, and grown to the same height and mass, probably trimmed up enough so that they do not get in the way of the lawn mower on the front of the border. This kind of planting usually means thinning and removing some of the plants.

Perhaps a neighbor's house or garage is considerably more prominent than it needs to be in your view and the planting there is either the wrong height or the wrong type to do the proper screening job. This is one of the places for addition of new material or material from somewhere else on the place. Where a view across neighboring country or to hills in the distance has been blocked out by shrubs that have grown too tall, an inspection of that piece of planting may show you that, although wrong where they are, they will be useful for screening out the neighbor's garage.

In this close inspection, if you are not too familiar with shrubs, you will probably run across some that you cannot identify, and you are not too sure exactly what they will do under other conditions and at other times of the year. It may be worth while to stop right at this point to learn their identity and ways, so that all of the plants on your own place are at least acquaintances, if not friends.

When you have gone over the planting enough to have a

fairly good idea of where it is inadequate or where it is over-
generous, you can decide how to go about correcting the difficulty. Unless you have an extraordinary memory some visible
aid in planning your operations will be a help. Strips of cloth
in three different colors, such as bright red, bright blue and
bright yellow are the first necessities. The bright red can mark
the shrubs that are to be taken out and thrown away, the
yellow indicate shrubs that are to be transplanted and the blue
show shrubs that are to stay where they are.

The reason for marking these latter shrubs at all is that as
you get more and more tags on things it is easier to have every
single plant marked somehow than it is to wonder if you really
meant to leave this, or if the red or yellow tag has gotten mis-
placed or removed by wandering children or the wind. Inci-
dentally, it is a good idea to put the pieces always on the same
side of the shrub, that is to your right or to your left as you
face the shrub from the front, so you at least know where to
look for them. If there are children about they should be as
high up as you can reach.

Deciding which shrub gets which color cloth is a difficult
problem sometimes. The easiest way to attack it is to take the
red ones first and go over all the planting, marking for removal all very unsightly or largely dead shrubs that have little
chance for recovery. Most of the needled evergreens which
through crowding or shade or bad care have lost their leaves
or whose leaves are of brownish, unhealthy looking color, will
not recover satisfactorily no matter what later care they are
given. Unless they are valuable from sentimental reasons or
rarity of variety, it is an economy to mark them to come out.
A red cedar, *Juniperus virginiana*, which is reduced to a trunk
with a tuft of green along one side or at the top, will not come
out in leaf again no matter how much feeding or care it is
given. A hemlock in a windy spot where the needles have all
been burned off on one side and look very brown and deadish
generally will never be a handsome specimen.

Broad-leaved evergreens respond much better to care and

feeding and, as they are rather expensive material to buy, the red strings had better be left off them to start with unless they are completely dead. In the deciduous material most of the flowering trees should be left for later consideration even though they may be badly broken by storms or ruined by crowding. Fast growing common shrubs like the mock orange, the weigela, the deutzia, that have been chopped back so that they are full of ugly stubs and rotten old wood are not worth much consideration and should probably be marked for removal.

When you have marked everything that you are sure needs to come out and be thrown away, the yellow strings are next. They mean that the plant is worth moving either because of its variety being rare or because of its beauty or its appropriateness in some other spot on the place. They go on most of the broad-leaved evergreens that are in fairly good condition but in the wrong place, and on the crowded flowering trees and any other shrubs that you are fond enough of to want to keep, or are in good enough condition to be worth moving.

The blue strings are the final ones and to start with should go only on the plants that you are certain can and should stay exactly where they are because of their shape or their variety or their general effect in the landscape. You will probably find that you have put the wrong color on some plants and that you cannot make up your mind in a crowded planting which are to be thrown away and which moved. Putting a strip of each color on the same shrub during the hour of decision may remind you that you have a question about this. It is easy enough to take off the wrong color later.

If the shrub border is crowded but has good varieties of material in it, you may find you have put yellow strings on enough plants for the whole neighborhood and that you simply have no room for all these shrubs. I have helped with places more than once where the owner has just brought an adjoining piece of property and we were able to plant it almost completely from an existing shrub border that had been done some years before and in which excellent material had been used, planted three or four feet apart instead of ten or twelve. On the other hand, I have been on many places where there was at least three times as much material as the place could possibly hold and, even though it was fine, it had to be disposed of. A living room so full of furniture that there is no room to move, no matter if the furniture is very valuable, is still neither comfortable nor attractive.

The dictionary description of a weed is that it is a plant out of place. It can apply just as well to a fine yew that is blocking all the air and light from the living room windows as it can to a dandelion in the lawn. If the yew is moved away from there to some other location where it is still a nuisance and is not needed, it is still a weed.

Sometimes it is not altogether a question of room for planting but a question of whether it is the right kind of material for the new location. One piece of planting may consist of lilacs, beauty bush, crabapples and cherries that are far too crowded. The only vacant place on the property is on the north side of big trees where no sun ever reaches. The overcrowded plants from the sunny borders are of no value because they will not grow in a shady location. If they are moved there they will only get less and less presentable and eventually have to be replaced with new planting for shade. If the yellow strings stay on plants, you not only have to decide whether they are worth moving but whether there is any place where they will grow well and where they are needed. If not, the yellow string should come off and a red one go on.

It takes considerable ruthlessness and determination to do the kind of drastic upheaval that face-lifting of a shrub border demands. A friend came to me not long ago and said flatly, "I wish you would come out and straighten out my shrub borders. I know they have to be pulled out and thrown away, but I simply haven't the nerve to do it." Her husband told me that she had been agonizing over those shrubs for several weeks, putting strings on and taking them off, putting them on and taking them off, and getting absolutely nowhere because her courage was not equal to her judgment when it came to throwing away useless shrubs.

After you think you have everything tagged properly the next visual help is to write down somewhere what happens to all the shrubs that have the yellow tags on them. Perhaps the surest way of doing it is to use wooden labels, probably the ten inch long size, and a wax China-marking pencil. At the base of each shrub stick a label on which is written the approximate new location. One may say, "Northeast corner of house." Next, "West border planting." A third, "Screen for garage." The directions should give merely the general vicinity in which the shrub is to go, not its actual location, except in case of specimens. When you are marking a lot of shrubs it is all too easy to figure out a place where you do need these shrubs and then in the general hurly-burly of transplanting completely forget where they were to go so that they go trundling around on a wheel barrow like lost souls.

Sometimes it is easier instead of marking the shrubs with labels to start in at one end of a certain border and list the things that are to be transplanted. Opposite each one you can note where it is to go. The advantage of doing things this way is that the list is less likely to get lost than the stakes are. It is also easier to check up in the peace and quiet of the house to see that you really have disposed of all the things to be transplanted. Doing both staking and listing is probably best of all. It has the added advantage of the list being available in the house where you can make further notes. In case you need new shrubs for a certain location it is helpful to check the list to find out exactly what is on hand for a new piece of planting and what else must be bought. The transplanting and the new planting is likely to be going on at the same time, and a complete list of new and old will make things simpler on the day of planting, in order to check orders and deliveries. If a nursery is doing the transplanting, at the same time they bring your new material by all means give them a fairly accurate list of the number of existing shrubs to be moved and how big they are, so that they will know what equipment to bring and what time to allow.

It is certainly advisable to have a nursery transplant any large or valuable material. It probably has been in place for quite a long time, is under more or less difficult digging conditions from being crowded and in order to minimize the shock of transplanting must be done carefully. It costs money to transplant big material, but if it is worth transplanting at all, it is worth doing so that it will survive the process without looking worse than ever for the next four or five years. Otherwise it is better to throw it away in the first place and buy a new young specimen of that particular thing.

It costs just as much to move a tremendously tall, broad forsythia as it does to move a very fine specimen of flowering crabapple. The cost of transplanting is in the time it takes to dig the proper sized ball. The forsythia has probably attained its size in six or eight years, while the crabapple may have taken twenty-five. In such a case I usually discard the forsythia, unless it is especially needed in some particular spot, and save the crabapple.

Sometimes it is even possible by throwing away four of the faster-growing and less expensive shrubs to leave a particularly fine specimen of a better variety right where it is, instead of moving all five of the plants just in order to get rid of the crowding. There are probably no real rules for determining what to leave, what to throw away and what to transplant, but the better you know your plants, how they respond to care, how they stand transplanting, and how rare they are, the more successful the face-lifting operation will be.

After the tagging and listing is all done, the actual operation of removal and transplanting can go right ahead. Getting rid of the things to be discarded is first. They should be taken out completely, roots and all. Just as sure as you decide that you can leave the roots of an old evergreen or a big shrub flush with the ground, that will be the one spot that another plant has to go when the transplanting is done. Furthermore, the ones cut to the ground will probably sprout up from the roots and you will have the same difficulty of a plant in the wrong place the following year. It may not be as big a plant but it will still be wrong. If they are very large and there are a number of them it will be an economy in the long run to have them taken out, with the help of the tractor and chain if you live in the country, or a truck with a winch on it from a nearby nursery.

Two men and a machine can take out in two days big plants that would take the same two men two or three weeks to get out by hand. If you are intending to have the removal done mechanically, they should not be cut down at all, as the man operating the winch truck is the best judge of how much trunk or height is needed on the shrub for him to get a good hold on it with his rope or chain. Sometimes you can arrange with the nursery that is going to handle the transplanting to do the removal the first thing when they arrive, load it on the trucks and dispose of it when they leave in the evening. In some sections of the country where work is scarce in the late fall and early winter months, you can get the removal done much more cheaply and all the debris cleared away from the property so that you have a much better idea yourself of what things look like. It is easier to remove most shrubs in the leafless season but, of course, before the ground is frozen hard.

When all the discards are out of the way the process of transplanting can begin. Just as in planting new material, the first things to be transplanted are the large ones, those for crucial positions. The same principles apply to transplanting that apply to moving new material in the nurseries. All large shrubs and flowering trees should be dug with a good ball and burlapped carefully. If they are flowering trees with heavy trunks they should probably also have a platform under them to which the ball is laced so that as little root disturbance as possible takes place. All evergreens and most of the big deciduous shrubs should be balled and burlapped, unless the root system is very fine and fibrous and the dirt holds well to them. Most of these shrubs have not been transplanted for some time so they have not made a particularly heavy root system with fine fiber roots like nursery-grown material. For that reason they will take a good deal of shock from transplanting and the older any shrub is, the harder it is to transplant. There is no gain in moving anything so carelessly or so badly that you have to spend more time and energy nursing it back into health than the saving in transplanting was worth, or cut the top back so it is an ugly short plant instead of a big specimen.

The cost of transplanting depends on the digging conditions; that is, whether it is sandy soil that digs easily, rocky or heavy clay soil that takes twice as long, and on the local price of labor. In fairly good garden soil a shrub ten feet high with a six or seven foot spread will take four men anywhere from three to five hours to dig and transplant properly. A flowering crabapple, hawthorn, dogwood, redbud, will take little if any more time, as it will need approximately the same sized ball and cost will be determined on the basis of the size of the ball needed for the plant. You may find when you estimate the cost of the planting that you have too many yellow strings on the shrubs and a great many of them are not actually worth the money involved.

In putting your own shrubs into their new home the same rules of having the holes considerably larger than the root system of the shrub, filling, watering, feeding and tamping apply as to nursery-grown material. Since these shrubs are probably actually in not quite as good condition as the ones from the nursery, care taken in the transplanting must be even more meticulous if they are going to do well. All too often a gardener or an untrained man seems to feel that these things did not cost anything because you already had them, and that you cannot kill the deciduous shrubs anyway. His slip-shod way of doing things may not actually kill them but it certainly can make them look very sick for a long time and even careless digging and transplanting takes time and therefore money.

Of course it is not necessary that all the face-lifting operations be done on a place the same season. Sometimes it is better if it is taken over a period of two or three years. Part of the removal can be done one year, giving room around a big plant that has to be moved later. Then that plant can be fed, possibly root pruned to make a new growth of roots and reshaped so that it is in better condition for moving a year or two later. This is certainly advisable where you have some really rare and valuable shrub or tree that is in bad condition and in the wrong place. You stand much less chance in moving it if it is healthy when you start the operation.

In some old shrub plantings that are looking shabby and down-at-the-heels, it may be less a question of transplanting than of merely bringing them back into condition slowly until you can find out how much of the shabbiness is due to hunger and how much of the crowding can be remedied by removal of every other shrub and feeding the rest of them to make them into handsome specimens. As the plants left in the border get better looking they may begin to crowd again and you can remove another third of the border.

There may be places where the planting is thick enough to serve some practical purpose, such as a screen or windbreak, but the material is uninteresting or there is too much of one certain variety in a planting. In such a situation removing all of it at once would show up the object you are trying to screen till the new material has a chance to grow, or leave you too much exposed to the wind. By taking out the front or the back of such a planting one year and replacing it with the new material you want, letting that grow until it is performing its purpose, then removing the other half of the border and replacing it with smaller material that has time to grow, will prevent unsightliness and in the long run save money on the whole operation.

But all of these long-time operations need to be planned in advance so that you know where you are going on every shrub you take out, transplant, or leave temporarily or permanently. A shabby house may look all the better for a complete new coat of paint, but on the grounds part of the charm is in age and in the plants looking as if they had always been in that location. If all of them are moved, pruned, transplanted and otherwise hauled about in one season, you are sure to have a rather meager set of leaves for a year or two and to have lost the feeling of permanence that established planting gives. The plants that are left in place will need to be pruned and fed and brought back into good condition. The ways of doing this, however, are exactly the same as for the care of new or any other sort of shrub planting, so they can be discussed in the following chapter.

CHAPTER XXIII

Care and Feeding of Shrubs

ALTHOUGH most shrubs will survive even under neglect, they will always, like any other living thing, respond to a good home and proper care and feeding. Like a child in a bad environment they can sulk and need a great deal of petting and nursing along. In such case the only thing to do is to correct the environment if it is not favorable, or move the plants out of it into a completely new one. If you have planted or transplanted everything into as nearly perfect location as you know how to give it, from then on it is a case of keeping the environment healthful and seeing that the shrubs are cared for.

In the wild, Nature does an excellent job of giving plants the kind of food they are best able to use. There is a certain amount of survival of the fittest in her treatment, and on the home grounds we are probably not willing to have one species of plant crowd out others. Certain plants do thrive in poor soil and get a sort of horticultural indigestion if the soil is made too rich for them. In looking over shrub lists any that are especially listed for poor soil should not be too heavily fertilized or fed. They are the ones to let take care of themselves in some spot where the soil is thin and we have neither the means nor the inclination to make it over into garden soil. This list is relatively small and anything outside of it needs to have the substances replaced which the growth of the shrub takes from the soil.

One of the best ways to do it is to imitate nature by letting decaying vegetable matter give back to the earth the elements that are being taken out. This is one of the chief values of mulches on all plant material. A layer of leaves, straw, hay, weeds (before they go to seed), strawy-manure, grass clippings, extending from the trunk of the shrub to the edge of the branches and added to from time to time as material becomes available, is known as mulch. The bottom of the material keeps rotting away and forming new rich soil, full of the elements plants need for growth. It is particularly valuable for new or transplanted material and its continued use keeps the shrubs in good health with little trouble. It always dismays me to see piles of leaves burning in the fall (I do like the fragrance) because so much plant nutrient is going up in smoke. Unless your place is as bald as a billiard ball, with no shrubs at all, the leaves of yours and your neighbors' trees should certainly be put to use. If you are in a windy location and they will not stay in the shrub borders it is well to weight them down or perhaps compost them for a few months and then put the half-rotted compost on for a mulch. This means handling all the material twice and is rarely necessary. A mulch can be left on shrubs throughout the year.

If your shrubs have a poor leaf color, or the leaves are unnaturally small, they are in need of food. A good mulch of partly decayed manure left to rot and feed the soil will bring them back very promptly. Manure is not advisable for acid-loving shrubs like the rhododendron family. Certain of the needled evergreens are particularly responsive to manure feeding. Their color deepens to a dark rich green within six months after the manure mulch is applied. I saw a yew hedge a year or two ago on which the owner had put the mulch half the length of the hedge the preceding fall. The two sections of the hedge looked almost like different plant material. The section nearest the house was thick rich green and the one farther away slightly brownish, thin of needle and quite anemic-looking.

If the plants are looking so badly that starvation is imminent, a quicker stimulant than the mulch treatment may be needed. Fertilizers are available especially mixed for shrubs. There is usually a high nitrogen and phosphorus content and a lower potash content. All these formulas have an analysis on the bag but you can buy them just as shrub fertilizers by some special trade name. The best method of application, particularly to a sick shrub, is by punching holes with a crowbar at the edge of the spread of the branches. It is fairly easy work unless you are in very stony soil. The holes should be one foot deep and one foot apart in a circle. A handful of food is put in the bottom and the soil filled back in the hole. The shrub must be watered thoroughly, as no plant can take food when it is dry, and most of the plant foods are available only in solution.

If the location of the plant or condition of the soil makes this hole method too difficult or inadvisable, fertilizer can be broadcast over the surface of the ground and thoroughly watered. It is usually better to water it in than to cultivate it, particularly on the broad-leaved evergreens, as there are feeding roots close to the surface and the process of cultivating is bound to break a great many of them. When a shrub needs feeding it needs every single little root that it has on it and a bruised or broken root under the ground can rot and cause all kinds of trouble. Rhododendrons and other acid-loving plants need special fertilizers known as acidulous fertilizers. Two to four pounds of fertilizer for a hundred square foot of bed or one to two pounds per specimen, broadcast over the soil underneath the shrub, is about the right amount. For the acidulous fertilizers the directions on the package should be followed.

The time of year for fertilization depends on your locality. It should usually be done either early in the spring before growth starts or late in the fall after the plants are dormant. In latitudes where there is freezing winter weather no feeding should be done after July. Later feeding is likely to cause soft growth which will winter-kill because it has not had time to harden up.

This "shot in the arm" kind of feeding is needed if the leaf color is poor, the flowers are small or the annual growth is far below normal. It is possible, however, to feed too much and too often so that you are forcing the shrub too fast. This may show up in very long, soft twig or branch growth or in very much over-sized leaves. If a valuable shrub is in really bad condition you will have better results by a light feeding in the spring, a mulch for the summer, another light feeding in the late fall, than you will in one heavy dosage the first spring with no further attention.

The sound kind of fertilizing is to keep the plant food available by as natural means as possible so that the plants grow at a normal rate and have a balanced diet, and little quick stimulant is needed.

PRUNING

There is probably no garden tool so dear to the hearts of the men of the family as the pruning shears. Nobody has ever satisfactorily explained whether it is atavistic instinct of chopping one's way through a jungle or just the small boy's sheer love of destruction, but pruning shears, pruning knives and pruning saws arouse more energy than any other kind of garden weapon. Unfortunately a great deal of this energy is misapplied and considerable damage results in the great burst of enthusiasm. An understanding of what, when and how to prune is essential if your planting is going to survive in anything like respectable shape. Where the growing season lasts twelve months in the year a great deal of pruning is almost always necessary. The closer we get to a tropical climate the nearer the plants come to taking on jungle ways. In other sections of the country if you have to wage a constant battle with your shrubs to keep them to the natural size and shape, it is almost sure to mean that you have the wrong shrub in that particular location. You will save yourself time and money by moving it elsewhere and replacing it with one whose size and shape is more suitable.

Any shrub compensates for drastic pruning by throwing an equal amount of wood at either the end of the cut or from the bottom of the shrub. Unless you are trying primarily to force the shrub to throw out more wood, you are only asking for twice as much work every time you cut off one piece of wood. Of course, if the shrubs are thin and you want to make them thicken up, pruning will sometimes do it but that is a very special kind of cutting, done for a special purpose.

The worst kind of butchery that goes by the name of pruning is the habit of cutting off the ends of things. We once had an old gardener from whom we had to hide all the pruning shears and saws. He was firm in his conviction that shrubs had to be "youngened" at least once a year. His method of doing it was to round off the top of everything, cutting back practically all of the new growth and all the flowers, so that every shrub on the place looked exactly like every other one. Two or three years of this kind of treatment and all that is left is a completely shapeless mass, full of ugly stubs and weak wild growth out from the ends. This kind of pruning dates from the early part of this century when driveways were marked with round balls of privet or hydrangeas and every shrub in the shrub border was ball-shaped from constant pruning.

Unless you have a trimmed hedge there is no need for big lopping shears used for hedges. Their very presence is too much of a temptation to do this unimaginative kind of pruning, which destroys all the variety and interest a planting should have.

The whole object of pruning is to remove dead or destructive wood and to help the shrub maintain its natural form. Most shrubs should be pruned immediately after their flowering period so as not to remove any wood on which they will flower the following season. A certain amount of pruning should be done all through the year instead of one great orgy in the late fall or early spring.

The first thing to remove on any shrub is dead wood. It is only an invitation to rot and fungus disease, which will spread to other healthy wood. If you see dead branches trace them back to the nearest crotch where the wood is completely alive and cut at that point. On old shrubs if this leaves a stem or trunk six inches to two feet above the ground with no leaves on it, it is better to take it directly to the ground than to leave this bare stub which may continue to die, and in any case will not look well.

After all the dead wood is out the next thing to look for are crossing or rubbing branches. These are particularly likely to occur on shrubs that have heavy trunks from the ground, or on the flowering trees like the crabapples and hawthorns. If two branches touch and rub constantly against each other, one or both of them will be damaged and eventually killed. It takes a certain amount of judgment to decide which of these rubbing branches needs to come out. Sometimes you will find that one main branch is rubbing in four or five places. In that case you can eliminate several sources of trouble by taking out the one branch. Another time you will see that one branch means very little in the general shape of the shrub while the other one will leave a tremendous hole if it comes out. Here again, the offending branch should be taken back to a crotch or, if necessary, to the ground. Short stubs should be avoided anywhere in any shrub or tree, both for looks and for the future health of the plant in inviting decay starting in at that point.

In most plants this should almost take care of the pruning with no further removal of wood. The exception is on the shrubs which have a great many stems from the ground and which left to their own devices will get too crowded in the center and not leave room for the new shoots to come from the bottom. Many of our familiar garden shrubs are of this type—the spireas, the mock oranges, the deutzias. The proper pruning of these means taking out the oldest canes from the ground and leaving the young wood to keep the shrub looking open and attractive.

If the shrubs are very old and have not been pruned for some time, removal of the old branches should be done over several seasons rather than in one major operation. A big weigela whose heavy wood is stubbed at the end and not too heavy in leaf toward the bottom of the shrub, can be rejuvenated by removing one or two of the heavy canes the first year, another third the second year, and the final ones a third year. During this process the shrub will still have size and some shape and at the end of the pruning will have no ugly stubs sticking up in the middle of its young growth. It is often questionable whether the plant is worth so much work. It may be better to take it out and put in a young one.

In pruning these old canes down it is important to get them literally just as close to the ground as you possibly can. This usually means a pruning saw rather than shears, if the plants are of any size. It is not an easy operation because it is hard to get you and your pruning saw into the middle of a big heavy heap of brush. If you do not take on too many at a time and do it carefully, it is amazing what results can be seen in two or three years.

Occasionally a shrub will throw out great long straggling branches that seem to be seeing how far they can go in one season. They should be removed any time they occur so that they do not take the full strength of the shrub in making this one long arm. They should, however, be cut to the point of origin—that is to the crotch from which they spring—just as in any other pruning.

Except for dead or crossing wood, evergreens need little or no pruning. If any is necessary, it should be done at the time the new growth is starting so the fresh leaves will cover the pruning damage. There is one special kind of evergreen pruning worth knowing about. On the yews, new growth is made in sort of three-fingered arrangement at the ends of the branches. If you are afraid the yew is going to grow too open and have too much long awkward-looking growth, the middle one of these three fingers should be pinched out while it is soft. If this is done at the right time you do not need pruning shears—your fingers are enough. The long growth is made on this middle branch and its removal will keep the yew shapely and fit.

Dead flower heads on the laurels, rhododendrons and azaleas can be removed. It is a debatable question whether this really helps make the blossoming mass heavier the following year or whether it is merely a matter of neatness and appearance of the shrub. If you have many of them you are likely to decide that it is not worth while as it is a tedious and time-consuming job. This is true also of some of the deciduous shrubs, like the lilacs, the weigelas, deutzias and other plants with heads of flowers at the ends of branches.

In order to do good pruning it is essential to have the proper tools. Everyone probably has his own pet pruner but few gardeners can get along with one type. The small hand pruners are best for light work or work in tight places. Those with a narrow long blade are usually best for shrubs. In addition to these there should be one pair of heavy duty pruners with a spring, so that your arms are not doing all the work. These come in three sizes and the different members of the family may find they need different sizes. The big ones are too heavy for most women to handle and men think the light ones are just a toy. In addition to these two types, a pair with long wooden handles and short narrow blades is useful for the brush-heap shrubs and particularly for the shrub roses or anything else with thorns. They mean that you can keep a discreet distance from the bush and still get in down at the bottom to get out the big canes. Some kind of pole pruners help a great deal for tall shrubs or flowering trees. A pair of snapcut shears on the end of a four foot or six foot pole is available. They are invaluable for the removal of seed heads on the top of tall shrubs. The regulation tree-pole-pruners are hard to operate unless you are used to them and calling in a tree man to do work high enough to require them is probably safer.

No matter how many pruning shears you have, they are all useless unless they are kept very sharp. A pair of dull shears can do far more damage than good. They will only chew the wood off the shrub, leaving a ragged uneven cut as an invitation to decay. Forming the habit of sharpening your shears after every use with a small emery stone or a fine file, keeps them in good shape. Most of the good ones come with directions on how to sharpen them and caution about maintaining the angle of the edge of the shears. It takes a little practice but there is no great trick to it and there is nothing that makes more difference in your results.

If you have planted your shrubs in the right location, given them the proper food, and know their natural shape and size, pruning is a very minor part of the garden hours. If you are spending more time pruning than you are in doing anything else on the place, you will be well advised to start analyzing the difficulty and correct things so that pruning becomes an occasional pleasure rather than a daily chore.

WATERING

Waving the hose around for an hour or so in the cool of the evening, may be fun for you but it is no help to the plants. It is about as useful as sprinkling the laundry instead of washing it. The place where water does some good is down in the ground at the roots of the plant. In order to get it there a sufficient quantity must be given that it can soak down deep where the small feeding roots are. Light sprinkling dampens only the very surface of the ground. It not only does no good, but may actually do considerable harm in encouraging the roots to come to the surface after water. They then burn out in a dry spell or in unusual heat. The first year or two years after the plants are moved is the critical period when thorough watering is imperative for survival.

If you have done a great deal of planting in one season, it will take a very careful schedule to make sure that all the plants get properly watered without spending your entire life doing nothing but watering. The best way to accomplish it is to make a program of watering one section on a certain day of the week, so that each plant or group of plants has two to three hours of steady watering before the hose is moved. Ground watering can be done all through the day but with sprays cannot be done in full sun without some danger of burning the leaves by the hot sun falling on the raindrops. In damp climates it is better not to water plants in the late afternoon, because the foliage will not dry out before evening and the dampness will encourage mildew or fungus diseases.

If overhead watering is done by sprinklers it takes proportionately a great deal more water, because a certain amount of it is blown away in all directions by the wind, more of it lodges on the foliage and comparatively little gets down to the ground under a heavy leafed shrub. It is better to remove the nozzle from the hose, turn the water down to a very slow, fine stream, and lay it under each shrub in turn until the ground has absorbed all the water it will hold without runaway. Placing the end of the hose on a flat piece of board will spread the water and you may be able to water several shrubs at the same time without getting a flood.

A canvas soil-soaker is invaluable in watering hedges, specimens or shrub borders. It consists of a piece of canvas, through which the water soaks slowly. It is attached to the end of the hose and there is never any danger of run or of wasting water. With a hedge you can lay it on one side of the hedge for two hours and then, without even turning off the water, shift it to the other side and leave it there for another two hours. If this is done once every ten days or two weeks, the hedge gets thoroughly soaked. For specimens putting it in a circle around the edge of the ball, or in two circles if it is long enough, gets the water down where the roots can reach it, in the loose soil at the edge of the ball. In an irregular shrub border it may take a little climbing around on the hands and knees to wind it among the shrubs, but once placed it can be pulled along to different sections in the border and insures a thorough soaking. There are other watering devices, such as a wand attached to the end of the hose, that are useful for reaching into the middle of borders or places where you do not want to climb through shrubs or over briars, and a water lance for thrusting into the ground and getting the water down deep at the bottom of large balls, for trees or specimens. The lance is useful only where the soil is light and soft so that it goes in easily.

If all your planting is well established and the season has normal rainfall, you may not need to do any watering at all. Unfortunately such conditions too seldom prevail. Most sections of the country seem to have a very dry season for a month to two months, sometimes during the growing year and it means at least part of the shrubs will have to have some water during that period if they are to thrive. If thorough watering cannot be done under such circumstances it is better not to do any at all. Giving plants a sip of water only makes them thirstier and they go through the dry season better with no watering at all than with teasers of sprinkles.

The amount of water the soil will absorb depends primarily on the amount of humus in it. If it is very light sandy soil, the water runs through and, as anyone who has lived near the shore knows, the hose has to be kept going almost constantly. If the soil is very heavy clay, the water runs off the surface and does not penetrate. The closer the soil comes to good garden loam, the less watering you will have to do and the better your plants will stand drought. Mulching cuts down considerably the need of watering and unless the mulch is very heavy, it is perfectly possible to give the additional water necessary right through the mulch. The moisture helps to rot the mulch and start it on its way to becoming humus.

It is surprising how many people seem to feel that as soon

as the weather gets cool it also gets moist, even though we may be in the midst of drought with no rainfall in the cool fall weather. The result of such a misunderstanding is that the plants go into freezing weather completely dry and winter losses may be very severe as a result. This is particularly true of any kind of evergreens, as they are giving off water all winter through their leaves and have no supply on which to draw. Two places side by side on Long Island illustrated this very graphically in 1943 and 1944. On one of the places the hose was going night and day all through September and October, on every evergreen on the place. The very cold, windy winter showed almost no burn and no casualties on this place the following spring. On the place next door, no amount of argument could convince the gardener that one or two light rains in early September were inadequate to give the planting the moisture that it needed. As a result in the spring of 1944 his losses were heart-breaking. Plants that did not actually die looked so brown and wind-burned and took so long to recover that the whole place was shabby most of that season.

There is no rule by which you can determine how dry the soil is short of digging a hole and finding out from first hand observation. Unless there has been an average of a half day's general rain once a week all through the growing season, the soil is not very moist. An August drought is not made up for by one day's rain in September. In the fall of 1945 around New York, the ground was powder dry down two and a half to three feet and some of the nurseries stopped digging material, because they could not hold the ball on it. After a three day almost steady rain, the moisture had actually only gone down about four inches, and below that the ground was still as dry as ever. This meant that hoses had to be used all through the fall on all planting that had been done in 1945, and all material to be moved had to be soaked artificially before digging.

If material is to be transplanted it is a very good idea to water it well a day or two in advance. This gives the roots and leaves the reserve of moisture that they need and also enables you to dig a ball on the shrub without the dirt all falling off in powdery dust. Sometimes when transplanting has to be done under very dry conditions, it will pay to fill the hole, where the shrub is to go, completely full of water before the shrub is set in it. After most of that water has soaked away, set the shrub in the hole and then fill it again, so you are sure the ball of earth is thoroughly soaked before the soil goes around it. It is almost impossible to give shrubs too much water by artificial means if it is applied slowly enough and the soil has enough humus material in it to act as a sponge.

Watering carefully and scientifically is really not much work and with the new plastic hose, even the chore of dragging heavy hose is done away with. Plants are exactly like people in their inability to survive without water. They cannot get their food for growth, except as water makes it available. Adequate watering means happy, vigorous plants.

Index

Abelia, Glossy (*Abelia grandiflora*), 63, 75, 181, 202, 203

Abelia grandiflora (Glossy abelia), 39, 63, 75, 181, 194, 202, 203

Acanthopanax sieboldianus (Five-leaved aralia), 45, 162

Acer rubrum (Red Maple), 53

Aesculus parviflora (Bottlebrush buck-eye), 47

Albizzia julibrissin (Silk Tree), 179

Amelanchier canadensis (Shadblow), 45, 56, 71, 108, 181, 198

Amelanchier laevis (Allegheny service-berry), 43

Andromeda, Japanese (*Pieris japonica*), 35, 37, 42, 71, 161, 181, 198, 203

Aralia, Five-leaved (*Acanthopanax sieboldianus*), 45, 162

Arboretum, 207-212

Arborvitae, Eastern (*Thuja occidentalis*), 157

Arborvitae, Pyramidal (*Thuja occidentalis pyramidalis*), 41, 133

Aronia arbutifolia (Red chokeberry), 31, 82

Aronia melanocarpa (Black chokeberry), 87, 88

Arrowwood (*Viburnum dentatum*), 91

Azalea arborescens (Smooth azalea), 73

Azalea calendulaceae (Flame azalea), 60, 74, 104, 108

Azalea canadense (Rhodora), 64

Azalea, Chinese (*Azalea mollis*), 60, 104

Azalea, Flame (*Azalea calendulaceae*), 60, 74, 104, 108

Azalea indica alba (White indica azalea), 57, 104, 118, 132, 181

Azalea, Kurume (*Azalea obtusa japonica* in variety), 64, 104, 181

Azalea, Magnolia (*Azalea mucronulatum*), 64

Azalea mollis (Chinese azalea), 60, 104

Azalea mucronulatum (Magnolia azalea), 37, 50, 64

Azalea nudiflora (Pinxter Azalea), 108

Azalea obtusa japonica in variety (Kurume azalea), 64, 104, 108

Azalea obtusa kaempferi (Torch azalea), 60, 88, 104

Azalea, Pinkshell (*Azalea vaseyi*), 62, 72, 88, 105, 134, 198, 199, 203

Azalea, Pinxter (*Azalea nudiflora*), 108

Azalea rosea (Roseshell azalea), 72

Azalea, Roseshell (*Azalea rosea*), 72

Azalea, Smooth (*Azalea arborescens*), 73

Azalea, Swamp (*Azalea viscosa*), 58, 118, 201

Azalea, Torch (*Azalea obtusa kaempferi*), 60, 88, 104

Azalea vaseyi (Pinkshell azalea), 50, 53, 62, 72, 88, 105, 134, 198, 199, 203

Azalea viscosa (Swamp azalea), 58, 118, 201

Azalea, White Indica (*Azalea indica alba*), 57, 104, 132, 181

Baccharis halimifolia (Groundsel-bush), 45

Balled and burlapped, 243

Bamboo, Heavenly (Nandina domestica), 46

Banana Shrub (Michelia fuscata), 179

Barberry, Japanese (Berberis thunbergi), 26, 31, 82, 88, 158, 160

Barberry, Warty (Berberis verruculosa), 34, 132, 161

Barberry, Wintergreen (Berberis julianae), 34, 132

Bayberry (Myrica pennsylvanica), 32, 135

Beautyberry (Callicarpa dichotoma), 86

Beautybush (Kolkwitzia amabilis), 44, 63, 74, 105, 201

Beech, Copper, 53

Beech, European (Fagus sylvatica), 156

Berberis julianae (Wintergreen barberry), 34, 132

Berberis thunbergi (Japanese barberry), 26, 31, 82, 88, 158, 160

Berberis thunbergi erecta (Truehedge columnberry), 158

Berberis verruculosa (Warty barberry), 34, 132, 161

Betula pendula (White birch), 30, 43

Birch, White (Betula pendula), 30, 43

Blackhaw (Viburnum prunifolium), 24, 78, 87

Bluebeard (Caryopteris incana), 61, 75, 202

Blueberry, Highbush, 26, 30, 77, 89, 135, 161

Blueberry, Lowbush (Vaccinium angustifolium), 89, 161

Botanical garden, 207-212

Box, Common (Buxus sempervirens), 158

Box, Tree (Buxus sempervirens arborescens), 41

Box, Truedwarf (Buxus sempervirens suffruticosa), 41, 132, 149, 158, 161

Broom (Cytisus in variety), 59

Broom, Scotch (Cytisus scoparius), 30, 43

Buckeye, Bottlebrush (Aesculus parviflora), 47

Buckthorn (Rhamnus carthartica), 87, 157

Buddleia in variety (Butterflybush), 61, 75, 201, 202

Butterflybush (Buddleia in variety), 61, 75, 201, 202

Buxus sempervirens (Common box), 129, 158

Buxus sempervirens arborescens (Tree box), 41

Buxus sempervirens suffruticosa (Truedwarf box), 41, 129, 132, 149, 158, 161

Callicarpa dichotoma (Beautyberry), 86

Calycanthus floridus (Sweetshrub), 47, 89, 134

Caragana arborescens (Siberian peashrub), 59

Carpinus betulus (European hornbeam), 156

Caryopteris incana (Bluebeard), 61, 75, 202

Cedar, Canaerts (Juniperus virginiana canaerti), 44

Cedar, Red (Juniperus virginiana), 42, 71, 133, 181

Cercis canadensis (Redbud), 50, 64, 73, 108

Cestrum nocturnum (Night-blooming Jessamine), 179

Chaenomeles japonica (Dwarf flowering quince), 71, 86, 134, 152, 161, 162, 197, 198

Chaenomeles lagenaria (Japanese flowering quince), 86, 105, 134, 160

Chastetree, Hardy (Vitex agnuscastus), 61, 75, 202

Cherry, Cornelian (Cornus mas), 59, 71, 197

Cherry, Higan (Prunus subhirtella in variety), 25, 62, 68, 71, 106, 198

Cherry, Manchu (Prunus tomentosa), 56, 71, 197

Cherry, Oriental (Prunus serrulata in variety), 56, 62, 69, 106, 198

Cherry, Sargent (Prunus sargenti), 56, 68

Chionanthus virginicus (White fringe-tree), 27, 47, 58, 74, 89, 162

Chokeberry, Black (Aronia melano-carpa), 87, 88

Chokeberry, Red (Aronia arbutifolia), 31, 82

Clerodendron trichotomum (Harlequin glorybower), 47, 75

Clethra alnifolia (Sweetpepper bush), 90, 118

Columnberry, Truehedge (Berberis thunbergi erecta), 158

Cornus amomum (Silky dogwood), 90

Cornus florida (Flowering dogwood), 42, 57, 82, 88, 102, 105, 108, 134, 181, 199, 203

Cornus florida rubra (Red flowering dogwood), 63, 73

Cornus kousa (Chinese dogwood), 58, 73, 82, 88, 102, 162, 200

Cornus mas (Cornelian cherry), 59, 71, 197

Cornus racemosa (Gray dogwood), 79, 86

Cornus stolonifera (Red osier dogwood), 30

Cornus s. flaviramea (Goldentwig dogwood), 30

Cotinus coggygria (Smoketree), 47, 88, 134, 203

Cotoneaster apiculata (Cranberry cotoneaster), 82, 203

Cotoneaster, Cherryberry (Cotoneaster zabelli), 181

Cotoneaster, Cranberry (Cotoneaster apiculata), 82, 203

Cotoneaster dielsiana (Diel cotoneaster), 45, 90

Cotoneaster, Diel (Cotoneaster dielsiana), 45, 90

Cotoneaster divaricata (Spreading cotoneaster), 23, 31, 83, 90, 134, 162

Cotoneaster foveolata (Glossy cotoneaster), 89

Cotoneaster, Franchet (Cotoneaster francheti), 162

Cotoneaster francheti (Franchet cotoneaster), 162

Cotoneaster, Glossy (Cotoneaster foveolata), 89

Cotoneaster horizontalis (Rock cotoneaster), 23, 83

Cotoneaster, Rock (Cotoneaster horizontalis), 83

Cotoneaster, Simons (Cotoneaster simonsi), 83

Cotoneaster simonsi (Simons cotoneaster), 83

Cotoneaster, Spreading (Cotoneaster divaricata), 31, 83, 90, 134, 162

Cotoneaster zabelli (Cherryberry cotoneaster), 181

Crabapple, Arnold (Malus arnoldiana), 66, 86, 107

Crabapple, Bechtel (Malus ioensis bechteli), 63, 67, 72, 106, 163

Crabapple, Carmine (Malus atrosanguinea), 65, 66, 84, 105, 199

Crabapple, Chinese Flowering (Malus spectabilis), 63, 67, 107

Crabapple, Cutleaf (Malus toringoides), 67, 84

Crabapple, Eley (Malus eleyi), 65

Crabapple, Hopa (Malus hopa), 65

Crabapple, Japanese Flowering (Malus floribunda), 66, 106, 107

Crabapple, Parkman (Malus halliana parkmani), 62, 66, 200

Crabapple, Rivers (Malus spectabilis riversi), 67

Crabapple, Russian (Malus niedzwetskyana), 65

Crabapple, Sargent (*Malus sargenti*), 24, 44, 67, 84, 107

Crabapple, Scheidecker (*Malus scheideckeri*), 67

Crabapple, Siberian (*Malus baccata*), 66, 84

Crabapple, Tea (*Malus hupehensis*), 67, 106, 163

Crabapple, Toringo (*Malus sieboldi*), 32

Crabapple, Wild Sweet (*Malus coronaria*), 42, 67, 118

Cranberry, European Highbush (*Viburnum opulus*), 32, 79, 85, 161

Cranberrybush, Yellow, 86

Crataegus crusgalli (Cockspur hawthorn), 41, 83, 107, 156

Crataegus intricata (Thicket hawthorn), 83

Crataegus nitida (Glossy hawthorn), 31

Crataegus oxyacantha (English hawthorn), 134

Crataegus oxyacantha pauli (Pauls scarlet hawthorn), 65

Crataegus oxyacantha rosea (Pink English hawthorn), 63, 105

Crataegus phaenopyrum (Washington hawthorn), 31, 79, 83, 89, 107, 181

Cryptomeria japonica lobbi (Lobb cryptomeria), 41

Cryptomeria, Lobb (*Cryptomeria japonica lobbi*), 41

Currant, Golden (*Ribes aureum*), 59, 119

Cytisus in variety (Broom), 59

Cytisus scoparius (Scotch broom), 30, 43

Daphne cneorum (Garland flower), 129, 199

Daphne, February (*Daphne mezereum*), 64

Daphne mezereum (February daphne), 64

Daphne somerset (Garland shrub),

39, 45, 62, 71, 118, 129, 140, 194, 199

Deutzia (*Deutzia* in variety), 57

Deutzia gracilis (Slender deutzia), 105

Deutzia, Lemoine (*Deutzia lemoinei*), 105, 161

Deutzia lemoinei (Lemoine deutzia), 105, 161

Deutzia, Slender (*Deutzia gracilis*), 105

Dewberry, American (*Rubus flagellaris*), 107

Dogwood, Chinese (*Cornus kousa*), 58, 73, 82, 88, 102, 162, 200

Dogwood, Flowering (*Cornus florida*), 42, 57, 82, 88, 102, 105, 108, 134, 181, 199, 203

Dogwood, Flowering Red (*Cornus florida rubra*), 63, 73

Dogwood, Goldentwig (*Cornus s. flaviramea*), 30

Dogwood, Gray (*Cornus racemosa*), 79, 86

Dogwood, Red Osier (*Cornus stolonifera*), 30

Dogwood, Silky (*Cornus amomum*), 90

Driveway entrance, 136

Duranta plumieri, 179

Elder, American (*Sanbucus canadensis*), 87, 107

Elder, Red-berried (*Sambucus racemosa*), 85

Eleagnus angustifolia (Russian olive), 37, 45

Eleagnus pungens, 179

Enkianthus campanulatus (Redvein enkianthus), 89

Enkianthus, Redvein (*Enkianthus campanulatus*), 89

Euonymus alatus (Winged euonymus), 24, 27, 43, 77, 83, 89, 134, 153, 162, 203

Euonymus alatus compactus (Dwarf-winged euonymus), 147, 152, 158, 161

Euonymus, Dwarfwinged (*Euonymus alatus compactus*), 152, 158, 161

Euonymus, Winged (*Euonymus alatus*), 24, 27, 43, 83, 89, 134, 162, 203

Evergreens, combinations with deciduous shrubs, 175
conditions favorable to growth, 177
foliage color of, 174
for southern use, 178, 195
in native planting, 224
use of, 126

Exochorda racemosa (Pearlbush), 46, 57, 105, 199

Fagus sylvatica (European beech), 156

Fall color, 82-91

Fences of shrubs, 151

Fertilizers, 249, 269, 271
chemical, 250

Firethorn, Laland (*Pyracantha coccinea lalandi*), 84, 130, 163

Flowering Almond, Pink (*Prunus amygdalus roseoplena*), 53

Flowering Almond, White (*Prunus amygdalus alboplena*), 53

Flowering shrubs, 49-75
color of bloom, 51
combinations of, 54, 70-75, 111, 232, 233
combinations with buildings, 54
combinations with garden flowers, 190, 197-203
combinations with trees, 53
effect in bloom, 50
in flower gardens, 188-203
texture of bloom, 52
time of bloom, 49

Foliage texture, 45-48

Forsythia in variety (Golden Bells), 59

Forsythia, Border (*Forsythia intermedia*), 91, 105

Forsythia, Fortune (*Forsythia suspensa fortunei*), 70

Forsythia intermedia (Border forsythia), 91, 105

Forsythia intermedia spectabilis (Showy forsythia), 70, 197

Forsythia, Showy (*Forsythia intermedia spectabilis*), 70, 197

Forsythia suspensa (Weeping Forsythia), 130, 154, 162

Forsythia suspensa fortunei (Fortune forsythia), 70

Forsythia, Weeping (*Forsythia suspensa*), 154, 162

Foundation planting, 120-135
corners of house, 128
country, 122
doorways, 127
proportion of, 124
seasonal effect of, 125
suburban, 123
under windows, 129

Franklinia alatamaha (Gordonia), 51, 58, 91, 179

Fringetree, White (*Chionanthus virginicus*), 27, 47, 58, 74, 89, 162

Fruit gardens, 182-187

Fruit trees, size of, 183
use of, 182

Fruiting shrubs, 79

Fruits, bramble, use of, 185

Fruits, bush, use of, 184

Garden entrance, 140

Garland Flower (*Daphne cneorum*), 199

Garland Shrub (*Daphne somerset*), 45, 62, 71, 118, 199

Glorybower, Harlequin (*Clerodendron trichotomum*), 47, 75

Golden Bells (*Forsythia in variety*), 59

Goldenchain Tree, Waterer (*Laburnum vulgare waterei*), 46, 60, 135, 163

Goldenraintree (*Koelreuteria paniculata*), 60

Goldflower (*Hypericum moserianum*), 60, 75, 202

Gordonia (*Franklinia alatamaha*), 51, 58, 91

Green gardens, 173-179

Groundselbush (*Baccharis halimifolia*), 45

Growth, rate of, 27

Habit, 22, 33
broadly oval, 25
pendulous, 25
picturesque, 24
spreading, 23
upright, 23

Halesia carolina (Silverbell), 43, 57, 73, 181

Hamamelis japonica (Japanese witchhazel), 59

Hamamelis virginiana (Common witchhazel), 60

Hawthorn, Cockspur (*Crataegus crusgalli*), 41, 83, 107, 156

Hawthorn, English (*Crataegus oxyacantha*), 42, 134

Hawthorn, English Pink (*Crataegus oxyacantha rosea*), 63

Hawthorn, Glossy (*Crataegus nitida*), 31

Hawthorn, Pauls Scarlet (*Crataegus oxyacantha pauli*), 65

Hawthorn, Thicket (*Crataegus intricata*), 83

Hawthorn, Washington (*Crataegus phaenopyrum*), 31, 79, 83, 89, 107, 181

Hedges, trimmed, 145-148, 156-159
untrimmed, 148-151, 160, 161

Hemlock, Canadian (*Tsuga canadensis*), 157, 203

Hemlock, Carolina (*Tsuga carolina*), 157

Hibiscus syriacus (Rose of Sharon), 58, 61, 63, 75, 135, 160, 202

Holly, American (*Ilex opaca*), 34, 71, 83, 133, 181

Holly, Convexleaf (*Ilex crenata convexa*), 34, 159, 181

Holly, Japanese (*Ilex crenata*), 87, 181, 203

Holly, Small-leaved Japanese (*Ilex crenata microphylla*), 34, 132, 159

Honeysuckle, Amur (*Lonicera maacki*), 84

Honeysuckle, Blueleaf (*Lonicera korolkowi*), 44, 63, 73, 84, 105

Honeysuckle, Fragrant (*Lonicera fragrantissima*), 118

Honeysuckle, Morrow (*Lonicera morrowi*), 118

Hornbeam, European (*Carpinus betulus*), 156

Humus, 249

Hydrangea, Bigleaf Blue (*Hydrangea macrophylla coerulea*), 61, 75

Hydrangea macrophylla coerulea (Bigleaf blue hydrangea), 61, 75

Hypericum moserianum (Goldflower), 60, 75, 202

Ilex crenata (Japanese holly), 87, 147, 181, 203

Ilex crenata convexa (Convexleaf holly), 34, 140, 149, 159, 181

Ilex crenata microphylla (Small-leaved Japanese holly), 34, 132, 159, 176

Ilex glabra (Inkberry), 34, 41, 87, 133

Ilex helleri, 23

Ilex laevigata (Smooth winterberry), 83, 90

Ilex opaca (American holly), 34, 71, 83, 133, 181

Ilex verticillata (Winterberry), 31, 83

Ilex verticillata chrysocarpa (Yellow-berried winterberry), 86

Ilex vomitoria (Yaupon), 37, 147

Inkberry (*Ilex glabra*), 34, 41, 87, 133

Jasmine, Winter (*Jasminum nudiflorum*), 130, 154, 163, 198

Jasminum nudiflorum (Winter jasmine), 130, 154, 163, 198

Jessamine, Night-blooming (*Cestrum nocturnum*), 179

Jessamine, Orange (Murraya paniculata), 179
Juniperus chinensis pfitzeriana (Pfitzer's juniper), 42
Juniper, Pfitzer (Juniperus chinensis pfitzeriana), 42
Juniperus virginiana (Red cedar), 42, 71, 133, 181
Juniperus virginiana canaerti (Canaerts cedar), 44

Kalmia latifolia (Mountain laurel), 35, 41, 108, 133
Kerria, Japanese (Kerria japonica), 30, 163
Kerria japonica (Japanese kerry), 30, 163
Koelreuteria paniculata (Goldenraintree), 60
Kolkwitzia amabilis (Beautybush), 44, 63, 74, 105, 201

Laburnum vulgare watereri (Waterer goldenchain tree), 46, 60, 135, 163
Larch, Japanese (Larix leptolepis), 70
Larix leptolepis (Japanese larch), 70
Laurel, Mountain (Kalmia latifolia), 35, 41, 108, 133
Lavender flowering shrubs, 61
Leaves, 36-48
    arrangement on stem, 38
    color of new, 36
    fall color of, 76
    foliage value, 39
    size of, 38
Leucothoe catesbaei (Drooping leucothoe), 72
Leucothoe, Drooping (Leucothoe catesbaei), 72
Ligustrum obtusifolium regelianum (Regels Privet), 32, 87
Ligustrum ovalifolium (California privet), 156, 181
Lilacs (Syringa in variety), 61, 72, 73, 200
Lilac, Common (Syringa vulgaris), 42, 119, 135, 161

Lilac, Common White (Syringa vulgaris alba), 57
Lilac, Japanese Tree (Syringa amurensis japonica), 48, 135
Lilac, Late (Syringa villosa), 135, 201
Lilac, Persian (Syringa persica), 46, 72, 200
Lilac, Persian White (Syringa persica alba), 57, 200
Linden, Small Leaved (Tilia cordata), 157
Lindera benzoin (Spicebush), 59, 70, 83, 90
Liquidambar styraciflua (Sweetgum), 76
Locust, Roseacacia (Robinia hispida), 46, 63
Lonicera fragrantissima (Fragrant honeysuckle), 118
Lonicera korolkowi (Blueleaf honeysuckle), 44, 63, 73, 84, 105
Lonicera maacki (Amur honeysuckle), 84
Lonicera morrowi (Morrow honeysuckle), 118
Lycium chinense (Chinese matrimony vine), 163

Maclura pomifera (Osage orange), 157
Magnolia, Saucer (Magnolia soulangeana), 135, 163, 198
Magnolia, Saucer Purple (Magnolia soulangeana lenni), 64
Magnolia, Saucer White (Magnolia soulangeana alba), 56
Magnolia soulangeana (Saucer magnolia), 48, 135, 163, 198
Magnolia soulangeana alba (White saucer magnolia), 56
Magnolia soulangeana lenni (Purple saucer magnolia), 64
Magnolia, Star (Magnolia stellata), 44, 56, 70, 118, 130, 163, 197
Magnolia stellata (Star magnolia), 44, 56, 70, 118, 130, 163, 197
Magnolia, Sweetbay (Magnolia virginiana), 48, 58, 201

Magnolia tripetala (Umbrella magnolia), 48
Magnolia, Umbrella (Magnolia tripetala), 48
Magnolia virginiana (Sweetbay magnolia), 48, 58, 189, 201
Malus arnoldiana (Arnold crabapple), 66, 86, 107
Malus atrosanguinea (Carmine crabapple), 65, 66, 84, 105, 199
Malus baccata (Siberian crabapple), 66, 84
Malus coronaria (Wild Sweet Crabapple), 42, 67, 107, 118
Malus eleyi (Eley crabapple), 65
Malus floribunda (Japanese flowering crabapple), 66, 79, 106, 107
Malus halliana parkmani (Parkman crabapple), 62, 66, 200
Malus hopa (Hopa crabapple), 65
Malus hupehensis (Tea crabapple), 67, 106, 163
Malus ioensis bechteli (Bechtel crabapple), 63, 67, 72, 106, 163
Malus niedzwetskyana (Russian crabapple), 65, 79
Malus sargenti (Sargent crabapple), 24, 44, 67, 84, 107, 152
Malus scheideckeri (Scheidecker crabapple), 37, 67
Malus sieboldi (Toringo crabapple), 32
Malus spectabilis (Chinese flowering crabapple), 63, 67, 107
Malus spectabilis riversi (Rivers crabapple), 67
Malus toringoides (Cutleaf crabapple), 67, 84
Manure, 248, 270
Maple, Norway, 53
Maple, Red (Acer rubrum), 53
Matrimony Vine, Chinese (Lycium chinense), 163
Michelia fuscata (Banana Shrub), 179
Mockorange (Philadelphus in variety), 58
Mockorange, Big, Scentless (Philadelphus grandiflorus), 106

Mockorange, Fragrant (Philadelphus coronarius), 119, 201
Mockorange, Hybrid (Philadelphus Virginal), 201
Mockorange, Lemoine (Philadelphus lemoinei), 74
Mockorange, Mt. Blanc (Philadelphus lemoinei), 74, 106
Mountain ash, European (Sorbus aucuparia), 46, 85
Mulches, 270
Murraya paniculata (Jessamine, Orange), 179
Myrica pennsylvanica (Bayberry), 32, 135

Nandina domestica (Heavenly bamboo), 46
Nannyberry (Viburnum lentago), 87, 91
Native planting, 100, 221-228
  contrast in, 225-226
  evergreens, 224
  fertilizers for, 227
Native plants, transplanting of, 228
Nurseries, 213-220
  ordering from, 243
  time to visit, 219
Nyssa sylvatica (Sourgum), 76

Orange, Osage (Maclura pomifera), 157
Oxydendron arboreum (Sourwood), 78, 89

Pachystima, Canby (Pachystima canbyi), 35, 181
Pachystima canbyi (Canby pachystima), 35, 176, 181
Parks, 207-212
Peach, Flowering (Prunus persica in variety), 69
Pearlbush (Exochorda racemosa), 46, 57, 105, 199
Peashrub, Siberian (Caragana arborescens), 59
Peat moss, 249
Pests, 116

Philadelphus in variety (Mock-orange), 58
Philadelphus coronarius (Fragrant mockorange), 119, 201
Philadelphus grandiflorus (Big scentless mockorange), 106
Philadelphus lemoinei (Lemoine mockorange), 74
Philadelphus lemoinei Mont Blanc (Mt. Blanc mockorange), 74, 106
Philadelphus Virginal (Hybrid mockorange), 201
Photinia glabra, 179
Photinia, Oriental (Photinia villosa), 84
Photinia villosa (Oriental photinia), 84
Pieris japonica (Japanese andromeda), 35, 37, 42, 71, 140, 149, 161, 181, 198, 203
Pink flowering shrubs, 62-65
Pinus mugho, 23
Planning the grounds, 237
Planting, after care, 256
  depth to plant, 252
  filling hole, 253
  preparations, 250
  size of hole, 252
  staking, 255
  watering, 254
Plum, Beach (Prunus maritima), 91
Plum, Flowering (Prunus triloba), 68
Plum, Purple-leaved (Prunus pissardi), 143
Privet, California (Ligustrum ovalifolium), 156, 181
Privet, Regels (Ligustrum obtusifolium regelianum), 32, 87
Pruning, 272
  amount needed, 274
  purpose of, 273
  tools for, 276
Prunus amygdalus alboplena (White Flowering Almond), 53
Prunus amygdalus roseoplena (Pink Flowering Almond), 53
Prunus maritima (Beach plum), 91

Prunus persica in variety (Flowering peach), 69
Prunus pissardi (Purple-leaved Plum), 143
Prunus sargenti (Sargent cherry), 56, 68
Prunus serrulata in variety (Oriental cherry), 62, 68, 69, 106, 199
Prunus subhirtella (Higan cherry), 53, 62, 68, 71, 106, 198
Prunus subhirtella pendula (Weeping cherry), 25
Prunus tomentosa (Manchu cherry), 53, 56, 71, 197
Prunus triloba (Flowering plum), 68
Prunus yedoensis (Yoshino cherry), 68, 198
Pyracantha coccinea lalandi (Laland firethorn), 84, 130, 163

Quince, Japanese (Chaenomeles lagenaria), 86, 105, 134, 160
Quince, Japanese Dwarf (Chaenomeles japonica), 71, 86, 134, 152, 161, 162, 197, 198

Redbud (Cercis canadensis), 50, 64, 73, 108
Rhamnus cathartica (Buckthorn), 87, 157
Rhododendron album elegans (White rhododendron), 58, 74
Rhododendron arbutifolium (Rockmount rhododendron), 65, 133
Rhododendron, Carolina (Rhododendron carolinianum), 72, 181, 199, 203
Rhododendron, Carolina White (Rhododendron carolinianum), 58
Rhododendron carolinianum (Carolina rhododendron), 72, 181, 199, 203
Rhododendron carolinianum album (White Carolina rhododendron), 58
Rhododendron, Catawba (Rhododendron catawbiense), 65, 200, 201

Rhododendron catawbiense (Catawba rhododendron), 65, 133, 200, 201

Rhododendron maximum (Rosebay rhododendron), 48, 73, 108

Rhododendron minus (Piedmont rhododendron), 65

Rhododendron, Piedmont (Rhododendron minus), 65

Rhododendron, Rockmount (Rhododendron arbutifolium), 65, 133

Rhododendron, Rosebay (Rhododendron maximum), 48, 73, 108

Rhododendron, White (Rhododendron album elegans), 74

Rhodora (Azalea canadense), 64

Rhus copallina (Shining sumac), 89

Rhus glabra (Smooth sumac), 32, 85

Ribes aureum (Golden currant), 59, 119

Robinia hispida (Roseacacia locust), 46, 63

Rosa blanda (Meadow Rose), 85, 167

Rosa centifolia (Cabbage rose), 119

Rosa harisoni (Harison yellow rose), 60

Rosa helenae (Helen rose), 119, 168

Rosa hugonis (Father Hugo rose), 39, 44, 46, 60, 72, 135, 149, 160, 168, 194, 200

Rosa moschata (Musk Rose), 170

Rosa multiflora (Japanese rose), 32, 74, 80, 85, 172

Rosa primula (Primrose rose), 60, 168

Rosa rubiginosa (Sweetbriar rose), 119, 169

Rosa rugosa (Rugosa rose), 48, 65, 80, 170

Rosa rugosa alba (White rugosa rose), 85, 160

Rosa setigera (Prairie rose), 26, 74, 85, 107, 167, 172

Rosa spinosissima (Scotch rose), 119, 168

Rose, Austrian Briar (Rosa foetida), 169

Rose, Cabbage (Rosa centifolia), 119

Rose, Father Hugo (Rosa hugonis), 38, 44, 46, 60, 72, 135, 160, 168, 200

Rose, Harison Yellow (Rosa harisoni), 60, 168

Rose, Helen (Rosa helenae), 119

Rose, Japanese (Rosa multiflora), 32, 74, 80, 85

Rose, Meadow (Rosa blanda), 85

Rose, Musk (Rosa moschata), 170

Rose, Prairie (Rosa setigera), 26, 74, 85, 107

Rose, Primrose (Rosa primula), 60

Rose, Rugosa (Rosa rugosa), 48, 65

Rose, Rugosa White (Rosa rugosa alba), 85, 160

Rose, Scotch (Rosa spinosissima), 119, 168

Rose, Sweetbriar (Rosa rubiginosa), 119, 169, 172

Rose of Sharon (Hibiscus syriacus), 22, 61, 63, 75, 135, 160, 202

Roses, floribunda, 171
  hybrid perpetuals, 171
  shrub, 167-172

Rubus flagellaris (American dewberry), 107

Russian Olive (Eleagnus angustifolia), 45

Sambucus canadensis (Elder), 87, 107

Sambucus racemosa (Red-berried elder), 85

Sapphireberry (Symplocos paniculata), 87, 163, 203

Screen planting, 130

Serviceberry, Allegheny (Amelanchier laevis), 43

Shadblow (Amelanchier canadensis), 45, 56, 71, 108, 181, 198

Shrub borders, distant, 95-108
  for property lines, 98
  nearby, 109-119
  quantities of plants for, 113
  rearrangement of, 258-268
  texture of, 116

Shrubs for cutting, 143

Silk Tree (*Albizzia julibrissin*), 179

Silverbell (*Halesia carolina*), 43, 57, 73, 181

Smoketree (*Cotinus coggygria*), 47, 88, 134, 203

Snowbell, Japanese (*Styrax japonica*), 24, 38, 44, 46, 181

Snowberry (*Symphoricarpos albus*), 32, 86

Soil, composition, 249
conditions, 115

Sorbus aucuparia (European mountain ash), 46, 85

Sourgum (*Nyssa sylvatica*), 76

Sourwood (*Oxydendron arboreum*), 78, 89

Specimens, use of, 140

Spicebush (*Lindera benzoin*), 59, 70, 83, 90

Spiraea arguta (Garland spirea), 56

Spiraea bumalda Anthony Waterer (Pink spirea), 65

Spiraea prunifolia (Bridalwreath spirea), 57

Spiraea thunbergi (Thunberg spirea), 56, 70, 90, 103, 199

Spiraea vanhouttei (Vanhoutte spirea), 26, 57, 73, 106, 149, 160, 201

Spirea, Bridalwreath (*Spiraea prunifolia*), 57

Spirea, Garland (*Spiraea arguta*), 56

Spirea, Pink (*Spiraea bumalda* Anthony Waterer), 65

Spirea, Thunberg (*Spiraea thunbergi*), 56, 70, 90, 199

Spirea, Vanhoutte (*Spiraea vanhouttei*), 57, 73, 106, 160, 201

Staking, 255

Stephanandra, Cutleaf (*Stephanandra incisa*), 46

Stephanandra incisa (Cutleaf stephanandra), 46

Stewartia, Japanese (*Stewartia pseudocamellia*), 58

Stewartia, Mountain (*Stewartia ovata*), 74

Stewartia ovata (Mountain stewartia), 74

Stewartia pseudocamellia (Japanese stewartia), 58

Styrax japonica (Japanese snowbell), 24, 38, 44, 46, 181

Sumac, Shining (*Rhus copallina*), 89

Sumac, Smooth (*Rhus glabra*), 32, 85

Sweetgum (*Liquidambar styraciflua*), 76

Sweetpepper Bush (*Clethra alnifolia*), 90, 118

Sweetshrub (*Calycanthus floridus*), 47, 89, 134

Symphoricarpos albus (Snowberry), 32, 86

Symplocos paniculata (Sapphireberry), 87, 163, 203

Syringa in variety (Lilacs), 61, 72, 73, 200

Syringa amurensis japonica (Japanese tree lilac), 48, 135

Syringa persica (Persian lilac), 46, 72, 200

Syringa persica alba (White Persian lilac), 57, 200

Syringa villosa (Late lilac), 135, 201

Syringa vulgaris (Common lilac), 42, 119, 135, 161

Syringa vulgaris alba (White common lilac), 57

Taxus baccata repandens (Spreading Yew), 23, 129

Taxus cuspidata (Japanese yew), 35, 41

Taxus cuspidata capitata (Upright Yew), 133, 157, 181

Taxus cuspidata nana (Dwarf Japanese yew), 23, 129, 159

Taxus hicksi (Hicks yew), 23, 159

Taxus hunnewelliana (Hunnewell Yew), 133, 159

Taxus media (Hybrid yew), 35

Taxus media hatfieldi (Hatfield yew), 159

Thuja occidentalis (Eastern arborvitae), 157

Thuja occidentalis douglasi pyramidalis (Pyramidal arborvitae), 41, 133

Tilia cordata (Small leaved linden), 157

Transplanting, 264

Tsuga canadensis (Canadian hemlock), 157, 203

Tsuga carolina (Carolina hemlock), 157

Vaccinium angustifolium (Lowbush blueberry), 23, 89, 161, 185

Vaccinium corymbosum (Highbush blueberry), 26, 30, 89, 135, 161, 185

Vaccinium vitis-idaea (Cowberry), 185

Values, 41-44

Viburnum acerifolium (Mapleleaf viburnum), 91, 175

Viburnum Burkwood (Viburnum burkwoodi), 119

Viburnum burkwoodi (Burkwood Viburnum), 119

Viburnum carlesi (Koreanspice viburnum), 62, 71, 91, 119, 135, 163, 199

Viburnum cassinoides (Witherod), 87

Viburnum dentatum (Arrowwood), 91

Viburnum dilatatum (Linden viburnum), 32, 79, 85

Viburnum, Doublefile (Viburnum tomentosum), 24, 42, 57, 73, 79, 91, 106, 135, 181

Viburnum, Koreanspice (Viburnum carlesi), 62, 71, 91, 119, 135, 163, 199

Viburnum lentago (Nannyberry), 87, 91

Viburnum, Linden (Viburnum dilatatum), 32, 79, 85

Viburnum, Mapleleaf (Viburnum acerifolium), 91

Viburnum odoratissimum, 179

Viburnum opulus (European highbush cranberry), 32, 79, 85, 161

Viburnum opulus xanthocarpum (Yellow cranberrybush), 86

Viburnum prunifolium (Blackhaw), 24, 78, 87

Viburnum rufidulum (Southern blackhorn), 78

Viburnum setigerum (Tea viburnum), 85

Viburnum, Siebold (Viburnum sieboldi), 48, 85, 135, 163

Viburnum sieboldi (Siebold viburnum), 38, 39, 48, 85, 135, 147, 152, 163

Viburnum, Tea (Viburnum setigerum), 85

Viburnum tomentosum (Doublefile viburnum), 24, 37, 42, 57, 73, 79, 91, 106, 135, 152, 181

Vitex agnuscastus (Hardy chastetree), 61, 75, 202

Wall shrubs, 129, 152-155, 162, 163, 172

Watering, 254, 277
tools for, 278

Weigela florida (Old-fashioned weigela), 63

Weigela, Old-fashioned (Weigela florida), 63

Weigela wagneri candida (White weigela), 57

Weigela, White (Weigela wagneri candida), 57

White flowering shrubs, 56-58

Windbreak, 97

Winter color, 30-32, 34, 35

Winter effect, 22-31, 96, 110

Winterberry (Ilex verticillata), 31, 83

Winterberry, Smooth (Ilex laevigata), 83, 90

Winterberry, Yellow-berried (Ilex verticillata chrysocarpa), 86

Witchhazel, Common (Hamamelis virginiana), 60

Witchhazel, Japanese (Hamamelis japonica), 59

Witherod, 87

Yaupon (*Ilex vomitoria*), 37, 147
Yellow flowering shrubs, 59, 60
Yellowroot (*Zanthorhiza apiifolia*), 90
Yew, Hatfield (*Taxus media hat-
    fieldi*), 159
Yew, Hicks (*Taxus hicksi*), 23, 159
Yew, Hunnewell (*Taxus hunnewelli-
    ana*), 133, 159

Yew, Hybrid (*Taxus media*), 35
Yew, Japanese (*Taxus cuspidata*), 35,
    41
Yew, Japanese Dwarf (*Taxus cuspi-
    data nana*), 159
Yew, Spreading (*Taxus baccata re-
    pandens*), 129
Yew, Upright (*Taxus cuspidata capi-
    tata*), 133, 157, 181

Zanthorhiza apiifolia (Yellowroot), 90